# Typical Men – Andrew Spicer

'One of the great strengths of *Typical Men* is its ability to dramatise the rise and fall, plenitude and exhaustion, of versions of masculinity in relation to the dynamics of social history … The detail within the broad overview is rich and fascinating' – *Bruce Babington, Journal of Popular British Cinema*

'*Typical Men* breaks new ground … an intriguing and interesting fast-track journey through British cinema by way of what Spicer considers the cornerstones of key male types and actors. It roots through an astonishing number and variety of films, and teases out a string of masculine constructions and their background context.' – *Stephen Guy, Contemporary British History*

'Andrew Spicer's *Typical Men* is a major intervention in debates about masculinity in the cinema. It takes a lot of intellectual risks, and locates cinematic stereotypes of masculinity in a cinematic and cultural context. It is trenchant and original, and redefines the field of gender representation.' – *Sue Harper, Professor of Film History, University of Portsmouth*

'The strength of this elegantly and wittily written book is that, in the precision of its detail about individual performances, actors and films, it never loses sight of its argumentative threads.' – *Brian McFarlane, Screening the Past*

# Cinema and Society Series

General Editor: Jeffrey Richards

Published and forthcoming:

# TYPICAL MEN

## The Representation of Masculinity in Popular British Cinema

Andrew Spicer

I.B. TAURIS
LONDON · NEW YORK

New edition published in 2003 by I.B.Tauris & Co Ltd,
6 Salem Road, London W2 4BU
175 Fifth Avenue, New York NY 10010
www.ibtauris.com

In the United States of America and in Canada distributed by
St Martins Press, 175 Fifth Avenue, New York NY 10010

First published by I.B.Tauris & Co Ltd in 2001

A full CIP record for this book is available from the British Library

ISBN 1 86064 931 9

Set in Monotype Garamond by Ewan Smith, London
Printed and bound in Great Britain by MPG Books Ltd, Bodmin

# Contents

# Illustrations

# General Editor's Introduction

It is a commonplace that as we enter the twenty-first century masculinity is in crisis. This is the product of the decline in the old heavy industries with their notions of the male breadwinner and the job for life, family breakdown which has undermined patriarchy, and the rise of feminism which has conducted a sustained assault on all aspects of traditional male dominance for upwards of thirty years. One of the manifestations of the crisis has been a record increase in the suicide rate among young males.

Since one of the most potent sources of male role models has been the cinema, the appearance of Andrew Spicer's *Typical Men* is timely. He sets out to establish a taxonomy of masculine types in British cinema since the 1940s. Drawing on a wide range of films from every possible genre, he traces the evolution of the different types: the gentleman, the professional, the adventurer, the everyman, the fool, the rogue, the criminal, the rebel, the damaged man, ending with a stimulating look at the contemporary male image in all its variety and complexity.

A rich and varied procession of British stars stride, strut, swagger, stumble, glide, creep, mince and tiptoe through his pages as he explains the image and significance of – among many others – John Mills, Stewart Granger, Dirk Bogarde, George Formby, Jack Warner, Kenneth More, Stanley Baker, Norman Wisdom, Albert Finney, Hugh Grant and Ewan McGregor.

By comparison with studies of women and femininity in cinema, there have been far fewer accounts of men and masculinity. This is therefore a pioneering work. It presents a rich picture of evolution and transformation, continuity and change, iconography and influence. It will be an essential starting point for anyone seeking to understand the nature of masculinity in Britain during the past half-century.

*Jeffrey Richards*

# Acknowledgements

This book began life about eight years ago as a PhD proposal that was prompted by watching *The October Man*. I knew I had to find out more about how and why such an extraordinary film came to be made. I should like to thank my doctoral supervisor, Vincent Porter, not only for his advice and guidance during the course of that research, but also for his kindness in commenting on a draft version of the radical revisions that have changed the thesis into *Typical Men*. I also wish to thank my external examiners, Jeffrey Richards and Sue Harper. Dr Harper has been astonishingly generous in her help with this book's production at several crucial stages; a generosity I now know to be entirely typical. Professor Richards encouraged me to develop the thesis as a contribution to the 'Cinema and Society' series and has been a comradely editor. Philippa Brewster at I.B. Tauris was persuasive in asking for the book to be 'brought up-to-date', despite my near panic. Tony Aldgate, Ian Conrich and Robert Murphy lent me copies of films that were difficult to come by. Ian and Robert kindly commented on a draft of Chapter 10 and their insights helped restructure that portion of the book. Naturally, I alone am responsible for the faults that remain.

I am grateful for the help received from staff at Bristol Central Library, the British Library, Bower Ashton Library at the University of the West of England and the Mass-Observation Library at the University of Sussex. I am particularly indebted to staff at the British Film Institute Library and at the National Film and Television Archive for patiently searching through their holdings, supplying Press Books or arranging numerous screenings and offering friendly support. Discussions with staff and students at South Bristol College, Cheltenham and Gloucester College of Higher Education, the Open University and the University of the West of England have helped focus and clarify my ideas. Guest lectures to postgraduate Film Studies students at Nottingham Trent University were important in refining the material on the 'maladjusted veteran'. I am grateful to the Faculty of Art, Media and Design at the University of the West of England for providing me with some teaching relief during the final stages of the preparation of the manuscript.

The illustrations in this book were purchased from the Stills, Posters and Designs Division of the British Film Institute and every effort has been made to obtain copyright clearance where copyright holders could be traced. If any have been omitted, I offer my apologies and would be happy to make any appropriate amendments to any future editions of this book.

I made many demands on the hospitality and tolerance of my sister Tina Benson and her family, and on my close friends Michael Burton and David Dorne and their families who allowed me to invade their homes on numerous visits to London in the pursuit of enlightenment and British cinema. David saw the completion of the thesis, but died before *Typical Men* could be finished. It is my fond hope that he would have enjoyed reading it.

My last and deepest thanks go to my partner Joyce Woolridge who has helped with every aspect of my work. Her ability to solve all the technological problems of word-processing the manuscript underlines the redundancy of the contemporary male. Without her perceptive insights about the films that she has sat through, occasionally several times, her comments on endless drafts of chapters and her willingness to discuss even the most recondite minutiae, this book would have been much poorer. Without her unfailing and unstinting love and support, it would not have been produced at all.

# Preface to the Paperback Edition

I have taken the opportunity of the paperback edition to make a few minor corrections and to update the bibliography.

*Andrew Spicer, Bristol*
*May 2003*

This book is dedicated to the memory of my parents:

Marjorie Grace Spicer (11 October 1916–18 July 1988)
and
George Wilmot Spicer (28 March 1913–17 August 1988)

# Introduction

Despite the strong resurgence of interest in popular British cinema, an extended study of the representation of masculinity has yet to be produced. *Typical Men* rectifies this neglect by providing an empirical but theoretically informed cultural history of the changing images of men in British cinema from the Second World War to the present. In order to do justice to the wealth and diversity of masculinities that have been produced, this study is organised through the detailed analysis of significant male cultural types.

Cultural types – such as the gentleman, the Everyman, or the rebel – are the staple representation of gender in popular fiction because they are easily recognisable and condense a range of important attitudes and values. Richard Dyer helpfully distinguishes between stereotypes which are rigid, limited and serve to stigmatise the group they refer to, and types which are much more fluid, flexible and 'open' in their meaning and can perform a range of narrative functions.[1] Cultural types are varied and unequal entities. They can be both specific social types arising at a particular historical moment like the Angry Young Man, or overarching archetypes, like the Fool, whose cultural history is extensive. Archetypes should be understood not as transcendent or unchanging, but historically, as complex, mutable signifiers whose meanings change over time through their deployment in different contexts.[2] Furthermore, the distinction between social types and archetypes is often blurred – the scientist, one of my 'civilian professionals', is always haunted by the spectre of the Frankenstein archetype – hence my use of the umbrella term 'cultural types'. Types are overlapping and *competing* constructions which struggle for hegemony, the version of masculinity that is most desirable or widely acceptable.[3] To achieve or maintain hegemony, types need to readjust ceaselessly to changing conditions. Even so, they can always be challenged by rival forms.[4] For instance, in the midst of the war, the restrained good form of the gentleman was challenged by the thrilling and subversive eroticism of the Byronic male, the renegade aristocrat who pursued pleasure.

As changing and competing forms, types allow us to understand gender in Foucauldian terms, as a cultural 'performance', which does not reflect 'reality' but is a discursive construction, the product of variable and historically specific sets of relations within particular contexts, and with a complex relationship to social change.[5] However, simply to identify the occurrence of a type tells us very little about its significance. *Typical Men* therefore examines both the textual configurations of the types in particular films and the contexts in which these films circulated. This requires careful analysis and interpretation of the film's narrative and visual style — types usually occur in specific genres where their repeated use allows them to evolve, often in quite subtle ways — and the role of the stars whose personae both embody and extend or refine cultural types, a process which helps give them currency and desirability.[6] Consequently, the performances of male stars are examined in some detail, the ways in which their looks, voices, movements, gestures and 'presence' are important for the meaning of the type.[7]

However, stars rarely have much institutional power, which resides, at least in the immediate post-war period, in the studios whose policies were carried through by producers. They took the strategic decisions about the ways in which males were represented, though there were clear exceptions where the creative input of the screenwriter and/or director was crucial. The British studio system started to unravel in the 1960s, when American finance allowed directors greater control. *Typical Men* therefore gives close attention to the shifting context of production that was subject to tight regulation and censorship, which only gradually and partially relaxed. But what exercised the censors gives important clues about representations of masculinity that were provoking unease.

Press Books and other forms of publicity provide a guide to the ways in which a type is being offered for consumption, but the context of reception is highly problematic. Broad shifts in cinema-going can be identified, but empirical evidence concerning audience preferences —

what male images were enjoyed and why – has been, and in many ways continues to be, sparse and debatable. Until its demise in 1960, *Picturegoer* was the most popular film journal and has therefore been used quite extensively.[8] Reviewers' comments are also cited frequently. While acknowledging their suspect status, reviews can, I believe, give important clues as to what might have been the currency of a type, or what was causing interest, alarm or offence about a new or radically altered version. Reviews, particularly where interpretations differ about the same film, therefore offer some indication of the *possible* impact of a particular representation from which audience reaction may be inferred. However, there were also numerous occasions when a film that was critically trounced was commercially successful, but this disjunction between reviewers and popular taste is then very revealing, particularly where it highlights gender differences. Trade reviews, which judge a film solely by their estimate of its potential commercial success, are another valuable resource. Where claims about a film's popularity are made, this has been based on the annual surveys of the main trade journals, *Kinematograph Weekly* and the *Motion Picture Herald*, though these are not wholly reliable.[9] In the later period more objective statistics about box-office grosses are available.

As *Typical Men* has such a broad canvas, its organising principles need to be made explicit. Throughout the book, I discuss what are identified as paradigm films, the ones that establish, reinforce, or significantly modify, an important male type, including those that initiated a cycle of films. Chapter 1 analyses the war years, concentrating on the crucial moment of change in male representations, *circa* 1943, and its consequences. This provides the foundations for the analysis of the particular types conducted in the subsequent chapters. Chapters 2 to 4 are devoted to the competing heroic types. The debonair gentleman was challenged by the modernising civilian professional, the trained expert, not the amateur. But the fortunes of both were chequered and fluctuating in a period when middle-class models lost ground to a rival Americanised form, the action adventurer. There was another rival, the ordinary Everyman, the hero of the People's War. As a consensual figure, the Everyman struggled to keep pace with a rapidly changing society where young men were becoming 'teenagers' with their own culture, rather than carbon copies of their fathers. It was an unequal struggle.

Peter Burke has suggested that popular culture produces three basic types: heroes, villains and fools.[10] If the heroes are the 'official' image of masculinity, the Fool, discussed in Chapter 6, is the 'unofficial' one, a comic Everyman. Rather than simply a figure of carnivalesque subversion, the Fool's ideological function is variable, but there is often an interesting tension between his propensity for anarchy and the conformist narratives into which he is inserted. The other great comic type, the Rogue, is striking by its sheer frequency. Audiences clearly took great pleasure in the ways in which Rogues, drawn from all strata of society, dodged responsibility. The importance of villains, the criminal types explored in Chapter 7, is also significant, especially given British cinema's reputation as dull and conformist. Criminals, of course, contest the authority of the state, as do the rebels, the subject of Chapter 8. In conservative cultures the rebel often has to assume an historical disguise, and British cinema made much use of Byronic rebels as well as social types. I had to extend Burke's model through a final type, the damaged man. The more familiar I became with the films, the more significant I recognised this type to be. Chapter 9 explores this extraordinary figure, incapable of resolving the problems of his fractured and flawed manhood whose actions create havoc.

The exploration of each type gives detailed attention to the 1945–60 period because British cinema was both popular and relatively sturdy, with a number of stable genres. The 1960s receive less attention because not only had attendances declined further, but, with the important exceptions of the horror genre, the 'Carry Ons' and the Bond films, film production became more fragmented and eclectic, only occasionally offering significant developments of existing types. Each chapter finishes around 1970, the date by which cinema had been undeniably supplanted by television as the central popular cultural medium. The television spin-offs that dominated the cinema box-office during the 1970s are best considered within a cultural history of television. Chapter 10 refers to the key developments that occurred in popular cultural types in the 1970s and 1980s, but its focus is on more recent British cinema which has seen a renewed attempt to create popular films at a time when cinema-going has undergone a significant revival. The radical differences in the male types in contemporary British films tell us much about current fears and anxieties, and the contrast with the types found in the earlier period serves to highlight the changes that have taken place. The comparison helps to define the preoccupations of both periods more clearly.

Although I hope I have acknowledged my debts to previous scholarship and built upon it, I must emphasise that there is no space in what follows to engage critically with others' work. As the book's focus is on dominant popular types, it has excluded discussion of the much more circumscribed and marginalised types of gay masculinity and varieties of regional or black British masculinity from 1940 to 1970. These varieties are the product of separate and complex histories that have been the object of detailed analysis and investigation.[11] Their importance means that, after much reflection, I have not attempted a summary account. Chapter 10, however, shows how important these representations have become in contemporary British cinema. *Typical Men* takes cognisance of these histories and explores extensively the relations between men, using Eve Sedgwick's invaluable concept of 'homosociality' to describe British culture's marked preoccupation with the bonds between men that are not necessarily overtly homosexual.[12] It also has much to say about men's relations with women, but without attempting a detailed discussion of female representation, already mapped in Sue Harper's 'buxom' history.[13] Within this framework, *Typical Men* concentrates on providing a cartography of varying masculinities, one that tries to account for their presence and the reasons for the changes that occur. I hope such a map will be both stimulating and provocative, encouraging debate about key issues and concerns.

# 1

# The War Years

B ritish cinema entered the war with two well-established male figures: the hegemonic form of the debonair gentleman complemented by an alternative working-class cheery buffoon, a comic Everyman. Both were continuations of the male types which had dominated British cinema in the 1920s and 1930s.[1] However, from the mid-point of the war, these figures were challenged by an emergent oppositional form of unexceptional ordinariness, the 'common man', the hero of the People's War.[2] At the same time a second oppositional figure, the Byronic male, based on residual cultural topoi, also emerged in Gainsborough's cycle of costume dramas. As the war entered its final phase a loose collection of criminals and misfits established themselves, products of the war's social and psychological dislocation.

These changes took place within the context of a radically altered cinema industry and film culture. Several studios were requisitioned by the government and the wartime production of British films dropped to roughly a third of the pre-war total.[3] However, the budgets for some first features, particularly those made by Rank's 'Independent Producers' and those for Two Cities led by Filippo del Giudice, were often lavish. There was a resurgent confidence in the capacity of a *national* cinema to make films that would match the production values of their Hollywood competitors while also offering resonantly British subject matter. These films were championed by a patriotic film culture which believed British cinema had come of age. The Ministry of Information exerted a strong influence on production policy, but could be resisted by recalcitrant producers, as at Gainsborough. Cinema-going became a more popular leisure pursuit, admissions rising by over 60 per cent.[4] Audiences seemed to enjoy British films, several of which were extremely popular.[5]

## Hegemonic Masculinity: The Debonair Gentleman

The perfect gentleman, the male ideal of the British ruling classes, was the product of a nineteenth-century synthesis of aristocratic style and bourgeois values.[6] Gentlemanliness combined an idealised medieval chivalry, the delicacy and sensitivity of the cultivated Man of Feeling, the athletic, vigorous manliness of 'muscular Christianity' and the Protestant success drive. Gentlemanliness was therefore a composite ideal that was romantic, ethical and practical.[7] This ideal was promoted by the public schools whose all-male communities provided an emotional disciplining and ethical training that stressed the formation of character rather than knowledge and expertise, and fostered the development of intense emotional relationships between men.[8] The core qualities of loyalty, teamwork, conformity, restraint, self-sacrifice and *noblesse oblige* formed the public school gentlemanly 'code', resulting in the characteristic product of the 'gifted amateur trained for nothing but ready for anything'.[9] The ideal of the gentleman was still dominant on the eve of the Second World War, as even hostile commentators acknowledged: '[he was] the cultural model of the best way to live … his habits, his tastes, his way of life have determined the conduct of all save a small handful of insurgent Englishmen'.[10]

The cultural hegemony of gentlemanliness had been achieved by its successful diffusion through a wide range of middlebrow and popular cultural forms, notably imperial adventure narratives which were central to this process.[11] The dominant version in British cinema during the 1930s, exemplified by Robert Donat and Leslie Howard, was the 'debonair gentleman' which combined the self-assured insouciance of the Man About Town with a sensitive but robust idealism.[12] Howard produced and starred in *Pimpernel Smith* (1941) and *The First of the Few* (1942), which together with his cameo role in *49th Parallel* (1941), offered the unworldly aesthete who, stung by the barbarian brutality of the Hun, rouses himself to defend civilised values. In *The First of the Few* Howard plays the Spitfire's inventor, R. J. Mitchell, as a romantic dreamer who comes to understand his destiny as perfecting the weapon that will win the war. He sacrifices his health and happiness in that cause, leaving

1. *The First of the Few*: David Horne, Roland Culver and Leslie Howard –
the debonair idealist (BFI Stills, Posters and Designs).

his practical self, Geoffrey Crisp (David Niven), to lead the squadron
to victory. Donat starred in Carol Reed's *The Young Mr Pitt* (1942) as an
idealistic and progressive democrat, the people's champion and a man
of peace, who also sacrifices his personal welfare to the cause of
overthrowing tyranny. *The Young Mr Pitt* vied with *The First of the Few* as
the most popular film of 1942. At this point, Donat and Howard
incarnated the ideal of, 'the unsullied Englishman, complete and typical,
polished, natural, and easy going, the Englishman's idea of an Englishman'.[13] Their charismatic performances were complemented by Hugh
Williams in *The Day Will Dawn* (1942), transformed from racing tipster
to war hero, and John Clements in Ealing's *Convoy* (1940) and *Ships with
Wings* (1941), who portrayed insouciant playboys redeemed through
gallant self-sacrifice.

These narratives reconfirmed the courage, poise and *sang froid* of a
reinvigorated officer class functioning effectively in its country's hour
of need, but the keynote was sacrifice, even more than leadership. In
the face of the pressure for a more inclusive and democratic repres-

entation of the nation at war, the officer hero, as in Two Cities' *In Which We Serve* (1942) initiated and scripted by Noël Coward, had to be one strand in a cross-class alliance. However, Coward's performance as Captain Kinross – paternal, saintly, infinitely caring about a crew he knows intimately – seems to have been too mannered and patrician for audience taste.[14] John Mills's Commander Taylor in Gainsborough's *We Dive at Dawn* (1943), was more modern and classless. Taylor, alert and determined, with his stubbly beard and crew-necked sweater, is ordinary and down-to-earth, almost the same as his men. *The Times*'s reviewer saw him as, 'by no means one of those carelessly heroic captains who can solve all difficulties with a studied flippancy and an order bellowed down the speaking tube. He is a man of nerves, which he can control, but not altogether conceal.'[15] Mills's more naturalistic performance style constructs Taylor as a tough man of action who has absorbed the democratic ordinariness of the People's War. Taylor is a competent, meritocratic professional, not a breezy amateur.

However, at this point, Taylor was a pre-emergent reconstruction. Neo-conservative British film-makers, conscious of the scale of the social changes taking place, opted for an elegiac mode in which the passing of the gentlemanly ideal could be offered as a profound loss. The most ambitious of these elegies were made by The Archers, bene-fiting from their exceptional creative freedom and high budgets as one of Rank's elite 'Independent Producers'.[16] The Archers' films, part of a Neo-Romantic movement that felt its cultural values were threatened, fused European high culture and a mystical English tradition.[17] *The Life and Death of Colonel Blimp* (1943) deflected its task of celebrating the rise of an efficient 'citizens' army', into a witty but nevertheless deeply serious threnody whose luxuriant visual style lovingly re-creates the vanishing glories of a chivalric European officer caste. Low's caricatured Blimp becomes the engaging and sympathetic Clive Wynne-Candy (Roger Livesey), united with his beloved adversary, the highly principled aristocratic Prussian Theo Kretschmar-Schuldorff (Anton Walbrook), in their detestation of Nazism and their belief in traditional values.

*A Matter of Life and Death* (1946) explicitly celebrated The Archers' ideal man. Debonair Squadron Leader Peter Carter (David Niven) fuses the twin selves of *The First of the Few*, both 'head and hands', artist and warrior, conscious that his world is changing. Carter can be read as a version of the legendary bomber pilot Richard Hillary who had experi-enced a miraculous resurrection after an horrendous crash.[18] Hillary was compared with Rupert Brooke, the ideal synthesis of physical beauty, cultivation and man of action from the previous generation. Carter undergoes a symbolic death just a week before VE day, which places him in a fantasy Arcadia where life and death, the virtues of democratic America and traditional England, can be miraculously united.

The Archers' allegorical elegies had a populist echo in Herbert Wilcox's *I Live in Grosvenor Square* (1945), whose slickly mid-Atlantic style offers a loving tribute to British patrician culture: benevolent to outsiders, self-sacrificing and chivalrous. Major David Bruce (Rex Harrison), a Dunkirk veteran, has to learn to lose gracefully, in politics (to a Labour candidate) and in love to democratic America in the person of Sergeant John Patterson (Dean Jagger), who wins the hand of Lady Patricia Fairfax (Anna Neagle). Harrison, whose persona had been created around portrayals of the effortless aplomb of the English upper classes with their well-bred sexual charm, displays, with great subtlety, the 'moral beauty of good form', even more charismatic in defeat and renunciation than in victory. However, *I Live* was careful to show shared sacrifice – Patterson dies saving the Fairfaxes' tied village – rather than social transformation.

The most celebrated elegy was Two Cities' *The Way to the Stars* (1945), another exercise in Anglo-American harmony. Screenwriter Terence Rattigan had affectionately debunked the gentlemanly ideal in *French without Tears* (1939) and *English without Tears* (1944), but *The Way to the Stars* has a deep sense of change in its undemonstrative commemoration of the *jeunesse dorée*, the Battle of Britain pilots whom the press dubbed the 'knights of the air'. Squadron Leader David Archdale (Michael Redgrave) is another warrior-poet, fearless in action but reflective, the diegetic author of 'For Johnny' with its beguiling mixture of pathos and the clear-eyed acceptance of fate. It becomes the memento that sustains 'Toddy' (Rosamund John), the sensible professional woman who bears him a son, after his death. It is immediately recognised by his replacement, American Johnny Hollis (Douglass Montgomery), the sensitive, pipe-smoking honorary Englishman, who understands that his destiny, as another 'bright star', is to sacrifice himself saving the quintessentially English village of Shepley from destruction. It is another Englishman, Flight Officer Peter Penrose (John Mills) – prosaic, ordinary, lower-middle-class, lacking the dash and flair of his social superiors – who represents change. Penrose emerges as a shy, awkward Everyman, eager to please, unsure of his role. For Penrose the events are an emotional training in the mysterious but accessible code of the gentleman, symbolised by his hesitant but sensitive reading of 'For Johnny', which encourages him to look to the future and to propose marriage to an ordinary girl, Iris (Renée Asherson), also representative of a changing England.

## The Action Hero

Laurence Olivier's famous physicality and dash made him a distinctive English star and his iconic roles as Nelson in *Lady Hamilton* (1941) and the warrior-king *Henry V* (1944) helped present English history as an engaging spectacle.[19] Shakespeare's play had been used in the First World War as a vehicle of patriotic and martial sentiment and Olivier's ambitious adaptation, thoroughly supported by del Giudice, was stylistically innovative and complex.[20] But it was also a patriotic swashbuckler that removed any of the play's criticisms of Henry's actions, presenting him as the ideal monarch whose athletic manliness and ardent love-making contrast with the decadent, febrile effeteness of the French aristocracy, especially the androgynous Dauphin.[21] Even in exhortation, Olivier's mobile camera gradually tracks back so that his speeches climax in a panoramic shot in which Henry is surrounded by his assembled troops excited by his ardour, thereby creating an image of the monarch as the centre of a unified nation. He is a democrat, mingling with the common soldiers on the eve of battle. Only Olivier could encompass a role which demanded virility and dynamism together with a delicate, 'feminine' sensitivity. As both classical actor and international star, he fused a debonair Englishness with the vigour and physicality of American swashbuckling stars, which women found sexually exciting.[22] The film was vigorously promoted as a major cultural achievement.[23]

Olivier's more populist and macho counterpart was Stewart Granger who offered a muscular eroticism. His arrogant, self-assured sensuality had transformed his dull role in *The Man in Grey* (1943) into something dynamic and sexually exciting.[24] Gainsborough, alerted to his potential, enlarged his role in *Fanny by Gaslight* (1944).[25] In *Love Story* (1944) as Kit Firth – engineer, damaged pilot and romantic hero – his athleticism was emphasised by diving off the Cornish cliffs and rowing skiffs bare-chested. In *Madonna of the Seven Moons* (1944) he was given a more exuberantly swashbuckling role as Nino, prince of the Florentine back streets. With shirts unbuttoned to the waist or gorgeously arrayed in his harlequin costume for the carnival, Granger was consciously fashioned as a new Valentino, the thrilling, hot-blooded Latin lover, fought over by two women.[26] Nino's capacity for generous devotion is expressed through his ardent and loyal love for his baffling sweetheart, Maddelena, on to whose dying body he throws a single rose. One of his female fans wrote: 'When Stewart Granger is kissing the heroine (in any film he has been in), I experience a real thrill … If only that could happen to you, something inside me seems to say.'[27] Granger had emerged as a modern matinée idol whose athletic virility contrasted with the usual 'effeminate type of juvenile'.[28]

## The 'Common Man' as Hero

The emergence of the heroic common man was one of the key ideological shifts in wartime. Representations of this figure formed part of the discourse of the People's War, promoted by a number of influential voices including the Ministry of Information.[29] The common man was the man of the future. *Picture Post*'s first issue of 1943 was entitled 'Changing Britain' and contrasted pre-war Britain – 'an old man's world' – with the progressive modern democracy that was being forged.[30] The quality film reviewers saw a new British cinema developing that was allied to these changes. *Millions Like Us* (1943) marked the 'coming-of-age of the British cinema', because of its sympathetic and rounded 'treatment of ordinary working people', no longer caricatured as 'clowns'.[31] However, the figure shows a profound split between a progressive idealism and a conservative stoicism, even in the same film.

## The Progressive Common Man

Michael Balcon, who had taken charge of production at Ealing Studios in 1938, believed in an educative role for cinema in the creation of a more progressive, egalitarian society.[32] Encouraged by MoI policy and the opinions of influential cultural elites, he began the process of replacing the popular gentleman heroes of *Convoy* or *Ships with Wings* with ordinary men as heroes in documentary-dramas.[33] *San Demetrio–London* (1943) faithfully follows the official account of an actual incident, issued as a special pamphlet by the MoI. The officerless crew who rejoin their stricken tanker represent a democratic consensus, a collective heroism. The stress is on calm professionalism and gritty determination.

The outsider –'Yank' Preston (Robert Beatty), arrogant and over-confident – has to learn to become a team player rather than an individualist and integrate with the group. Balcon judged the film to be, 'the best example of the final descent from tinsel which the film industry can make without any misgivings on the part of the shareholders'.[34]

For all its social-democratic impulses, *San Demetrio*'s crew are stoics rather than idealists. Ealing's more progressive films were those scripted by J. B. Priestley. Priestley's popularity, particularly through his BBC broadcasts in 1940–41, made him the wartime voice of a robust socialist populism that emphasised the ability of 'ordinary British folk' to triumph through a form of commonsense rather than revolutionary change.[35] His screenplay *The Foreman Went to France* (1942), again based on an actual incident, looks back to 1940 as the moment of change. Ordinary works foreman Fred Carrick (Clifford Evans), acting on his own initiative in the face of red tape and indifference, proves himself capable of extraordinary feats of daring, courage and resourcefulness in retrieving vital machinery from under the noses of the advancing Germans. Carrick is an actively heroic version of the common man, dynamic, knowledgeable and decisive, often photographed in the Soviet 'heroic style' with low-angle shots to emphasise his size and dominance as he gazes into the distance. Carrick has no political dogma, just puts into practice 'plain good sense'. He combines a robust practicality with (a notably undefined) idealism: 'We've been half asleep … We're waking up at last. It's not too late.' His dynamism is offered as sexually attractive through the rather unconvincing figure of the American (Constance Cummings), and commands the loyalty of the representative working-class figures. *They Came to a City* (1944), adapted from Priestley's own play, offered a visionary account of a reconstructed Britain as a socialist Utopia, rejected by businessmen and landowners, yearned for by the lower-middle-class who cannot make the plunge, but warmly embraced by the working-class ship's stoker, Joe Dinmore, played by John Clements, deliberately cast against type.

Charlie Forbes (Eric Portman), a munitions factory foreman, was another commonsensical idealist in *Millions Like Us* (1943), Launder and Gilliat's attempt to provide a comprehensive drama-documentary about the war effort at home. Forbes, the archetypal blunt Northerner, is a calm, authoritative expert who seems to run the factory without much reference to the bosses. His apparent self-sufficiency and macho arrogance excites the upper-crust Kensingtonian Jennifer Knowles (Anne

Crawford) whose feisty independence and well-bred sexual allure attract the misogynist Charlie. It is an unlikely alliance, both in terms of class and geography, a product of the strange social distortions of wartime, but convincingly built up through a succession of antagonistic encounters in which they are well matched. The key scene comes near the end when they discuss what might happen when the war is over. It is the film's only rural episode, a hilltop prospect, symbolising both a pastoral idyll and their gaze into an uncertain future. Characteristically, Charlie eschews romance for plain speaking: 'The world's roughly made up of two kinds of people – you're one sort and I'm the other. Oh, we're together now there's a war on – we need to be. What's going to happen when it's all over? Shall we go on like this, or shall we slide back? That's what I want to know.' Through Charlie, *Millions Like Us* seems to demand an egalitarian post-war society but without the confidence that it will necessarily happen or could last.

John Baxter had built up a reputation for films which sympathetically depicted working-class life, alternating between broad comedy and social realism. As a Christian Scientist, he believed in the classes 'getting on' rather than struggling for supremacy.[36] His wartime films at British National included *Love on the Dole* (1941), finally bringing Walter Greenwood's famous novel to the screen with Clifford Evans as the sympathetic socialist activist Larry Mead. Like *The Common Touch* (1941), it ends on a note of hope that post-war reconstruction will sweep away inequalities and deprivation. *Let the People Sing* (1942), adapted from a Priestley novel, celebrated the transformative powers of popular entertainment to unite classes against vested interests. In *The Shipbuilders* (1943), Baxter's adaptation characteristically submerges the novel's critique of a class-ridden society and its sense of Clydeside militancy into an argument for a patriotic union of the classes which overrides differences.[37] Clydeside riveter Danny Shields (Morland Graham) remains loyal throughout the miseries of unemployment during the Depression to his ex-employer Leslie Pagan (Clive Brook), with whom he had served in the First World War as his batman. Shields's principal quality is stoicism – when his son dies heroically saving his ship he responds, 'It's not altogether bad news. I'm glad he stuck to his job' – and an obstinate faith that Pagan and his class will rise to the challenge in wartime. The final Soviet-style montage sequence is a hymn, not to the power of the workers, but to the glories of Churchill and the monarchy. In Baxter's eyes, the possibilities of the 'new commonwealth' and the 'rights and freedom of the common man' lie in a traditional beneficent paternalism.

Two Cities' *The Way Ahead* (1944) also celebrates the collective resourcefulness of the common man, the unexceptional 'Tommy Atkins of Today': 'Your husband, my brother, their son, the man next door … He was a civilian, he became a crusader.'[38] The key creative figure behind the film was the left-wing writer Eric Ambler. His documentary, *The New Lot* (1942), which formed the basis for the film, centred entirely on the lower ranks and contained a delightful cameo by Robert Donat which parodies officer heroics. In the feature film the cast was widened to encompass an assortment of civilians drawn from all walks of life, whose differences are submerged in the collective endeavour. However, Rank, the major financier, insisted on a star presence and a key role had to be created for David Niven.[39] Niven plays Lieutenant Jim Perry, a garage mechanic who has worked his way up the ranks, serving as a sergeant at Dunkirk before getting his commission. His sympathetic, sensitive leadership is contrasted with the rule-bound drilling of the old sweat Sergeant-Major Fletcher (William Hartnell). The key moral exhortation about the need for discipline, responsibility and fighting courage to maintain the honourable traditions of the regiment, originally assigned to the sergeant, was given to Perry.[40] Thus Perry emerges as the film's chief focus and Niven plays the role with all the debonair urbanity that constituted his established persona.

It can be seen from this discussion that the representation of the progressive common man was deeply problematic for British film-makers; there was a tendency to slide into a quiescent stoicism or a residual paternalism. Audiences also found the image of the idealist unappealing. Neither *San Demetrio–London* nor *The Foreman Went to France* was successful, except with metropolitan middle-class audiences.[41] *They Came to a City*, patchily distributed and without a West End showcase, seems to have been, like the Boultings' *Thunder Rock* (1942), a *succès d'estime* rather than popular.[42] A recent revisionist account of the 1940s has argued persuasively that it was the public-spirited middle classes that were interested in progressive change, not the working classes.[43] This is corroborated by the popularity of a competing group of films that unreservedly celebrate lower-class stoicism and steadiness.

## The Stoics: The Suburban Paterfamilias and the Boy-next-door

The image of the common man as the suburban paterfamilias had deep cultural roots going back to that English folk hero, the sturdy yeoman.[44] Before the war the paterfamilias was often a comic figure, his pretensions and vanities the butt of music-hall humour and satire. He was depicted as dull and predictable, obsessed with order and routine, and caricatured as 'the pipe-smoking, slipper-loving archetype'.[45] Robertson Hare played this version in Ben Travers's Aldwych farces, including *A Cup of Kindness* (1934).

However, with the onset of war this image could be reconstructed as heroic, transforming 'John Citizen into John Bull'.[46] In Warner-British's *The Briggs Family* (1940), mild-mannered paterfamilias Charlie Briggs (Edward Chapman) – the conventional archetype, with his brush moustache, wing-collar and bow-tie, bowler hat, pipe and shapeless coat – becomes a special constable. British National's *Salute John Citizen* (1942), based on Robert Greenwood's popular 'Mr Bunting' novels, was very similar, but uses actuality footage of the Blitz to make the stoical resilience of George Bunting (Edward Rigby) and his family, and their love of routine, heroic. This reconstructed image offered, 'the association of ordinary courage with extraordinary danger. The average man or woman in a war film had only to behave naturally to become a hero or heroine. We accepted them as dramatic heroes; yet we recognise them as the men and women we met everyday.'[47] Bunting's heroism comes from 'seeing it through', enduring the disruptions as best he can, carrying on stolidly and steadfastly and making sure that the family stays centred and united. His eldest son, Ernest (Jimmy Hanley), converts from pacifism to commitment, joining up to make the world a decent place for his new-born son to live in. This figure of the young man prepared to do his duty and loyally supporting his father or father-in-law became the complementary archetype of stoical ordinariness: the boy-next-door.

*Salute John Citizen*'s popularity was limited by its obviously frugal budget, and uncharismatic central star. It was Noël Coward's two films for Two Cities, *In Which We Serve* and *This Happy Breed* (1944), which gave these figures currency as representative images. *In Which We Serve* offered CPO Hardy (Bernard Miles) and 'Shorty' Blake (John Mills) as admirable images of masculinity, the lower-class complements to Captain Kinross, and audiences responded enthusiastically. *This Happy Breed* dispensed with the problematic upper-middle-class altogether. Coward's earlier account of the interwar years, *Cavalcade* (1933), was rewritten as the fortunes of a London suburban lower-middle-class family, the Gibbons, offered as emblematic of the nation as a whole. Nearly all the action consists of the minutiae of everyday family interaction.

The casting of the charismatic Robert Newton as paterfamilias Frank gave the type greater strength, vigour and virility.[48] Although Frank is loyal and affectionate towards his wife Ethel (Celia Johnson) and occasionally shares the domestic chores, he expects her to be the main workhorse: 'I said to myself, she may not be much to look at, but there's a worker if ever I saw one.' Frank is a 'fond daddy' to his children, not the Victorian patriarch, but tempers his sentiment with exhortation. He is the mouthpiece for Coward's gradualist philosophy where England is a 'nation of gardeners' who have, 'got our own way of settling things'. As suburban sage, Frank connects the family's situation with the public events that punctuate their lives: the Empire Exhibition, the General Strike, George V's death, the abdication, and finally the Munich crisis. Each becomes a moment for Frank to reaffirm what the family stands for: patriotism, loyalty and the ability to see things through, including enough manly 'guts' to stand up to the appeasers and prepare for another war. When son Reg (John Blythe) and father are on opposing sides during the General Strike, Frank's amicable chat mingles pathos and stern advice: 'I belong to a generation of men most of whom aren't here any more. And we all did the same thing for the same reason no matter what we thought about politics … It's up to us ordinary people to keep things steady. And that's your job and just you remember it.' 'Keeping steady' means to accept things as they are and make an enduring marriage. Marriage will settle Reg as it has Sam Ledbitter, whose communist politics were relinquished when he married Vi Gibbons.

Frank's problem is Queenie (Kay Walsh), the 'wayward woman', who, in a plot device straight out of nineteenth-century melodrama, exposes the perils of misplaced sexual desire by running away with her dancing partner. Her 'recovery' creates a decisive moral role for the boy-next-door, Billy Mitchell (John Mills), whose love and loyalty eventually reclaim Queenie and reunite the Gibbons family. Billy is also a surrogate son, after Reg's accidental death, and cements the union of Frank with his neighbour Bob Mitchell (Stanley Holloway), a comrade-in-arms, another of that denuded generation which survived the First World

War and whose one desire is to be settled and 'steady'. Mills's role is almost identical to his earlier one as 'Shorty' Blake. Both roles draw upon the 'cheerful Cockney' stereotype: good-humoured, irrepressibly optimistic, but resistant to change.[49] Coward's deployment of the type, coupled with the sincerity and boyish charm of Mills's performance, invest the figure with a new dignity, charisma and dramatic weight which took it beyond the conventional stereotype and helped make *This Happy Breed* the top-grossing British film of 1944.

## Alternative Masculinities: Fools and Rogues

The Fool and the Rogue are the two basic comic types and have long and complex cultural histories. Enid Welsford argues that their primary function is to act as a safety-valve, freeing audiences from shame about human frailties, weaknesses and failures, removing, through laughter, the moral burden of behaving responsibly and heroically.[50] George Orwell saw that their appeal was to 'your unofficial self, the voice of the belly protesting against the soul'. This 'unofficial self' is cowardly, lazy, preoccupied with looking after Number One, and celebrating bodily pleasures, but is only 'a harmless rebellion against virtue'.[51] As 'unofficial selves', both Fools and Rogues occupy a liminal, licensed space on the margins of society for 'unacceptable' masculine traits, which can include deviousness and incompetence. Their ideological function varies, but they can be empowering for subordinated groups as their resourcefulness, ingenuity and resilience often expose the arbitrariness of social systems.

   In modern British culture, music hall was the training ground for the stars who gave these types their particular and instantly recognisable incarnations. British cinema drew extensively on this pool of talent. During the war the established stars of the 1930s – George Formby, the Crazy Gang, Will Hay and Arthur Lucan – were joined by new ones: Arthur Askey, Tommy Handley, Frank Randle and Tommy Trinder. As Fools or Rogues they battled the pompous, the pretentious, the bullies and the kill-joys; audiences responded, as they always had done, with 'unabashed delight and approbation'.[52] They had the licence to mock constituted authority – barking sergeants, braying majors, stolid policemen and bombastic bureaucrats – in the name of cheery 'common sense'. As populist entertainers, their films were either ignored or ridiculed by the critical establishment and their films did not get a West

End release; but they offered what Mass-Observation thought was vital for public morale in the 'dark days' of the war: comic relief.[53] They represented pleasure, having fun, keeping cheerful, and their individualism was always subordinated to images of community spirit, of pulling together and seeing it through. In the four Flanagan and Allen films directed by John Baxter – *We'll Smile Again* (1942), *Theatre Royal* (1943), *Dreaming* (1944) and *Here Comes the Sun* (1945) – utopian communities were created, even in prison. Through judicious deployment in service comedies or spy farces, these stars emerged as unlikely patriotic heroes.

However, from 1943 onwards, the popularity of these comedians started to decline appreciably. Like the debonair gentlemen, they could not be identified with the social changes that were unfolding. A brief analysis of the three most popular stars – Formby, Askey and Trinder – will indicate the reasons for this decline.[54]

Formby's early war films, *Let George Do It* (1940) and *Spare a Copper* (1941), continued the successful deployment of the star's persona as a well-meaning proletarian Everyman who triumphs over various humiliations to make a genuine contribution to the war effort. The former included a fantasy sequence that was particularly enjoyed where he descends from a balloon to interrupt a Nazi rally and punch Hitler on the nose.[55] Formby's desire to play more serious characters led to a rift with Ealing and a move to Columbia British in 1942.[56] But *Get Cracking* (1943) and *Bell Bottom George* (1943) show few differences. In *Bell Bottom George* his song 'It Serves You Right' creates an instant camaraderie with the other recruits who recognise their own subjection to rules and regulations. George's songs and his effervescent desire for fun and laughter allow him to transcend social barriers, to mix with the admiral, revealed as decent and unstuffy, and to win the heart of the sensible girl who has always recognised the sterling qualities beneath his bumbling shyness.

However, problems arose when attempts were made to align Formby with social change and reconstruction. *He Snoops to Conquer* (1944) teamed town hall odd-job man 'George' with two London reporters and an eccentric inventor (Robertson Hare) to expose a supine and corrupt local council flouting the regulations about post-war planning. Formby's character is much the same, but the film was not popular. A new team of writers was employed for *George in Civvy Street* (1946), which tackled the urgent issues of demobilisation and readjustment to a peacetime existence. 'George' returns to the representative hamlet of Tumbleford and battles against ruthless property sharks to resurrect his father's traditional pub. Some strong songs, including the plangent 'We've Been a Long Time Gone', quite lively slapstick and George's victory resulted only in a decisive box-office failure that ended Formby's screen career. Clearly, 'George' could not be associated successfully with a projected future, but was trapped in his earlier ideological role as a comforter in times of crisis and doubt.[57]

Askey's persona as the diminutive, mischievous, wickedly innocent schoolboy or man-child, was a lower-middle-class version of the Fool. Askey's soubriquet was 'big-hearted Arthur', always irrepressible, trying hard to bring fun and good cheer to those around him.[58] Gainsborough exploited this persona in a series of wartime films beginning with *Band Waggon* (1940), a straight transference to the screen of his popular radio show. In *I Thank You* (1941), 'Arthur' makes light of the tribulations of life in the Underground shelter through a robust cheeriness determined to make the best of things. But in *Back Room Boy* and *King Arthur was a Gentleman* (both 1942), one commentator detected a move away from the 'irresponsible fooling' of his earlier roles towards the Everyman: 'a "little man" with aspirations, trapped by red tape and feelings of inferiority … The writers' idea is to make us feel that we know many humble clerks with immortal longings who would behave in just the same way and to make us laugh with him instead of at his misfortunes.'[59] However, this Everyman is preoccupied with anxieties about manliness.[60] In *King Arthur was a Gentleman*, 'Arthur' is obsessed with the legendary sword which will endow him with the phallic potency he craves, prove his worth to his sweetheart (Evelyn Dall) and to the scoffers in his regiment.

Part of this fear, also present in *Miss London Ltd* (1943), is of attractive, capable but bossy women who have a tendency to try to run things on their own. In *Bees in Paradise* (1944), Askey's final wartime film, fears of feminine authority take on epic proportions. 'Arthur' and his three comrades crash-land on an uncharted island under the rule of the 'monstrous regiment' which demands that men commit suicide two months after their wedding night. Arthur spends his time in flight from the blonde virago, Rouana (Anne Shelton), who looks about to fulfil all his worst castration nightmares. In the process of graphically dramatising male fears and anxieties, *Bees in Paradise* also allows a voice to masculine resentments about 'liberated', powerful women. After 'Arthur' mistakenly plummets through a skylight into the queen's bedchamber, he recovers himself sufficiently to climb on her bed and scold her for presiding over a distaff tyranny in which males cannot win no matter how they behave. However, he is defeated, losing out to the debonair male in the contest for Jani (Jean Kent) and is recaptured by Rouana as he tries to row away from the island.

This was a strangely downbeat image on which to end Askey's wartime roles. 'Arthur', offered as Everyman, is no longer a figure of fun and confidence, but a man in flight. These later films did not recapture the popularity of *I Thank You*. Clearly, cinema-goers preferred Askey in his role as cheerful zany; he was not a figure who could acceptably embody masculine fears about the future.

The comic Rogue was a more problematic type in wartime because of its emphasis on individualism rather than community values. Max Miller, the supreme individualist, made only one wartime film, *Asking for Trouble* (1942), where his engagement to an upper-crust girl cements class alliances and transforms social behaviour: 'I tell you what we're going to do. We're going to sing and dance and I want you to let yourselves go.' Tommy Trinder's stage persona was a brashly confident version of the wisecracking, know-it-all working-class Cockney cock-o'-the-walk.[61] This image was softened on screen, becoming the irrepressible cheery optimist. As Tommy Towers, pierrot entertainer, in British National's *Laugh It Off* (1940), he finds his service niche as the organiser of camp concerts. His first film for Ealing, *Sailors Three* (1940), begins with a cheerful celebration of a sailor's life, but allows the rogue element, the man on the make, to become more pronounced. He tells a Spanish beauty in Granada, 'The name's Taylor, that's T-A-Y-L-O-R. It's pronounced "Success".' His role as national hero comes inadvertently. When he wakes up with a terrible hangover on board a German battleship, his means of saving his own skin is to use his ready wits to circumvent the blundering enemy whose ship is captured by the British.

Balcon may have been uncomfortable at this individualism and both *The Foreman Went to France* (1942) and *The Bells Go Down* (1943) carefully subordinate Trinder's role to communal demands. In the former, his mildly insubordinate private rattles around northern France with a truck-load of curry powder to liven up the major's suppers. Trinder has a muted role, with few wisecracks and only one, chaste, song, delivered to the 'nursery' which has been accumulated in the back of the truck. In *The Bells Go Down*, his lovable East End rogue, Tommy Turk, dies heroically when he tries to save the local hospital. Revealingly, the narrative had established no definite role for Tommy once the war has ended. The future is left to the respectable lower-middle-class professional, Ted Robbins (James Mason), now settled emotionally by the death of his rival.

*The Bells Go Down* symbolically expelled the Rogue from Ealing's vision of the future and his final two films were set in the past. Cavalcanti's celebration of music hall, *Champagne Charlie* (1944), offered an apposite role for Trinder as George Laybourne, the greatest exponent of the music-hall 'swell'. The swell was the knowing working-class dandy, a parody and appropriation of gentility and masculine display which celebrated proletarian success.[62] However, Laybourne's spirited stage combats with the Great Vance (Stanley Holloway) sit oddly with his off-stage role as an innocent Everyman who lacks confidence and is unsure of his role. The film draws the teeth of the swell, subordinating the image to a fantasy of community presided over by a beneficent aristocracy. This was probably the result of Balcon's reluctance to endorse an image of a self-assured and devil-may-care working-class masculinity; the final screenplay is more anodyne than an earlier script which emphasised working-class deprivation and drew attention to the seditious messages of some of Laybourne's songs.[63] This sanitised, middle-class image of the music hall gained critical approval, but failed to attract working-class audiences. *Fiddlers Three* (1944) had a contrived script, lacklustre décor and leaden direction by a Harry Watt. Within its laboured fantasy of Ancient Rome, the only gem is Trinder's parody of Carmen Miranda, transferred from his Palladium act, involving some highly suggestive byplay with the lecherous Nero, a camp performance by Francis L. Sullivan. *Fiddlers Three* was uneasy and unsure about what would happen once the war is over. Tommy's song 'You Never Can Tell' is, Nero remarks, 'as prophecy somewhat defeatist'.

## The Byronic Male

Nineteenth-century popular melodrama had created two male archetypes, the virtuous hero and the Gothic villain.[64] The Gothic villain was a strikingly handsome, tall, dark and pale misogynist who, exuding an unfathomable mysteriousness, had more energy, daring and charisma than his morally pure but lacklustre opponent. The Byronic male was a development of the type, drawing upon Shakespeare's hero-villains and European Romanticism's cult of the 'fatal man'.[65] The Byronic male embodies contradictory qualities. He is lonely, melancholy, corrupted by a secret guilt, but retains traces of a noble spirit and the ability to inspire

2. *The Man in Grey*: James Mason – the Byronic male: sex and sadism (BFI Stills, Posters and Designs. By courtesy of Carlton International).

love.[66] He embodies an unfettered aristocratic sexual and social power that is cruel and sadistic, but also fascinating and erotic.

The type's eruption into wartime British cinema resulted from the assessment of Mark Ostrer, studio head at Gainsborough, that by the end of 1942 audiences wanted fantasy and escape rather than realism and exhortation.[67] Executive producer Edward Black, whose background was in showmanship, was responsible for implementing this policy, aided by writer-producer R. J. Minney who thought 'blood and thunder' melodrama popular entertainment *par excellence*.[68] Unlike Tod Slaughter's old-fashioned barnstormers, Gainsborough's costume melodramas were modern and sophisticated, 'the writing is sober, the acting restrained' and the cinematography polished.[69] Their stylish spectacle offered a highly charged emotional experience in which women cinema-goers were encouraged to identify with the female protagonists and their compulsive attraction to ruthless and sexy male aristocrats.[70] The adaptation of *The Man in Grey* (1943) changed the novel's well-meaning and honourable Marquis of Rohan into a Byronic figure played by James Mason. Rohan is the unreformed Regency aristocrat concerned only with his own appetites and the ruthless preservation of his rank and title. His addiction to violent pleasure – duelling, dog-fighting and whipping – finds its greatest piquancy in possessing a woman, Hester (Margaret Lockwood), his wife's companion, as ruthless as himself: 'You take what you want and to the devil with the consequences. So do I.' Approaching the trembling Clarissa (Phyllis Calvert) on their wedding night, or in the [in]famous final scene where he advances towards Hester riding crop in hand to exact terrible vengeance for the dishonour of the Rohan name, he represents the fearful, forbidden but overpowering object of female desire, incarnating an '"unspeakable" dark sexuality'.[71] One woman spectator found the film, 'enjoyable and stimulating. At night I kept seeing the terrifying look on James Mason's face as he beat Hester to death. I could not get it out of my dreams for some time.'[72] As *Picturegoer*'s leader writer remarked, Mason's appeal lay in attracting sympathy for such a villain, the strong man who is violent but also vulnerable.[73]

*The Man in Grey* established Mason as the new matinée idol and Gainsborough restructured their production policy to concentrate on costume dramas in which Mason could repeat his performance.[74] In the adaptation of Michael Sadleir's popular novel *Fanny by Gaslight* (1944), directed with style and feeling by Anthony Asquith, Mason played the dark and unnaturally pallid Gerry Manderstoke, a man with brooding hatreds and a 'savage gleam' in his eyes who ruthlessly pursues a life of dissipation and sensuality. Manderstoke is the Regency rake still at large in mid-Victorian society. In *The Wicked Lady* (1945), Mason appeared as the daring, sexually voracious highwayman, 'Captain' Jerry Jackson. As the masked 'gentleman of the road', Jackson is invested with all the allure of the romantic swashbuckling outlaw, sensual, swaggering and irrepressible, most obviously displayed in his grandstanding defiance to the assembled crowd at Tyburn.

Despite the huge success of *The Wicked Lady*, audiences did not respond as strongly to Mason in that role; they preferred him as the sadistic but vulnerable hero of the Boxes' *The Seventh Veil* (1945) which takes place in a timelessly opulent world of upper-class artistic refinement.[75] Nicholas (Mason), is again dark, pale, brooding and cruel, he even has a Byronic limp. But his loneliness, melancholia and misogyny result from his deep psychological wounding by his beautiful but faithless mother whose portrait dominates the main room of his elegant Belgravia home. Nicholas's cruelty and his desire to dominate his hapless ward Francesca (Ann Todd) arise from this emotional damage, which could be easily linked with war trauma. In the film's highly contrived dénouement, her choice of Nicholas is based on a sense of the nobility that he has revealed through his own piano playing. The film's appeal came from this combination of danger, suffering and pathos.

## Damaged Men and Criminals

Hints about psychological damage pervaded Eric Portman's roles after his rise to stardom as the result of his performance as the Byronic Nazi in *49th Parallel*. In *We Dive at Dawn* (1943), his Leading Seaman Hobson is a troubled man, truculent, cynical, acerbic, almost misanthropic, referred to as someone who has 'made a mess of his life'. Hobson is a misfit on the verge of marital break-up, but in this story he can be made whole by heroic action. No such solution is offered in The Archers' *A Canterbury Tale* (1944). Portman's Thomas Colpepper is both the voice of the film's mystical sense of Englishness and the demented 'glue man', venting his sexual frustrations, born of contempt and revulsion, on the local women. In the original script he slashes girls' dresses with a knife.[76]

These hints about psychological and social damage were developed in RKO's *Great Day* (1945) which introduced the figure of the maladjusted veteran unable to integrate socially or emotionally into civilian society. Portman played John Ellis, an ex-First World War officer who cannot recapture the importance and fulfilment of his wartime role in peacetime, nor come to terms with his diminution in status and esteem.[77] When not gazing at the flight of the windhover, which symbolises his longings for space and freedom, Ellis fans his withering ego by acting the role of 'hail fellow' county squire while his wife Liz (Flora Robson) scrimps and saves, desperate to maintain the fiction of their gentility. Ellis's bar-fly bonhomie proves to be his undoing when he is caught stealing a ten-shilling note to buy his own round. The scene is beautifully photographed by Erwin Hillier, using low-angles, mirror images and shots through distorting bottles, so that Ellis appears to drift somnambulistically, under a stronger compulsion than his conscious will, towards his humiliation, thereby retaining the viewer's sympathy. His subsequent arrest forces him to articulate the way in which he has been an emotional stranger to his wife and daughter, trying desperately to act out what he has been brought up to believe is the male role, living a fiction whose impossible demands have finally been exposed: 'I was never frightened in war but I was frightened in peace ... petrified at the thought of a wife being dependent on me and then a child.' In the scene which follows, also evocatively beautiful, he shambles off towards a pool where his reflected image, fractured by swirls and ripples, symbolically mirrors his broken identity. But, in a major departure from Lesley Storm's play, his suicide is forestalled by his daughter whose strength, together with her mother's competence and refusal to give in, pull Ellis together. The family unit is restored and he is reintegrated into the community celebrating its 'great day'.

Portman's role presaged an important cycle of post-war films, as did Stewart Granger's spiv, Ted Purvis, in *Waterloo Road*. The spiv was the dark version of the Rogue, the symbol of the licentiousness and criminality released in wartime, an image of that 'other war', conducted by amoral opportunists and shirkers, that threatened the values of order and community. Purvis uses the considerable income from his ownership of an amusement arcade to fashion himself as the lower-class dandy. His soft trilby set at a rakish angle, smart suit with its padded shoulders and the loud bow-tie, were the conventional image of the type, an appropriation of the glamorous style of the Hollywood gangster.[78] Purvis's war effort, as summed up by his discarded mistress Toni (Jean Kent), consists of jitterbugging, dog racing and going to the cinema, 'to get a few hints from Victor Mature' about love-making. But the film retains a sneaking admiration for the spiv in its half-affectionate caricature and Granger's engagingly flamboyant performance. The threat the spiv posed had not yet crystallised and he could be defeated by John Mills playing the decent ordinary soldier Jim Coulter.

By the end of the war Mills had emerged as the new Everyman, a masculine ideal of stoicism, steadiness and modest hopes for the future. Unlike the Fool, he could be associated with gradual change. It was not a radical new image of masculinity, but a renegotiation of the debonair ideal, a democratised version of the same values. But his triumph was not absolute. It had to compete with the charisma of the fading debonairs, with Mason's erotic aristocrats, Portman's tormented misfits and Granger's spiv and action men, all of which gave clear indications of other needs and desires. Wartime culture proves to have been more heterogeneous than is often argued.[79] In the chapters that follow I shall trace the fluctuations of these types over the next quarter century.

# 2

# The Twilight of the English Gentleman

As I have shown, the hegemony of the debonair gentleman was challenged by the emergence of the ordinary man as hero, but the image retained considerable currency with audiences through its tragic romanticism. In the post-war period two important producers, Herbert Wilcox and Alexander Korda, acted as if no changes had occurred in films that were clearly residual. But a more powerful strand led by Michael Balcon tried to reconstruct the figure as a meritocratic professional that could absorb the gritty stoicism of the People's War but within the ethical framework of middle-class endeavour. The persistence of the gentlemanly ideal was demonstrated by the popularity of Dirk Bogarde and Kenneth More, but they too were overtaken by the pressure from more radical reworkings of the type.

## Plus ça change: Wilcox and Korda

The success of *I Live in Grosvenor Square* (1945) gave Wilcox the confidence to produce further films in what became the 'London' series. All five films used a highly polished but undemanding visual style, economically achieved by a small, self-contained team of creative personnel that gave a consistent look and address.[1] *Piccadilly Incident* (1946) was simply a delayed war film, another passionate central romance larded with tragedy, but with Michael Wilding replacing Rex Harrison as the chivalrous and unprejudiced aristocrat, Captain Alan Pearson. Tall, slender and broad-shouldered, Wilding produced a less patrician incarnation of the debonair archetype, while retaining its soft-spoken charm and romantic ardour. Although his character was thought to be clichéd, the new lead displayed, 'the looks and bearing of Lord Louis Mountbatten ... like Leslie Howard, Wilding possesses that rare quality labelled charm'.[2] The film's huge popularity suggested that Wilding continued Howard's appealing synthesis of style and patriotic fervour.

*The Courtneys of Curzon Street* (1947) was more confident and ambitious, rewriting the history of the first half of the twentieth century, not as the story of suburban stoicism, but as the idealised union of gentleman-democrat Sir Edward Courtney (Wilding) and the independent and energetic working-class Kate O'Halloran (Anna Neagle), which eventually triumphs over prejudice and adversity. Their marriage complements Courtney's traditional role as warrior hero, defender of homeland and empire, arrayed in a series of becoming uniforms which, as always, flatter the height and slender legs of the perfected aristocratic male body.[3] Courtney's ideals are handed down to his son, Edward – when they meet they recite Rupert Brooke together – and their lives emphasise sacrifice rather than privilege or glory: Edward is killed on imperial service. As the film circles back to another New Year's Eve, 1945, the Courtneys unhesitatingly welcome their grandson Edward, just returned from active service, and his fiancée Pam, a factory worker. The only impediment to their wedding might be her parents' inverted snobbery. Toasting their fortieth wedding anniversary, Edward asks his grandparents, 'to go on being, well, just as they are for the next forty years'. The message is nicely hesitant, but clear and reassuring: things have changed, but they are just the same.

Critics dismissed Wilcox's 'curious piece[s] of nobbery' as a Hollywood fantasy.[4] Unrepentant, Wilcox argued that his films fulfilled a social need for, 'open pictures, happy unclouded pictures. We do not want sadism, abnormality and psychoanalysis. That is no good for the average audience – they don't understand it and in most cases don't want it.'[5] In a brilliant manoeuvre, the final two films of the series, *Spring in Park Lane* (1948) and *Maytime in Mayfair* (1949), audaciously resurrected the epitome of the 'unclouded' debonair style, the Man About Town, with all its, 'charm, sense of humour, suavity and sex appeal'.[6] These upper-class romantic light comedies gave Wilding a much more active and energetic role.

*Spring in Park Lane* remade *Come Out of the Pantry* (1935), Wilcox's vehicle for the pre-war embodiment of West End elegance, Jack Buchanan. Wilding demonstrated the same lightness of touch and graceful movements as the urbane, impeccably groomed, perfectly attired metropolitan sophisticate able to overcome any obstacle in an easy-going manner.[7] As Lord Richard, the aristocrat-in-hiding, Wilding moves between upstairs and downstairs, street-wise and shrewd as well as romantically charming. His decision to boogie on his night off with Judy (Anna Neagle) at the Camden *palais de danse* acts as a populist equivalent to their 'dream dance' sequence which also emphasised Wilding's physical strength and grace of movement. Nicholas Phipps's witty and fast-paced script provided Lord Richard with an ever-ready riposte, including an excuse for his well-known 'Cockney act' as he dispatches the spiv art forger Streaky Bacon (Nigel Patrick) with a deft descent into the demotic: 'Scarper! Keep walking. Go on will yer? I'll 'ave yew lumbered.' Lord Richard is thus an attractively liminal figure who can move effortlessly between classes, at home in both. His fluid, self-adjusting masculinity is carefully contrasted with the antiquated snobbery of his elder brother, the Marquis of Borechester, and the superficial *arriviste*, Basil Maitland (Peter Graves). These contrasts make Wilding appear charming, gracious, quick-witted and attractive without being mannered, foppish, vulgar or anachronistic. He becomes a fitting partner for Anna Neagle's new incarnation as the independent pro-fessional woman.

*Spring in Park Lane* was the most popular British film of its release year, revealing widely shared longings for a world of lavish spectacle and 'unclouded' fantasies of romance, pleasure and success in a drab 'austerity' world. One of *Picturegoer*'s readers wrote in to comment: 'I should think the majority of picturegoers would rather forget rationing and relax in supplies of luxury and fantasy.'[8] Such 'supplies' were even more abundant in *Maytime in Mayfair*, the first 'London' film to be made in colour. Wilding plays another Man About Town, Michael Gore-Brown, who inherits a dress-shop run by the competently professional Eileen (Neagle) whom he rescues from the clutches of the foppish D'Arcy Davenport (Graves), head of a rival firm, and the repeated *faux pas* of his slow-witted partner Sir Henry Hazelrigg (Nicholas Phipps), the 'silly ass'. The skimpy narrative fails to provide a reason to be interested in the affairs of the *beau monde* other than as sheer romantic spectacle, a virtual procession of costumes and dance numbers. It does not provide any fantasies of class mobility, or aristocrats resuming their rightful place in the scheme of things. Lacking that resonance, *Maytime in Mayfair* was less successful than *Spring in Park Lane*, and indicated the exhaustion of the cycle and with it the unmodernised construction of the Man About Town. Wilcox's romantic comedy *Into the Blue* (1951), with Wilding as the debonair gentleman-on-the-run, failed at the box-office, as did Wilcox's two Errol Flynn–Anna Neagle sub-Novello fantasies, *Lilacs in the Spring* (1954), and *King's Rhapsody* (1955) with its creaking Ruritania.

The other powerful producer who continued to deploy the resonance of the debonair ideal was Alexander Korda, 'a confirmed Anglophile' who saw the gentleman as the apex of civilised masculinity.[9] Korda preferred to use the past to celebrate the national character, because an historical setting afforded most opportunity for his characteristic visual style, sophisticated and pictorially beautiful, with lavish settings, décor and costumes. Korda observed that, 'men, in particular, look ten times handsomer in the more colourful clothes of other ages'.[10] Korda's reconstituted London Films, buoyed up by a massive government loan, had the financial and cultural space to mount expensive cosmopolitan and cultivated films such as *An Ideal Husband* (1948), which exploited a middlebrow taste for Wilde's comedies. It was Michael Wilding's first outing as the fashionable Man About Town, the affably capable Viscount Goring. Elsewhere, Korda's resurrections of a charismatic aristocracy were often maladroit. His eclectic use of assorted creative personnel resulted in an unevenness of style and address in *Anna Karenina* (1948), and also in *Bonnie Prince Charlie* (1948) where David Niven's soft-spoken urbanity was not equal to the part of the dynamic Highland *chevalier*. Neither film was popular.

*The Elusive Pimpernel* (1950) was Korda's third reworking of Baroness Orczy's fantasy of aristocratic courage and cleverness. Sir Percy Blakeney/the Scarlet Pimpernel is man of action and dandy, a blend of masculine and feminine characteristics.[11] But the post-war version was riven by the creative clash between Korda's partner Samuel Goldwyn, who wanted a straight Hollywood-style remake, and Michael Powell's increasingly uncompromising desire to make a European *Gestamkunst-werk*, which elevated style over plot and character. The resulting film's knowing archness and visual pyrotechnics often displace rather than enhance Niven's performance, which could not recapture the confident brio of Leslie Howard. Anthony Steel fared no better in *Storm Over the Nile* (1955), a CinemaScope version of *The Four Feathers* (1939), which re-used existing location footage and R. C. Sherriff's screenplay. Pre-war audiences found Harry Faversham's purgatorial journey from cowardice to heroism – towards an understanding of 'a tradition, a code which we must obey even if we don't believe in it' – inspiring. But by 1955 reviewers were wondering, 'what will the younger generation used to the toughness of a film like *Mr Roberts* think of these old-fashioned heroics?'[12] The answer came in the film's box-office failure.

## The Debonair Aesthete: Dirk Bogarde

One way in which the gentleman could be preserved was as the romantically tragic Englishman. Dirk Bogarde's appeal to women was based on a strong continuity with the beautiful losers of the wartime elegies. His slim frame and sensitive looks reminded audiences of Leslie Howard or Ivor Novello. *Picturegoer*'s Donovan Pedelty thought Bogarde was a star for one reason: 'He looks romantic. His attitude suggests there is no hope of happiness in it. He *provokes* us into *wanting* that contradictory prediction to be wrong.'[13] These qualities are to the fore in his early roles: as the neurotic young pianist in the 'Alien Corn' episode of *Quartet* (1948); the romantic artist hero of *So Long at the Fair* (1950); and his embodiment of Guy Gibson in Mayflower's *Appointment in London* (1953). His performance was diametrically opposed to Richard Todd's later incarnation; Bogarde emphasised youth, combat fatigue, neurasthenia and romantic vulnerability. Once the 'Doctor' films had made him a popular star as the modern Everyman (see Chapter 5), Bogarde was pressed into a series of debonair roles. In Powell and Pressburger's *Ill Met by Moonlight* (1957), he played Leigh Fermor/Philedem as the epitome of the insouciant English gentleman amateur. Betty Box's *Campbell's Kingdom* (1957) tried to combine the appeal of the tough action thriller with a wistful romanticism, with Bogarde as a shy, bookish weakling, harbouring an 'incurable' disease, reluctantly fighting for his inheritance amid the magnificent scenery of the Canadian Rockies. Bogarde was the most popular male star for his performance with *Picturegoer*'s readers, indicating that his appeal was to women rather than to men.[14]

Typically, Bogarde's major war film, *The Wind Cannot Read* (1958), included hardly any action and was marketed for women as, 'love that was forbidden but could not be denied', with Bogarde in his 'greatest romantic role'.[15] Bogarde played a sensitive and thoughtful pilot whose war largely consists of falling in love with his beautiful language tutor (Yoko Tani) and wandering round tourist India with her. Her fatal illness obviates the need to deal with problems of miscegenation, so their love story can sustain a note of high romance throughout, suffused by a poetic wistfulness rather than overt eroticism. One reviewer thought Bogarde offered, 'the wry smile, the imperceptibly quivering stiff upper lip, the spaniel pathos in the eyes. He is still prowling the screen, demanding mother love from his millions of female fans.'[16] If these traits irritated the critics, they were highly effective. Bogarde was again *Picturegoer*'s readers' first choice in 1959, the last year in which a star poll was taken.[17]

He came second for his revival of one of Ronald Colman's great tragic roles, Sydney Carton, in Box's *A Tale of Two Cities* (1958). The role of the wan, wistful, dissipated upper-class wastrel, whose hopeless love for Lucie Manette (Dorothy Tutin) can express itself only in the one great gesture of sacrifice, was an obvious choice. Most reviewers thought that Bogarde did not attempt the high heroic style of Colman, showing a more dejected, 'quizzical and reserved', ironic anti-hero.[18] This was an indication that the debonair ideal had lost its capacity to be inspiring, but still retained an appeal for women as a solely tragic figure, although *The Doctor's Dilemma* (1959) was too high art for his fans.

## The Meritocratic Professional Officer

Bogarde's appeal as the tragic gentleman was based on a residual feminine taste, one that was largely excluded from what became the dominant image of 1950s masculinity, the meritocratic professional officer.[19] As noted, the type had emerged in wartime in John Mills's Commander Taylor in *We Dive at Dawn*. This construction was extended in Ealing's *Scott of the Antarctic* (1948) where Mills starred as Captain Scott. Scott was one of the most famous of the British imperial figures who became moral exemplars and role models, the paradigm case of the heroic explorer whose courage, indomitability and martyrdom created a secular saint around whose memory a cult could be created.[20] Ealing's film became another moment of veneration. Balcon was determined, despite the difficulties and expense it would entail, that 'this great story' would form a centrepiece in the studio's 'projection of the true Briton to the world'.[21] As the continuation of Ealing's wartime 'semi-documentaries', *Scott* was a meticulously accurate reconstruction right down to the printing of the wrappers round the bars of chocolate taken by the expedition.[22] The use of colour was thematic rather than spectacular, contrasting the euphoria of the early scenes with the virtually colourless ones showing the bleak return from the Pole.[23] The cast, including John Mills, was chosen because of a supposedly strong physical resemblance to the originals.

For all its authenticity, Scott is offered as the exemplary and inspirational leader of the legend, drawing heavily on his own *Journals*. He is disciplined and indomitable, exuding sober middle-class virtues rather than aristocratic style. He retains elements of the inspired amateur who feels that an Englishman should be first to the Pole – not that 'damned unsporting' Norwegian, Amundsen – but his expedition is also an efficiently organised scientific mission. Above all, it is a supreme test of the close-knit disciplined male group, the key image of Ealing at war. Though occasionally boisterous, indulging in a bit of 'horse play' or impromptu soccer, at key moments the accent falls on restraint and control, the conscious suppression, not of emotion, but of its inappropriate expression and utterance. The film gives enormous emphasis to unspoken masculine accord, to a spareness of words and dialogue. When Scott informs Lieutenant 'Teddy' Evans (Kenneth More) of his decision not to include him in the final party, few words are uttered so the dramatic weight falls on an extended close-up of Teddy's face suppressing tears. This is followed by a lengthy point-of-view shot as he gazes after the disappearing figures in the chosen group. The male figures have absorbed, but in an undemonstrative, 'manly' way, the 'feminine' emotions of loss and disappointment as they, like the women on the quayside, watch their loved companions depart.[24] The chosen group grow ever closer as they have to accept disappointment, defeat and the knowledge of their certain death. In the final frostbitten days the survivors are shown, 'almost as if telepathically united'.[25] Oates's 'magnificent gesture', itself the stuff of legend, is shown as immediately understood and sanctioned by Scott who restrains Bowers from pursuit. Scott's final voice-over, drawing on some of the most famous passages from his *Journals*, provides an elevated tribute to his 'gallant companions' as the tent becomes their shrine.

As an inspiring national saga, *Scott* was vigorously promoted, and was chosen for the (third) Royal Command Performance. Any revisionist account of the 'Scott myth' was more than a generation away and reviewers were either fulsome in their praise or disappointed that *Scott* was not more heroic. It was almost uniformly read as reinvigorating a wounded national psyche: 'at a time when other races speak disparagingly of our "crumbling Empire" and our "lack of spirit". It should make those who have listened too closely to such talk believe afresh that ours is the finest breed of men on earth. And so it is.'[26] Audiences responded too: *Scott* was a box-office success.[27] This indicates that as well as making a clear bid for the hegemony of the professional middle-class, it mobilised popular nationalism, reaffirming national greatness in a period of disquiet, and was able to allay post-war fears of change, bewilderment and a possible sense of Britain's diminishing role as a world power.

However, the ability of imperial stories to function in this way became increasingly problematic. It was the cycle of war films, from around 1950 onwards, that replaced imperialism as the source for epic and inspiring stories about British male endeavour and the national character. Although the earlier films in the cycle use debonair heroes – *Landfall* (1949, Michael Denison) and *Appointment with Venus* (1951, David Niven) – the dominant successes deploy the Scott paradigm. Their visual mode was a subdued, neutral realism, with a preference for location shooting and an emphasis on quotidian detail as a means of authentication. As in *Scott*, masculine comradeship is the dominant relationship, virtually excluding women altogether. Like *Scott* they marginalise working-class characters who return to their subordinate pre-war screen roles as humorists, grumblers (but with hearts of gold) and stooges.[28] The middle-class officers therefore become the admirable heroes whose hegemony is justified by their combination of intellect and practicality.[29]

The masculine bonding at the heart of these films is shown primarily through the induction of the young new recruit, always middle-class, into the fighting team, a process which becomes his passage into manhood. The new recruit, the principal figure for audience identification, was the 'eternal cadet': 'grown-up boys, trusting, vulnerable, decently worried and ready aye ready … [in whom] … obedience and manliness, loyalty and maturity are perfectly compatible', and who defer to the authority of the older 'stern father' figure.[30] It was a tribute to Mills's flexible persona that he could play both roles: officer-'father' in *Morning Departure* (1950) and *Above Us the Waves* (1955), eager cadet in *The Colditz Story* (1955) opposite Eric Portman as the stern but loving 'father'. The dominant star, Jack Hawkins, played the 'father' to various cadets, John Gregson in *Angels One Five* (1952), Alec Guinness in *The Malta Story* (1953), and Donald Sinden in Ealing's *The Cruel Sea* (1953).

3. *The Cruel Sea*. Donald Sinden and Jack Hawkins – the eager cadet and the stern father (BFI Stills, Posters and Designs. By courtesy of Canal +Image UK).

*The Cruel Sea* contains Hawkins's defining performance, as Lieutenant-Commander Ericson, a tough, seasoned ex-Merchant Navy professional who has to assume the burden of war's cruelty and apparent futility. In the film's most memorable scene, always cited in reviews, Hawkins's scarcely mobile face sheds silent tears at the loss of the drifting British merchant seamen, blown up by his decision to depth-charge a suspected submarine. This overt display of masculine emotion was strong enough to worry the puritanical Balcon.[31] But it serves to strengthen the admiration of the cadet, Lieutenant Lockhart (Sinden), who recognises it as the expression of a vulnerable and sensitive humanity. After Ericson collapses from exhaustion, strain and drink, Lockhart puts him tenderly and lovingly to bed. The war film is a genre which can foreground intense relationships between men, providing 'a licensed space for the otherwise inexpressible'.[32] The love of Ericson and Lockhart, expressed through looks and glances not overt display, allows both to acknowledge and overcome the negative emotions of fear and doubt amid the annihilating rigours of the North Atlantic campaign. It softens and controls Ericson's penchant to become brooding and obsessive, a latter-day Captain Ahab, and is the force which facilitates Lockhart's growing maturity as he gradually understands the difficulties of, and yet the necessity for, emotional discipline.

The centrality of the male bond requires the virtual exclusion of women. Eric Ambler's screenplay lacks the waspish misogyny of Monsarrat's novel, but also removes Ericson's wife. Women are most often seen as a threat – they may be over-anxious wives or good-time girls – but Julie Hallam (Virginia McKenna), the belle of Operations, is the preferred figure because she is engaged on war work as well as being chaste and tolerant of male friendship. In the one romantic scene with Lockhart, her role is to listen thoughtfully to the harrowing account of his uncontrollable crying at the loss of the *Compass Rose*. Not only does Julie, clearly positioned as a indication of how women in the audience should respond, accept and approve of his grief, she also understands that his deepest emotions and loyalties must be to Ericson, with whom he wants to finish the war. He tells her they are like 'David and Jonathan. Does it sound silly? ... It's about the only personal relationship war allows you.' Given biblical sanction, the homosocial bond of comradeship displaces the usual centrality of heterosexual coupling.[33]

Lockhart has also been clearly established as the most deserving cadet, the one who can become a true image of his 'father'. The working-class ex-used car salesman First Lieutenant Bennett (Stanley Baker) is the first to be rejected. His essential vulgarity takes the form of a coarse, authoritarian bullying and his boorish attitudes grate on the more refined sensibilities of the middle-class officers. When he returns, drunk, from his shore leave, he is shown framed in the doorway, the gross outsider, as seen from the point-of-view of the sober middle-class group. He succumbs to stomach cramps, which may be psychosomatic, an indication of the basic unreliability of the uppity lower orders. Lieutenant Ferraby (John Stratton) is the oversensitive neurasthenic, becoming a long-term hospitalised psychiatric case after the sinking of the *Compass Rose*. He lacks the moral fibre of the true cadet, too dependent on his wife's proximity and therefore unable to draw strength from the male group. Lieutenant Morell (Denholm Elliott), the most upper-middle-class, displays a careless and barbed insouciance which hides nagging doubts about his wife's fidelity. Like Lieutenant Manson (Nigel Patrick) in *Morning Departure* (1950), the debonair gentleman is fundamentally unfitted for the rigours of modern warfare and falls by the wayside. Lockhart's triumph is that of ordinary, unexceptionable middle-class decency, capable of mastering technology, but which has to be moulded and stiffened by the rigours of a long campaign under the watchful eye of Ericson. In a society that, as will be shown, had become preoccupied with the disaffected working-class young man (the 'delinquent'), the cadet was being offered, by a number of British producers, as the responsible figure of young manhood with whom male adolescents should identify. In the process they were being powerfully socialised into a middle-class ideology of deference, respect for their parents and their country's institutions and achievements. In reproducing the masculinity of the officer 'father', the cadet represented a powerful generational continuity of masculine style and values.

*The Cruel Sea* was the top-grossing film of 1953. One commentator argued that Hawkins appealed to the whole family: 'Father likes him because he's a man's man, so level-headed, just like father fancies himself to be; mother likes him because he's dependable and at the same time quietly romantic; daughter likes him for much the same reason as mother, and especially for his good looks; son likes him because he's the born-leader type, virile and tough.'[34] Another celebrated that 'rocky frame [which] has become a national institution, a kind of male Britannia'.[35] As the 'male Britannia', an appropriately re-gendered national icon, Hawkins embodied what Angus Calder has defined as the 'myth of the Blitz', a compensatory myth that celebrated the 'moral preeminence' of the national character as a unified entity.[36] As a hostile commentator argued, Hawkins and the other war heroes inhabited 'an *imaginary present* in which we can go on enjoying our finest hours … The H-bomb looms ahead and we daren't look at it so we creep back to the lacerating comfort of "last time" … [where] subject, film-maker and audience were at one.'[37] War films were one genre where audiences showed a very marked preference for British rather than American pictures.[38] Despite their middle-class bias, they succeeded across class divides. A Rank audience survey showed that the films actually appealed more strongly to lower-income groups through their display of guts and toughness.[39]

This powerful hegemonic form of masculinity dominated the mid-1950s, but the Hawkins synthesis of the modern no-nonsense professional and the traditional British hero, the saintly father and the virile tough guy, became increasingly difficult to sustain. The puritanical rigidity of the stiff upper lip became evident in ABPC's *The Dam Busters* (1955) in which Richard Todd's Guy Gibson showed a further development into a near instrumentality, starting to lose both the cadet's boyish charm and the father's moral centrality. When we see a touch of 'horse play' from his squadron, Gibson is not involved and assures his senior officer that he will break it up and get the men to bed. We never see his wife, nor does the screenplay acknowledge that he was even married. His one moment of emotion, at the death of his dog 'Nigger', is quickly contained. Gibson, like the bomb's inventor Barnes Wallis (Michael Redgrave), is an obsessive, dedicated solely to the success of this one mission. Both men are a world away from the dreamy, sporting, inspired amateurism of Leslie Howard and David Niven in *The First of the Few* (1942) and showed the distance which had been travelled. The tension in their relationship, between the necessity to win and its human cost, is left unresolved. This was symptomatic of the forces which were threatening to destabilise the moral certainties of the war film and its version of the hero. But one star managed to postpone its demise: Kenneth More.

## The Edwardian Hero Revived: Kenneth More

More's success was based on a complex synthesis of the debonair ideal with a contemporary blokeishness which shed all the unacceptable class elements. More was not tall, handsome or elegant enough to be a classical English leading man. His face and physique had a pugnacious quality which suggested a robust well-being and confidence, always active and outgoing rather than thoughtful or introspective, 'a sense of rugged spiritual health'.[40] More's emergence as a popular star came with the role of Ambrose Claverhouse in *Genevieve* (1953) which blended Ealingesque eccentricity with fashionable American marital comedy. It celebrated the Edwardian age through its vintage car rally, but its young professional couples were distinctively modern, 'contemporary people', free from the constraints of 'high class refinement'.[41] The exclusively fashionable world of the 'London' series was reconstructed, in William Rose's original screenplay, as a new 'executive class', a celebration of a broader appropriation of aristocratic style.[42] Ambrose has securely adjusted to an increasingly affluent consumerism, describing his profession as an advertising agent as 'tedious, but lucrative'. More's reworking of the bachelor cad in pursuit of the feisty Rosalind (Kay Kendall) alternated boisterousness – the braying laugh, 'old sport' banter and the big Spyker car recklessly driven – with quieter, more introspective moments. It made Ambrose, as many reviewers judged, a sympathetic, rounded character rather than a caricature. *Genevieve* clearly caught a new mood of confidence within the middle classes to whom the film's celebration of modern but still elegant living appealed strongly.[43]

More's popularity was increased by the success of *Doctor in the House* (1954) where he re-created Ambrose as Grimsdyke – ebullient and mildly outrageous in his procession of gaudy waistcoats – a similar updating of the Edwardian Man About Town.[44] In Wendy Toye's *Raising a Riot* (1955), More's Tony Kent, spruce naval officer and disciplinarian, is humanised by his unruly children who make fun of their despotic father 'busting with duty' and his iron regime imposed while their mother is absent. He develops a more easy-going tolerance sustained by a funda-mental good-naturedness and commonsense, prepared to acknowledge the burdens of domesticity. Unlike Hawkins, who looked uncomfortable in the domestic comedy *Touch and Go* (1957), More's robust, confident masculinity could accommodate mickey-taking. *Films and Filming* thought he had become, 'almost a symbol of everything that we like to think of as English ... More is of the upper middle classes whether as under-graduate or naval officer. But he has all of the virtues and none of the vices of his class. Whatever our politics or whatever our prejudices, Kenneth More on the screen is a man we cannot help liking.'[45]

His symbolic centrality was emphasised and deepened by his role as a national icon, Douglas Bader, in *Reach for the Sky* (1956). Bader, the most famous Battle of Britain fighter pilot, had been canonised in Paul Brickhill's hagiographic memoir, an instant bestseller since its publication in 1954. Bader's story, like Scott's, exemplified 'the victory of a man's own spirit creating strength and hope out of disaster'. *Reach for the Sky* narrates the literal smashing of the breezy, overconfident pre-war debonair gentleman and his reconstruction as the tenacious modern professional officer whose grasp of tactics as well as his courage are vital to the Allied cause. Bader's manly virtues, his indomitable will-power, ability to endure almost unimaginable suffering and lead by example, are complemented by a more vulnerable, sensitive side. In a finely judged performance, More gives weight to moments of quiet and tenderness as well as to those where he displays ebullience and breezi-ness. In the much praised scene when he departs from the nursing home, he gives Nurse Brace one chaste kiss, murmuring, 'The others took me apart, but you put me back together.' Dilys Powell felt that More was 'able, within the limits of national under-emphasis, to show

4. *The 39 Steps* – Kenneth More, the 'characteristically self-mocking modern gentleman' (BFI Stills, Posters and Designs. By courtesy of Carlton International).

a good deal more emotion than without either falsity in the performer or embarrassment to the audience can usually be expressed in the cinema'.[46]

The huge success of *Reach for the Sky* made More the only star in the late 1950s whom *Kinematograph Weekly*'s critic thought 'unquestionably a big draw', able to 'turn an ordinary film into a box-office success mainly on the strength of his name'.[47] The first of these was a revival of J. M. Barrie's 1905 satire *The Admirable Crichton* (1957). More had reservations about the role until the director, Lewis Gilbert, persuaded him that the key was to play the butler, 'as a likeable, human, contemporary man', once he had assumed leadership on the deserted island.[48] Thus, the class contrast between the inadequate, febrile aristocrats and 'Guv' becomes a contrast between the unacceptable aspects of Edwardianism and More's capable modernity, energetic and utterly self-assured. *A Night to Remember* (1958) was a revisionist account of the 1912 *Titanic* disaster. However, its emphasis fell not so much on the plight of the steerage passengers or the chivalric courtesy of the upper classes, but on More as the omni-competent, cool and calm, no-nonsense professional Second Officer Lightoller, shown working endlessly, to good effect, throughout the film.

*The Sheriff of Fractured Jaw* (1958), a comedy-western, was an Anglo-American production, co-starring Jayne Mansfield, with More instantly recognisable to American audiences as the eccentric Englishman. His Jonathan Tibbs is a skit of the eager beaver Edwardian gentleman-inventor, willing to attempt the conquest of the American market on behalf of his family firm with a new form of retractable firearm. His impeccably English good manners and refusal to adjust his deportment or dress whatever the circumstances create the comedy. More's two films for Rank, *The 39 Steps* (1959) and *North West Frontier* (1959), were less facetious, but the star's performance had a light and knowing touch. *The 39 Steps* ostensibly updated John Buchan's 1915 novel – the secret is a ballistic missile formula – but critics detected a reassuring period feel to the visual style with More as the pipe-smoking sporting gentleman in a flat cap, 'play[ing] Hannay with a kind of tweedy casualness and dare-devil insouciance'.[49] *North West Frontier* was an expensive epic 'Eastern'. In the troubled India of 1905 riven by religious conflict, More's exploits as Captain Scott are presented as a last-ditch effort of honour-able mediation and protection, the struggle to 'keep order'. The script provides many opportunities for derring-do and capable manliness amid the grandeur and sweep of Geoffrey Unsworth's acclaimed CinemaScope location cinematography, but a slightly tongue-in-cheek tone is detect-able. Scott laughs in approval when the Hindu prince's young governess (Lauren Bacall) scoffs at British tea-drinking inactivity. His attempt to keep up the spirits of the faithful Gupta, driving the escape train, through a robust rendition of the 'Eton Boating Song', is character-istically self-mocking.

Some of the rumblings of discontent about More's characters in the quality reviews became much more pronounced in the reception of this film. Derek Hill denounced this 'Male Britannia' in 'an appalling film. Appearing at this time it can only be interpreted as a defence – and as an encouragement – of the Suez mentality.'[50] However, others relished his portrait of the imperialist, 'calm, cocky, self-assured, Sandhurst from wavy hair to polished toecaps'.[51] Several commentators detected a possible middle ground: 'Imperialism is represented by Mr. More with amiable toughness, unpretentious urbanity – his is an imperialism very much to the modern taste.'[52] Despite some reservations, by this point More had 'become an institution'.[53] Isabel Quigly described the More persona as, 'a sort of generalised national image of Englishness ... the medium, middling, middlebrow Englishman'.[54] As the contemporary Edwardian, he combined modernity with tradition, combating the insecurities and anxieties of the present by relocating them in a time that has consistently functioned in post-war English culture as a comfortingly nostalgic reference point, innocent, ordered and secure and which was particularly welcome after Suez.[55] However, More's wholesome persona probably excluded most of the key sixteen to twenty-four-year-old group as his female fans were, 'under fifteen and over thirty ... the others all go for a handsome bloke like Bogarde'.[56] It is likely, therefore, that More appealed to older, more traditional cinema-goers and their offspring, rather than the single adolescent, and that he was a middle-class icon rather than a working-class hero. More's final success was as the capable martinet Captain Jonathan Sheppard in *Sink the Bismarck!* (1960), another Anglo-American production. His emergence from the Admiralty bunker back into the everyday world at the end of the film, task completed, now appears richly symbolic. This was the last appearance of the unflappable, indefatigable officer hero, and the last major role for Kenneth More. His stardom, and the masculinity it radiated, was now decisively on the wane. His career plummeted after this point.[57]

## The Decline of the Gentlemanly Ideal: Blimps, Neurotics and Victims

More's consensual wholesomeness was fighting against a strong tide as the 1956 Suez crisis had helped to undermine the credibility of the national greatness which the officer hero incarnated. The more characteristic modern gentleman was Trevor Howard whose performances in *The Clouded Yellow* (1950), *Outcast of the Islands* (1951), *The Heart of the Matter* (1953), *The Stranger's Hand* (1954), *Manuela* (1957) and *The Key* (1957) were recognised as innovative in the degree and intensity with which he was prepared to explore weakness, failure and despair.[58] Derek Hill marvelled at Howard's ability to project an 'extraordinary inner tenseness that makes [him] perhaps our greatest screen actor'.[59] Hill's sensibilities, revolted by Kenneth More, warmed to the man who could encapsulate the tragedy of a *decaying* middle class in films that explored the price paid for the demands of service and duty. Here, sympathetically presented, was the man who could not live up to the self-assurance of the gentlemanly ideal. Columbia's *The Key*, scripted by the left-wing American writer Carl Foreman, dwells on the flaws in Chris Ford (Howard). He gets by on nerves, controlled panic, drink and his love for Stella (Sophia Loren). Stella is the most enigmatic *femme fatale* in post-war British cinema, who transfers her loyalty from one skipper to another with baffling equanimity: 'It's as if we're all the same man and I don't know which one. I don't know which one, and I don't care,' says Ford despairingly. Dilys Powell, Howard's most eloquent admirer, was entranced by 'That sad, seamy rueful air, that doomed look – I can think of no other actor who wrings my heart in quite the same way. All leather on the surface, but beneath wrestling with fear.'[60] However, *The Key* hedged its bets by offering William Holden as a more conventional hero, even if he too cannot fathom the motivations of this modern siren.

Columbia also produced *The Bridge on the River Kwai* (1957), another Foreman adaptation, from Pierre Boulle's ironic novel that satirised the stiff-necked, unyielding and irrational British blimp officer, Colonel Nicholson. However, in the film's rewritten screenplay, Alec Guinness's Nicholson is a softened, less satirical portrait.[61] Like The Archers' Clive Wynne-Candy, Nicholson becomes a just and honourable man whose values have become antiquated. His attachment to the mystical significance of the officer code, to the superiority of British know-how and team-spirit, is eventually allowed to become tragic as he gazes out over the tranquil waters from the triumphant solidity of the bridge, philosophising about the life of a soldier. His final action is shown with a deliberate ambiguity. Is his destruction of the bridge inadvertent, or a moment of revelation? The liberal English officer, Major Warden (Jack Hawkins), ex-Cambridge don and self-deprecating reluctant combatant, watches in perplexity and fear, conscious of his own powerlessness, guilt and responsibility. As in *The Key*, an alternative hero is offered. The novel's ex-cavalry officer is transformed into 'Major' Shears, an American 'swab-jockey' played by William Holden, a rugged, sceptical individualist whose bared, muscular torso dominates the latter half of the film. Shears is the voice of unprejudiced democracy, equally contemptuous of both Warden and Nicholson whom he sees as infected with a military code that prefers honourable death to victory: 'How to die like gentlemen, how to die by the rules, when the only important thing is to live like a human being.' The film's moral and emotional complexities, and the neat sidestepping of any judgement – Major Clipton (James Donald)'s anguished cry of, 'Madness! Madness!' captures the requisite note of bewilderment – allowed all sorts of allegiances and identifications for audiences. Unlike *The Key* – too enigmatic, inward and forlorn for popular taste – *The Bridge on the River Kwai*, photographed in David Lean's sumptuously epic style, was highly successful.

Other post-Suez war films displayed a similar ambivalent scepticism, showing men-on-the-edge. Their visual style was an 'uncompromising, unromantic … gritty, sinewy realism', exposing the dirt, sweat, drunkenness and hysterical outbursts which combat entailed, emphasising the necessity for rugged action not rules and moral niceties.[62] The favoured terrain was no longer the crack unit on a daring raid or the stable microcosm of a ship or an air-force base, but the jungle or the desert where units were trapped, lost, or abandoned to their own devices. In ABPC's desert film, *Ice Cold in Alex* (1958), John Mills played Captain Anson, an ex-POW suffering from exhaustion and combat neurosis, no longer sure why he is doing what he is doing and held together by drink, nervous energy and the ministrations of his faithful NCO (Harry Andrews). Mills himself thought that the role, 'did one marvellous thing for me – it destroyed that ridiculous stiff upper lip image I had been stuck with'.[63] Captain Williams (John Gregson) in Tempean's *Sea of Sand* (1958), the rule-book disciplinarian, is an anachronism who has to be schooled into the prevailing guerrilla mentality by bearded Captain Tim Cotton – Michael Craig playing the Holden role. In Hammer's *The Steel Bayonet* (1957), Leo Genn's Major Gerrard was another indomitable middle-class officer, but there was a pervasive atmosphere of gloom and despondency in his battle-weary platoon which is given a virtual suicide mission. His relationship with the new recruit Lieutenant Vernon (Michael Medwin), is but a ghostly echo of Ericson and Lockhart. Stanley Baker's performance in *Yesterday's Enemy* (1959), discussed in Chapter 4, finally demolished the type.

However, there was one other important reworking of the paradigm, David Lean's *Lawrence of Arabia* (1963). T. E. Lawrence was another legendary British hero.[64] Korda's attempt to film his life in 1937 starring Leslie Howard, had been aborted for political reasons, like Rank's 1955 version starring Dirk Bogarde, because of the cost.[65] The filming of Columbia's version became its own epic, as has been extensively documented.[66] The key to Lawrence's continuing fascination and currency was his ambivalence, a fact not lost on producer Sam Spiegel: 'We did not try to solve the legend of Lawrence of Arabia. We tried to perpetuate it.'[67] Dissident writer Robert Bolt's screenplay was psychological rather than political, concerned with the complex identity of the 'blond Bedouin'. In becoming an Arab hero, El Aurens, Lawrence rejects British culture, yet through the colour of his skin he can never fully inhabit that adopted culture. He is a hybrid figure outside the orthodoxy of imperial exemplars.[68] Lawrence is part soldier-hero, part sceptical non-conformist and renegade, part femininised aesthete. Perhaps, as Prince Feisal (Alec Guinness) chides, he is just another eccentric Englishman, in love with the desert which can be used to mortify the flesh. Lawrence's masochism and ambiguous sexuality further complicate his fractured identity. The film leaves the famous 'defilement' at Deraa equivocal and inconclusive, characteristic of a generic hybrid, both imperial epic and modernist psycho-biography. Lean's panoramic visual style was at once overwhelming and alienating; foreclosing intimacy and offering a critical distance. As Lawrence, Peter O'Toole's frail, etiolated physique convincingly incarnates a figure held together by will-power and a vision that is itself paradoxical. Is he the Arabs' saviour and liberator, or an egotist who enjoys power? At the massacre of the Turkish troop train at Tafas he displays a trembling excitement, half ecstatic, half appalled. But whatever Lawrence is, he is preferable to an opportunistic British establishment led by General Allenby (Jack Hawkins), engaged in Machiavellian *Realpolitik*.

As in *Kwai*, *Lawrence*'s creative combination of iconoclasm and epic heroism elicited both critical praise – 'an epic with intellect behind it'[69] – without alienating a wider public; *Lawrence* was very popular and established O'Toole as a major star. More successfully than *Zulu* (1962) or the underrated *Khartoum* (1965), it mobilised scepticism about the imperial mission with a compelling story of heroism that could interest working-class males not usually engaged by stories of middle-class failure. As Graham Dawson argues, this was the final moment in which a residual imperial sentiment could be mobilised without conscious nostalgia.[70] *The Battle of Britain* (1969), with its parade of left-overs from a 1950s war film, was precisely that: an exercise in nostalgia. The 200-year hegemony of the gentleman hero was finally over.

# 3

# Heroes of Modernity: Civilian Professionals

## The Growth of Professionalism

The figure of the civilian professional became one of intense interest because of the pace and complexity of the social changes that faced British society. The war itself stimulated the demand not only for scientists and technologists, but also for doctors and social scientists.[1] This process accelerated after 1945 to meet the needs of a modernising welfare state that attempted 'a more coherent interventionism in wide areas of social life than ever before'.[2] Professionalism became the ideal of a carefully managed post-war reconstruction which required not 'gifted amateurs', but meritocratic experts whose value lay in their accumulated knowledge, skills and specialised training.[3] This chapter will explore the shifting patterns of the representation of the three central groups of civilian professionals: doctors, police inspectors and scientists. Scientists present the most complex paradigm as, historically, their role has fluctuated constantly from saviour to monster, a characteristic that intensified after the war into a radical instability.[4]

## The Professional as Social Crusader: Doctors

Various progressive egalitarian professionals were offered in films of the immediate post-war period, notably campaigning provincial journalists:

John Mills in Rank/RKO's *So Well Remembered* (1947) and Norman Wooland in Wessex's *All Over the Town* (1949); progressive, dedicated teachers: Robert Flemyng in the Boultings' *The Guinea Pig* (1948) and Jack Hawkins in *Mandy* (1952); and Cecil Parker as a transformed social worker in Ealing's *I Believe in You* (1952). However, doctors were always the dominant image of the admirable crusading professional, based on the modern archetype of Robert Donat's Andrew Manson in MGM-British's highly successful *The Citadel* (1938), reissued in 1948, the year in which the profession was nationalised. Manson, a young man of idealism and selfless dedication, was the heir to the image of Victorian doctors as, 'crusaders embodying bravery, patience, modesty, reverence and chivalry'.[5] Manson is susceptible to the temptations of success and wealth, but rehabilitates himself as the people's champion, a middle-class moderniser opposed to vested interests and the hidebound prejudices of his own profession. Three films – British National's *Green Fingers* (1947), London Films' *Mine Own Executioner* (1947) and ABPC's *My Brother Jonathan* (1948) – reworked this image during Clement Attlee's administration that was, '[the] last and most glorious flowering of late Victorian liberal philanthropy'.[6] *Green Fingers* and *Mine Own Executioner* were modestly budgeted films, flatly photographed, but *My Brother Jonathan* was the flagship of ABPC's relaunched post-war production, an accomplished and expensive-looking adaptation, handsomely photographed, of Francis Brett Young's popular novel. In essence it is a symbolic contrast between two brothers. Harold Dakers (Ronald Howard) is the debonair playboy – good-looking, carefree, sporting and gregarious – for whom life is a smooth success not a struggle. His elder brother, Jonathan (Michael Denison), is unglamorous and dedicated to medicine. He smokes a pipe, that symbol of sobriety, self-control and middle-class reliability. When their father's death shatters the Dakers's economic security, it is the self-sacrificing Jonathan who abandons his hopes for a career as a London surgeon so that Harold can continue at Cambridge. His enforced choice becomes the spur for a latent idealism as he takes up general practice in an impoverished working-class district in a Black Country town where he perceives, 'I had two main enemies to fight, ignorance and poverty. And I had only one ally, the courage, the amazing courage, of these people. What they really wanted was something I could never give them in a bottle: sunshine, decent houses and good, wholesome food.' His hopes, with their unmistakable echoes of Beveridge, have to be fought for against corrupt commercialism, the entrenched views of the old guard and a

5. *White Corridors* – James Donald, the modern professional: the hero
in a white coat (BFI Stills, Posters and Designs. By courtesy of
Carlton International).

compromised medical establishment. Jonathan becomes the people's
champion, instrumental in establishing a hospital for the genuinely needy.
His only weakness, the common fallibility of the ardent young doctor,
is a lingering romantic attachment to a beautiful but superficial socialite,
whom he marries when he finds she is pregnant with his dead brother's
child. Her death releases Jonathan to settle down to a true partnership
with an unglamorous but devoted wife, Rachel (Dulcie Gray), the
daughter of his partner, who loves and admires him for his skill and
integrity. His dedication is finally rewarded when Harold's son, just
returned from active service in the Second World War, is inspired by his
surrogate father's life story to take up medicine as his civilian career.

*My Brother Jonathan*, adroitly updated, and shorn of all the self-doubts
and downbeat ending of the novel, was a major success. Denison was
clearly Donat revived, soft-spoken, restrained and chivalrous. He was
the debonair gentleman as dedicated professional, purged of the carefree
insouciance of the playboy.

An important reworking of the type came with James Donald's

performance as research bacteriologist Neil Marriner in Joseph Janni's *White Corridors* (1951) which combined the doctor with the scientist. Ex-documentarist Pat Jackson's functional *mise-en-scène*, particularly in the drab, awkward clutter of Marriner's laboratory and his use of naturalistic sound, reinforces the hard-pressed, undemonstrative exactitude of this modern professional in his stained white coat.[7] As a researcher whose primary role is to push back the frontiers of medical knowledge through experimentation with the effects of gamma rays from cobalt obtained from a nearby atomic plant, Marriner exhibits an obsessive dedication. He never relaxes, hardly eats or sleeps, is often moody and irascible and has difficulties in forming relationships. To the importuning of his fiancée, surgeon Sophie Dean (Googie Withers), he replies with wary scepticism: 'Dr Kildare labours on, sacrificing his romantic dreams to science.'

However, as a practising doctor Marriner is caring and gentle – adept at reassuring young nurses and relaxing young patients – and also a practical idealist. He places his own health and career at risk to test his unproven serum. His courage saves a boy's life, disarms the criticisms of the hospital's Old Guard and secures Sophie's loyalty. As Marriner is not vulnerable to the lure of wealth and fame, it is she who undergoes the paradigmatic conversion from ambitious careerist to selfless dedication in an unfashionable provincial hospital. But this point is underlined by the failure of the playboy, charming Dr Richard Groom (Jack Watling). His carelessness and irresponsible womanising nearly cause a patient's death. He is admonished by his father, the august senior surgeon (Godfrey Tearle), who reminds his errant son of the unrelenting vigilance and exacting responsibilities which the profession requires.

Though made on a small budget and without much support from Rank, *White Corridors* was highly successful. One reviewer identified Donald as the film's 'greatest asset ... an actor who is subtly simple, mutely eloquent, and unobtrusively brilliant. He is one of the few stars who can play a doctor or an engineer and *seem* like a doctor or an engineer.'[8] His performance was significant because it reworked the Donat image into a more meritocratic, sober ordinariness, the perfect embodiment of post-war paternalist welfarism.

However, *White Corridors* marked the end of the popularity of middle-class reformism. Michael Frayn identifies the 1951 Festival of Britain as an important watershed in which the 'radical middle-classes – the do-gooders ... The Herbivores, or gentle ruminants' who wanted reform

and social amelioration, lost hegemony to the more ruthless and predatory Carnivores which were quite willing to let the weak go to the wall.[9]
Subsequent films about crusading doctors – *Windom's Way* (1957), *Behind
the Mask* (1958), *Life in Emergency Ward 10* (1959) – were not popular
despite the presence of attractive male stars Peter Finch, Tony Britton
and Michael Craig respectively. The last was a television spin-off, but it
could not reproduce the popularity of the ATV series which ran through
until 1967. An audience survey revealed that the increasingly influential
young working-class cinema-goers did not like pictures about caring,
problem-solving professionals.[10] They preferred to see the paternalistic
professional mocked or discomfited, as in Betty Box's irreverent 'Doctor'
films discussed in Chapter 5.

## From Father Figure to Tough Guy: Police Detectives

The dominant image of the police inspector in the immediate post-war
period has been identified as a gentle and kindly father figure who
pursued his suspect, 'more in sorrow than in anger'.[11] Inspector Conway
(Roland Culver) in *Wanted for Murder* (1946) is unruffled and gentlemanly.
Tapping his pipe on the ornate mantelpiece of his room, he spreads the
tails of his tweed jacket to warm himself at the fire as he ruminates on
the strange ways of men. This image solidified into the avuncular
ordinariness of Jack Warner in *Dear Murderer* (1947), *It Always Rains on
Sunday* (1947), *Valley of the Eagles* (1951) and *Emergency Call* (1952). Warner,
of course, played an ordinary bobby in *The Blue Lamp*, but Bernard
Lee's Inspector Cherry in that film was exactly the same. These detectives
were deeply reassuring: calm, middle-aged, good-natured, slow to anger
but righteous and tireless in their pursuit of malefactors. They helped
contribute to the dominant image of the policeman as, 'the ideal model
of masculine strength and responsibility'.[12]

This paternal image was retained but modified by Jack Hawkins as
Superintendent Tom Halliday in Ealing's *The Long Arm* (1956). Halliday,
in parallel with Hawkins's officer roles, is younger, harder, tougher, less
idealistic, more weary and resigned to the vices of a fallen world, than
Warner's inspectors.[13] He is also more professional, the head of a team
of disciplined experts who use the latest technology. However, Halliday
remains a father figure, provided with a stable home life which emphasises the strained finances of the middle-class suburbanite struggling
to raise children – 'a scholarship will make a lot of difference' – on an

income which does not seem an adequate reward for their dedication. Halliday has a surrogate son (a 'cadet') in Detective Sergeant Ward (John Stratton). As in the war films, Ward must be schooled into the necessary toughness: trying to extract information from a dying man which may provide the vital clue. Critics admired the film, but it was not successful, a further indication of cinema-goers' increasing apathy towards dedicated professionals. In Columbia British's *Gideon's Day* (1958), based on the successful series of novels by J. J. Marric and directed by John Ford, Hawkins part parodies his own idealised image.

This 'herbivore' construction lost out to a more 'carnivorous' reworking of the inspector as a modern tough guy. The beginnings can be detected in Rank's *Lost* (1956) through its use of the virile David Farrar. Farrar's Inspector Craig has the paternalist's calm authority in dealing with the hysterical parents of the missing child, but is also a loner, abrasive with his subordinates who speculate on when he will develop an ulcer and remark about his unattractive furnished rooms in Earls Court. John Mills's Inspector Mike Halloran, in Columbia's *Town on Trial* (1957), introduced the working-class hero, a hard-bitten self-made professional, 'from the London Polytechnic'. He prowls the leafy lanes of the Home Counties town in a shabby, battered raincoat, no longer the protector of a community but its scourge. Halloran stalks his suspected serial killer with a vindictiveness and loathing that suggests his own inner turmoil and frustrations. *Town on Trial* seems to have been in tune with the times, 'making a deep impression on the high as well as the low class box-office'.[14]

However, the actor who played out the tensions between the paternalist and the tough guy most evocatively was Stanley Baker. *Violent Playground* (1958) was Dearden and Relph's deliberate response to the cosiness of *The Blue Lamp*, set in the 'tough and vital community' of Liverpool whose young offenders' scheme had caught their imagination.[15] Harry Waxman's bleak black and white cinematography presented this unfamiliar urban landscape in 'a harsh, raw visual style'.[16] It attempts to show Detective Sergeant Truman's transformation from macho, authoritarian tough guy into caring modern professional. Baker plays Truman as a cynical, rather boorish bachelor who believes in 'an old-fashioned wallop' as the solution to youthful indiscipline and deeply resents being switched from the manly certainties of orthodox CID work to the unmanly role of juvenile liaison officer. But his responsibility for the Murphy twins and his love for their sister Cathy (Anne Heywood) release those qualities of kindness and compassion that he has been repressing. Cathy, initially hostile, comes to understand him as the transplanted good shepherd (the work of his father and grandfather), uneasy in the face of modern urban life, a complex and strangely vulnerable figure in need of reassurance and acceptance. Truman's failure is with the brother, Johnny (David McCallum). Although they strike up a guarded rapport at the sports track – a shared masculine sense of the need to save face, of doing only what you can succeed in – this is shattered when Johnny returns to his flat and leaps into a rock 'n' roll jive, deliberately sexually provocative, enticing Truman into a forbidden world, both sensuous and threatening, from which he feels he can only walk away. This is the key moment, as John Hill argues, at which Truman's project of patient, rational reform is shattered.[17] The film's discourse becomes more authoritarian, showing the inadequacies of the saintly paternalists, Father Laidlaw (Peter Cushing) and Headmaster 'Heaven' (Clifford Evans), in favour of Truman's robust, no-nonsense condemnation. In the final shot Truman, now a community policeman, equipped with his new family, Cathy and the twins, is pictured holding the hand of the black child who had earlier spurned him. But it is a resolution made possible by excluding what was ostensibly the main concern, the delinquent, and shows clearly the limitations of Truman's tolerance.[18]

Joseph Losey jettisoned the paternalist paradigm altogether in *Blind Date* (1959), using Baker's self-made Inspector Morgan to highlight the class conflicts in British society. Morgan, the son of a chauffeur, is contemptuous of how Deputy Commissioner Sir Brian Lewis (Robert Flemyng) and his acolyte, Inspector Westover, rely on the 'old school spirit' and the 'deeper meaning of public service', to protect the reputation of the corrupt Sir Howard Fenton. In contrast to their debonair assurance, Morgan, in his ill-fitting suit, an incongruous deer-stalker rammed on his head or pushed roughly backwards, is, as he announces, 'no gentleman'. Lighting up a cheap cigar, not the middle-class pipe, his working-class Welsh accent thickened by a heavy cold, Morgan is rough, incipiently brutal, unafraid to manhandle his suspect. But if Morgan is admirably honest and free from class prejudice, the film also shows his puritanical and intolerant misogyny and his philistinism.[19] It is his contempt for women and for art which separate him from the romantic painter Jan Van Rooyen (Hardy Kruger), whom he can help but not understand. What unites these two outsiders is a shared criticism of the clubland gentlemen who still run Britain.

The ambivalence and incipient violence of the modern policeman were taken further in Hammer's *Hell is a City* (1960). As in *The Day the Earth Caught Fire* (1961) and *80,000 Suspects* (1963), writer-director Val Guest offers the figure of the hard-bitten professional as a necessary part of an increasingly lawless and violent society, authenticated by the grubby documentary realism of the visual style which had a 'newsreel quality'.[20] The bleak settings in and around Manchester and hard, harsh cinematography give a raw, edgy quality to the *mise-en-scène* that is mirrored in the tense, irritable touchiness of Baker's performance as Inspector Harry Martineau. The self-made professional Martineau is like a caged bear in the confines of his genteel suburban semi-detached, constantly quarrelling with his middle-class wife Julia (Maxine Audley). His milieu is the street, the pub and roughing up suspects, where the barely suppressed violence that characterises Baker's performance threatens to explode. But it is precisely these qualities that make him capable of defeating his *Doppelgänger*, vicious hardman Don Starling (John Crawford). Martineau opines, 'I know how his mind works. I grew up with him. We went to the same school together, fought in the same war.' This blurring of moral boundaries, the disturbing mirroring of policeman and villain, continues even after Starling's capture. At the moment of his execution, Martineau blurts out, 'I'm on the edge, Julia. Can't you see I'm on the edge?' *Hell is a City* destroys the paternalist paradigm where crooks are evil and the policeman can return safely to his family, replacing it with alienated modern urban man, a detached, unstable loner who can only feel at home on the night-time city streets.

However, Martineau was ahead of his time. Astonishingly, Guest used Jack Warner in *Jigsaw* (1962), and John Gregson offered a Hawkins-esque performance in *The Frightened City* (1961). As Robert Murphy has shown, the police inspector was not a figure of particular importance in 1960s crime films, displaced by the criminal anti-hero or caper films that are uninterested in detailing the processes of detection.[21] Rank's *The Informers* (1963) introduced the spectre of police corruption only to dismiss it, but *The Strange Affair* (1968) was much more disturbing. The film shows a deracinated London, a hodge-podge of concrete office blocks, multi-storey car parks, scrubby wastelands and anonymous pubs. Its inhabitants include a middle-class couple distributing pornography and an amoral flower-child. The 'cadet', PC Strange (Michael York), is gullible and tainted, becoming the pawn of Detective Sergeant Pierce (Jeremy Kemp) who has become unbalanced in the excess of his righteous loathing of Quince, an ex-detective turned drug baron. Both policemen are destroyed in the process.[22]

## The Scientist-Inventor

During the war the scientist was either Leslie Howard's mystical idealist in *The First of the Few*, or the comic boffin, Felix Aylmer's eccentric inventor in *Time Flies* (1944). But in a rapidly changing post-war society this image changed: 'The boffins had captured the public's imagination: the stereotype of the absent-minded professor had been transformed into the keen-eyed inventor in a white coat of radar and artificial harbours.'[23] Here indeed was C. P. Snow's 'new man', the rational expert whose knowledge was the instrument through which modern civilisation could be forged. *School for Secrets* (1946), scripted, directed and co-produced by Peter Ustinov for Two Cities with the full co-operation of the Air Ministry, celebrated the discovery of radar.[24] Ustinov depicted the boffins as a varied collection of idiosyncratic ordinary men. Collectively they exhibit what Robert Jones has identified as the key characteristics of the boffin hero: pedagogism, obsessiveness, unworldly innocence and a classless, ambivalent status, both insiders and outsiders.[25]

At the end of *School for Secrets*, two of the boffins go off to help bomb Japan. It was precisely this disarming innocence about the re-percussions of Hiroshima that made *School for Secrets* outmoded by the time of its release. The scientist's image as an heroic moderniser and apostle of progress, celebrated in *No Highway* (1951), became overladen with anxieties about the Atomic Age in which the scientist could be a fearful figure, the witting or unwitting agent of disasters let loose by atomic energy, and a pawn in sinister government 'initiatives' and Cold War rivalries.[26] The Boultings' *Seven Days to Noon* (1950), an urgently topical quasi-documentary using a high proportion of location shooting, was the first film to explore these renewed fears of the 'mad scientist'. The mild paternal boffin, Professor John Willingdon (Barry Jones), balding and absent-minded, is transformed into a fanatic by the knowledge that his atomic research has turned evil: 'I saw in science a way of serving God and my fellow men. I wanted to serve. Now I see my life's work used only for destruction, the dream becoming a nightmare.' Jones manages the difficult task of giving substance and credibility to this obsessive, unstable maverick, retaining the conventional eccentricity but also conveying a steely determination as the man-with-a-mission, unable to communicate his fears except through threats of annihilation. The danger is overcome by paternalistic policing, courageous political leadership and an orderly population, revealing a profound nostalgia for a wartime unity.

*The Sound Barrier* (1952) combined the fear and fascination of modern science in a rich and tense ambivalence. It exploited the intense interest generated by a nationalistic popular press about the wonders of the Jet Age, a field in which Britain was considered to be 'out in front'.[27] *The Sound Barrier*, a major Korda project nearly two and a half years in the making, was driven by the technocratic fervour of David Lean who wanted a story about modern explorer-heroes that would capture 'the wonderment and fascination of a new element. It is a new world like the North Pole or the planet Mars is a new world.'[28] This sense of the marvellous comes through in the film's justly acclaimed aerial sequences that convey the thrill and the excitement of speed, together with majestic and seemingly limitless space. But Lean's fervour was counterpointed by the questioning scepticism of Terence Rattigan's screenplay. Rattigan presents the inventor John Ridgefield (Ralph Richardson) as a divided figure. In his own eyes Ridgefield is a man of destiny, a modern Prometheus, the name he gives to his new aeroplane prototype. He tells his daughter Sue (Ann Todd) that his drives come not from the needs of the moment, but from an inexplicable and profound sense of the mystical destiny of the English: 'I could talk of national security, beating the enemy bombers or flying to New York in two hours. But that's not the real reason. The real point is, it's got to be done. What purpose did Scott have in going to the South Pole?' It is a destiny that requires sacrifice; first his son Chris (Denholm Elliott) who fails to share his vision, then his son-in-law Tony Garthwaite (Nigel Patrick), the inspired amateur, the Battle of Britain ace who lacks the brains to cope with the new technology. It is the 'new man' who succeeds, the quiet, un-demonstrative Philip Peel (John Justin), the methodical technical expert.[29]

This achievement demands a high price. After his climax in 'pene-trating' the sound barrier, Peel breaks down into hysterical weeping. During the test itself Ridgefield cannot bear to be alone, imploring his despised daughter to stay and reassure him that his life's work has not been in vain: 'Can a vision be evil, Sue? Can it? Can it?', he cries, close to breakdown. Richardson's intelligent, nuanced performance, for which he won a BFA award, gives great intensity to this moment of disclosed dread, making the insecure inventor a near tragic figure. Sue is the key presence. Outside the male domain her probing intelligence tries to explore the recesses of the male drives for new inventions, speed, achievement, 'penetration'; drives which they themselves cannot explain. When asked why he must continue testing, Peel echoes her dead husband's words: 'I don't know. It just has to be done.' But having consistently shown the justice of her questioning, the film draws back from a fundamental challenge to the male quest and the inventor's purposes. Conscious of her father's lonely suffering, Sue returns to the patriarchal home bringing with her Ridgefield's grandson, another Tony, born on the night of his father's death. The film ends in his observatory where, to their approving gaze and with the model Prometheus and the phallic telescope optimistically pointing towards the stars, Ridgefield pledges to continue the fight against a 'hostile and unfriendly' universe with, 'the only weapon we have, imagination', thereby combining the technocrat with the creative artist in a higher synthesis.

Anthony Asquith's rival project *The Net* (1953) showed a similar structure of feeling.[30] James Donald built on his performance in *White Corridors* to produce another image of technological man, Michael Heathley, both inventor and test pilot, who argues that his supersonic plane, by obliterating distance, can create a closer and more harmonious world. But his idealism has, as its complement, an obsessiveness and inability to communicate. His vision is not shared by his patient and supportive wife Lydia (Phyllis Calvert) who finds it soulless and rather terrifying. One reviewer identified Heathley as: 'The Atomic Age lover … A hero in white overalls or baggy tweed; a scientist and/or aviator who pores over his algebra, with a half-chewed sandwich lying among the litter of pencils and protractors, and never remembers to kiss his wife goodnight.'[31]

*The Net*'s rather clumsy futurism and Cold War machinations scuppered its box-office chances, but *The Sound Barrier*, despite some critical carping about the ending, was embraced as a new national epic by reviewers: 'its great merit … is that it attempts to deal seriously with one of the great subjects – at once scientific and dramatic – of our times'.[32] Audiences concurred, making it one of the most successful films of 1952.[33] But this celebratory moment was short-lived. A series of disasters with the Comet contributed to an increasing disillusionment with Britain's technological achievements and no subsequent films could rekindle that optimism.[34] In the longer term, the film's importance, as John Baxter states, was 'to offer the suggestion that a new technological society had been born, a group of people to whom emotional and social allegiances were of little importance'.[35]

These modern technological heroes were ambivalent figures and their triumphs of rational invention always came at a cost. It was not so much, as Baxter suggests, that their emotional needs were of little importance, but that they *denied* their importance, always subordinating them to the drive for success. Even a retrospective war film, *The Dam Busters* (1955), showed the inventor, Barnes Wallis (Michael Redgrave), as neurotic; one who treads a fine line, as he admits himself, 'between inspiration and obsession'. Redgrave's absorbing performance – stooped, hunched, distracted, living on will-power and nervous energy, with jerky movements like a marionette – expresses this ambivalence. And in the end it is Wallis who registers his emotions, who grieves at the sacrifice of so many young lives; though here this also serves to absolve the instrumentality of Wing Commander Guy Gibson.

The films analysed so far were isolated projects, but the interest generated by the scientist-inventor was, by the mid-1950s, incorporated into the development of science fiction films as a significant popular genre, one which offered handy formulae for smaller production companies with an eye for the already existing American market and which borrowed frequently from known television successes.[36] The cruder films dispensed with the ambivalence of the technological hero, representing the figure as either courageous hero or madman. In Eros's *The Strange World of Planet X* (1958), whose opening voice-over announced the perils of scientists probing the unknown in this 'new and terrifying age', Forrest Tucker played the physicist as an action hero who relies more on his fists than his protractors to overcome deranged Dr Laird (Alec Mango) whom cosmic rays have sent mad. These clean-cut heroes, often played by fading American stars, were uniformly dull action adventurers, but the mad scientist could attain kitsch status. Fortress's *Womaneater* (1958) was graced by George Coulouris's Dr Moran, returned from the Amazon with a tree which devours the flesh of voluptuous young women, having first ripped off their clothing, to produce a liquid which will restore the dead to life. It all comes to no good.

However, Hammer, which had churned out similar fare in *Spaceways* (1953), developed the two key figures that embodied the fear and fascination of science, the contemporary inventor-hero Professor Quatermass and the archetypal mad scientist Baron Frankenstein.

## The Sceptical Rationalist: Quatermass

Quatermass was the creation of Nigel Kneale in three television serials broadcast by the BBC between 1953 and 1958 which have been identified as, 'the first TV SF in Britain to be aimed at adult viewers'.[37] Kneale, who acknowledges the influence of popular Gothic traditions, 'always looked for an idea that seems to contain contradictions'.[38] These contradictions were played out in a dialectic between an idealistic and progressive vision of modern science, and its potential destructive abuse. Kneale's Quatermass was a rationalist who admitted the possibilities of forces beyond his comprehension, making him an anxious, self-questioning liberal. However, this subtle characterisation was simplified in Richard Landau's adaptation of *The Quatermass Experiment* for Hammer, in order to make it more familiar and acceptable for the American market. The imported fading American star, Brian Donlevy, plays Quatermass as an brusque, authoritarian tough guy.[39] Any wordy self-doubt is replaced by steely determination and decisive action. He shows little sign of remorse at the death of two of the astronauts or compassion for the survivor, Victor Caroon (Richard Wordsworth): 'Dead or alive, they'll be heroes.' When Caroon's wife confronts Quatermass with his responsibility for her husband's condition, 'You've destroyed him like you have everything else', he tells her flatly: 'There are no personal feelings in science … Some of us have a mission.' In contrast to the BBC version, where Quatermass triumphs through an earnest appeal to Caroon's residual identity, Hammer's Quatermass fries the monster through the electric current from Battersea power station. He strides off past a bemused Inspector Lomax (Jack Warner), the film's marginalised figure of earnest middle-class concern, to start work on his next rocket. Donlevy's flat performance threw attention on to what this contemporary Frankenstein has created. Caroon is unable to control a body that has been fatally damaged by his encounter with space, helplessly metamorphosing from the conventional clean-cut astronaut hero into an alien being, violently destructive. Richard Wordsworth's poignant performance creates a figure of immense pathos, and the scene in the bleak Deptford landscape where he decapitates the child's doll would have reminded viewers of Boris Karloff's monster.

Aggressively marketed as adult entertainment, *The Quatermass Experiment* was highly successful, and led to further productions.[40] Kneale was invited to collaborate with director Val Guest on the sequel, *Quatermass*

*II* (1957). However, in this film there is even less sense of Quatermass as the self-questioning visionary inventor, though the 'food plant' at Wynerton Flats is a perversion of his plans for a moon colony. Instead he becomes the lone tough guy, the only one capable of dealing with the alien threat that has penetrated into the upper reaches of the British Establishment, and who leads the enslaved workers in a revolt against their alien colonisers.

In many ways it was the intervening film, *X the Unknown* (1956), with a specially commissioned story and screenplay by Jimmy Sangster, that approximated more closely to Kneale's vision. Dr Adam Royston, played by the avuncular American actor, Dean Jagger, was a more convincing figure of the liberal scientist. Although he is obsessive and self-absorbed, Royston succeeds by an imaginative solution based on an attempt to understand a different form of life, with an evolved intelligence of its own, rather than naked force or populist revolt.

Kneale's liberal idealist was used by Hammer but in the figure of Dr John Rollason (Peter Cushing) in *The Abominable Snowman* (1957), Kneale's adaptation of his 1955 BBC play *The Creature*. Here the American tough guy Tom Friend (Forrest Tucker) is a boorish adventurer who regards a scientific quest as an opportunity for the extension of his previous activities of gun-running, smuggling and fraud. He is determined to turn the Yeti into a televised circus attraction and is killed in the attempt. Rollason survives because he has the courage and the imagination to speculate about other forms of life: 'suppose we're the savages … perhaps we've been in the dark ages. Perhaps not *homo sapiens*, thinking man – what has our thinking brought us to? – but *homo vastans*, man the destroyer.' Contact with the Yeti subdues Rollason's potential hubris, forcing him to accept a limitation to scientific inquiry, to acknowledge boundaries and the forbidden. His 'progress' is to accept the wisdom of the aged, all-wise Lama, a complete rejection of western scientific rationalism and explicitly anti-authoritarian.

However, the wordy liberalism of *The Abominable Snowman*, despite Arthur Grant's majestic 'HammerScope' cinematography, and *X the Unknown* did not appeal to adolescent cinema-goers. Hammer did not return to this paradigm until *Quatermass and the Pit* (1967), released nearly ten years after the BBC original. This time, Kneale's own adaptation keeps Quatermass, sensitively played by Andrew Keir, much closer to his original conception, but plays up the elements of terror and vulnerability that exist alongside his commitment to scientific rationalism.

Kneale subtly contrasts the clinically controlled logic of Dr Matthew Roney – another convincing performance by James Donald – with the more intuitive, rather feminised Quatermass who, even though he wants to deal in known facts, has a large measure of doubt. His susceptibility to the emanations of the unknown, a quality he shares with the woman scientist Barbara Judd (Barbara Shelley), allow Quatermass to acknowledge the need to go beyond rationality, to understand the importance of history and folklore and that, 'We're the Martians'; these alien 'demons' are 'the inheritance within us', not a conquerable external threat. The genocidal brutality of the mob unleashed by the promptings of this race memory is a far cry from the resurrected Second World War unity invoked by *Seven Days to Noon*. Despite Roney's heroic sacrifice, the film ends with a sense of exhaustion rather than victory. Kneale was responding to changed times and shrewdly dropped the television Quatermass's paternalistic appeal, delivered direct to camera, to control 'the ancient destructive urges in us' and forge a better world.

*Quatermass and the Pit* was as much about male fears and paranoias as rationality, typical of the 1960s where 'the scientist's self-confidence … has gone and all that is left is a state of perpetual uncertainty'.[41] Anglo/ Independent Artists' *noir* sci-fi *Unearthly Stranger* (1963), a typical alien 'invasion' narrative, takes the celibate bachelordom of the male scientist and shapes it into a nightmare. The beautiful young wife of Dr Mark Davidson (John Neville) turns out to be an alien, part of a force which has been arriving for twenty years. This memorably embodied how far fears of alien invasion and women meshed together, a deep-seated fear of women's sexuality, signified as *the* irrational or uncontrollable element.[42]

## The Overreacher: Frankenstein

Another reason for Hammer's abandonment of contemporary sci-fi was the success of *The Curse of Frankenstein* (1957). Frankenstein's story, the scientist as monstrous overreacher attempting to create life itself in his own laboratory, has taken on the status of a modern myth with a remarkable capacity for change and transformation.[43] Jon Turney argues that the myth incorporates an unresolvable ambiguity about the work of the scientist at its most exciting and most dreadful; in the late 1950s this interest was heightened by popular fears that atomic radiation could

6. *The Curse of Frankenstein*: Peter Cushing – the scientist
as overreacher (BFI Stills, Posters and Designs).

create mutations.[44] For *The Curse of Frankenstein*, Jimmy Sangster's screen-play discards the bland and self-pitying student experimenter of Mary Shelley's novel in favour of, 'a magnificently arrogant aristocratic rebel, in the direct Byronic tradition'.[45] As I have shown, the Byronic male was a figure of fear and fascination, both ruthless and noble in the pursuit of his desires. Frankenstein (Peter Cushing) disdains the bour-geois respectability of his friend and former tutor Paul Krempe (Robert Urquhart) in favour of unconfined experimentation: 'Nature puts up her barriers to confine the scope of man. We've broken through those barriers.'

Hammer's period films were a coherently mixed mode whereby some elements were realistic (acting and set dressing), while others (lighting, colour and costume) were highly stylised.[46] Despite budgets of under £80,000, Hammer's tightly-knit production team created a handsome and innovative visual style; even its detractors noted the film's carefully composed *mise-en-scène*, the solid palpability of Frankenstein's laboratory, designed with imagination and skill by Bernard Robinson, where Cushing conducted his 'symphony in sound and light'.[47] The use of colour provided a freshly graphic, visceral depiction of horror, creating a highly controlled Grand Guignol in which Frankenstein's grotesque creation is all the more frightening and invasive. These elements were given maximum weight by Terence Fisher's balanced, measured direction, complemented by Cushing's precise performances.

Cushing's slim, high-cheekboned good looks coupled with his crisp, direct, authoritative performance style created a Byronic charisma and a convincingly high-minded experimenter animated by a noble purpose. He was equally credible as the altruistic rationalists Van Helsing in the 'Dracula' films, and Sherlock Holmes in *Hound of the Baskervilles* (1959). While working-class audiences may have been relatively uninterested in his performance as a liberal scientist, they could respond enthusiastically to his sexy Baron. *Curse* builds to a gripping finale in which Frankenstein confronts his creation. His 'superior man', mechanically assembled, is monstrous, a function of his egotism and hubris, the part of himself he did not wish to recognise, his hideous and uncontrollable *doppelgänger*. In his portrayal of the monster, Christopher Lee manages to evoke, in his brief but highly charged appearances, a disturbing pathos and tragic quality, the sense of an intelligent and suffering man trapped in an alien body that he cannot control. His piteousness, like Caroon's, serves only to underline the inhumanity of Frankenstein, prepared to murder even his old tutor, Professor Bernstein, the epitome of civilised wisdom and a kindly father figure, to pursue his obsession.

With its Byronic rebel hero, sympathetic monster and fresh visual style, *The Curse of Frankenstein* was highly successful. The film offered a 'double appeal': sufficient time had lapsed since the Universal films of the 1930s to make Frankenstein both nostalgic for older viewers and 'a curiosity value for an enormous number of young cinemagoers'.[48] Hammer made a further six Frankenstein films through to *Frankenstein and the Monster from Hell* (1973) where his purpose is to explore and re-create the recesses of the human psyche. These films had various degrees of inventiveness and success, but Pirie is surely right to emphasise that through the series as a whole Cushing's characterisation 'reaches a level of subtlety that can be compared interestingly with the most equivocal of nineteenth-century anti-heroes'.[49]

## The Decline of the Professional Ideal

What the Quatermass and Frankenstein films demonstrate is the declining confidence in the scientist who is to unable to control the forces that his experiments unleash. Both show an increasing concern with the 'alien within', the rational scientist's fear of his own sexuality, and the 'alien without', the sexuality of women. These fears are also strongly present in Hammer's 'Mummy' cycle – *The Mummy* (1959), *The Curse of the Mummy's Tomb* (1964), *The Mummy's Shroud* (1967) and *Blood from the Mummy's Tomb* (1971) – which all punish the invasive archaeologist for his hubris and presumption.[50] In the last and best, Christopher Wicking's screenplay uses the figure of the monstrous woman, the Goddess Tera, Queen of Darkness, whom the priests fear, kill and maim. Her spirit takes possession of Margaret Fuchs (Valerie Leon), daughter of Professor Julian Fuchs (Andrew Keir) who has been obsessed since his youth with Tera and whose expedition to her tomb unleashes the 'curse'. He has spent the rest of his life keeping from his daughter her 'true' inheritance, but Fuchs and those who accompany him are driven mad or destroyed.

Less graphically than the scientist, the other two types of the professional also exhibit increasing stresses and strains as the belief in the authority of the professional, based on Victorian philanthropic idealism, declined. Indeed, the overweening rational paternalism came to be seen as the source of the problems, a cover for monstrous desires that hinged on the fear of women.

# 4

# The Action Adventurer

I n the post-war period, the action adventurer was always a rival image of the hero, competing and also overlapping with the gentleman and the professional. Where the gentleman was primarily a middle-class construction emphasising duty and *esprit de corps*, the action adventurer embodied the core American masculine myth of successful, competitive individualism.[1] It was a democratic and classless ideal: the adventurer's worth is proved by deeds not birth or privilege and his success celebrates gutsy resourcefulness. The dynamic energies of the action adventurer made him a potentially disruptive figure; a restless, rootless loner, seeking confrontation and danger.[2] It was always difficult for British production companies and British stars to compete with the hegemonic Hollywood version and they concentrated on ambivalent heroes. The exception to this was Connery's James Bond, that extraordinary synthesis of the tough guy and the debonair.

## The British Swashbuckler

Stewart Granger extended his wartime action roles in four further period adventures: *Caravan* (1946), *The Magic Bow* (1946), *Captain Boycott* (1947) and *Saraband for Dead Lovers* (1948). Ealing's *Saraband* deliberately tried to revise the conventions of the historical costume film in a ponderously elaborate re-creation of Hanoverian *Realpolitik*. Its anti-romanticism required Granger to make a 'dignified farewell to history in his powerful and *restrained*' performance as the impoverished and ambivalent soldier of fortune Count Philip von Königsmark.[3] *Saraband* was an ambitious misfire; its reworking of generic conventions was too pronounced; audiences wanted Granger to be dynamic and athletic not restrained. By contrast, Gainsborough's *The Magic Bow* created a role carefully tailored to exploit Granger's persona as the proud, quick-tempered but talented violinist Paganini whose proletarian energies allow him to defy social conventions and class barriers.[4] For Individual Pictures' *Captain Boycott* he was also popular as another fiery and truculent young man, Hugh Davin, championing the rights of the oppressed Irish tenantry against the English yoke. Granger's presence shifted sympathies away from Boycott, and romanticised Davin as a rebel and a dashing lover.

*Caravan* was the most complex role as it transferred the schizophrenia associated with female figures in Gainsborough's wartime films – *Madonna of the Seven Moons, The Wicked Lady, The Seventh Veil* – to the central male figure, Richard Darrell (Granger). Unusually for a swash-buckler, *Caravan* is as much about male identity as male achievement. The film is preoccupied with the antithetical pulls of the rational north, embodied by the impoverished English aristocrat Oriana Camperdene (Anne Crawford), versus the passionate south, embodied by the sensual Spanish gypsy Rosal (Jean Kent). Darrell is responsive to both because he is a hybrid figure, combining the bourgeois respectability and work ethic of his father, an altruistic English doctor, and the Mediterranean sensuality of his Spanish mother. His childhood is spent in a liminal world between the Camperdene country estate and the 'wild wood' where the gypsies live. Thus, although there is ample scope for Granger's athleticism – in the first scene he overpowers two London garrotters – the central scenes show him wounded, his memory gone, refashioned by Rosal as Ricardo, dressed like a matador whose exotic eroticism resembled Valentino's.[5] In the end his disciplined northern puritanism triumphs and he is reunited with Oriana. This is offered as the recovery of his 'true' identity, but *Caravan* was unusual in the weight and sympathy it gave to the passionate south where women dance, and bathe naked. Critics thought *Caravan* would delight a female audience that 'throbs at every exposure of Stewart Granger's torso'.[6] However, its masculine perspective, its interest in male psychology and its amnesiac narrative could also have provided an identificatory space for male viewers, now returned from their own wartime sojourns and possible infidelities.

Sydney Box's *The Man Within* (1947) with its introspective and divided hero, and its homoerotic central relationship, was more challenging but failed to win over audiences without the compensating pleasures of Granger's athletic elan. With his departure to America, British film-makers could not compete against the two Hollywood swashbuckling cycles: the chivalric one initiated by *The Black Rose* (1950) and the pagan one begun by *The Vikings* (1958).[7] ABPC's *The Moonraker* (1958), with George Baker as the eponymous Cavalier hero, was a successful pastiche of Hollywood, but the main British line explored ambivalent protagonists. Rank's *Dangerous Exile* (1957), a return to the lush pastures of the 'prestige film', reworked the myth that the boy king Louis XVII survived the Revolution. This elegant and sophisticated film, beautifully designed and photographed, had two male leads, the Duc de Beauvais (Louis Jourdan) and Colonel St Gerard (Keith Michell). Both are introspective men, ambivalent about their actions. Joseph Losey's *The Gypsy and the Gentleman* (1958) also explored a divided protagonist, Keith Michell's Sir Paul Deverill. Writer-director John Gilling's *The Scarlet Blade* (1963), for Hammer, had its conventional dashing hero, Edward Beverly (Jack Headley), fighting the sadistic ruthlessness of Cromwell's turncoat tyrant Colonel Judd (Lionel Jeffries), but its real energies went into the self-questioning figure of Captain Sylvester (Oliver Reed). Michael Reeves's *Witchfinder General* (1968) also used a Civil War setting, but his more modern sensibility abandoned a clear sense of opposing sides for a shifting, fluid, anarchic situation, made all the more shocking by its setting in an idyllic East Anglia. The sinister amoral Witchfinder Matthew Hopkins (Vincent Price) exploits the superstition and easily activated violence of the populace. His adversary, the young Roundhead Cornet Richard Marshall (Ian Ogilvy), has all the outward trappings of the swashbuckling hero, but he is corrupted by the pervasive lawlessness, and is goaded into madness by Hopkins's possession of his fiancée Sara Lowes (Hilary Dwyer). His dedication to Christian chivalric values becomes a dark surrender to violence, revealed in the apocalyptic final scene where his manic axe blows to Hopkins are his only means of release. 'You took him from me. You took him from me,' he screams at the comrade who shoots Hopkins.

MGM's *Alfred the Great* (1969) offered Alfred (David Hemmings) as another modern hero, torn between reason and the need for violence. His quest, like that of T. E. Lawrence, was as much to understand himself as his cause.[8] Alfred is divided between the scholarly contemplative virtues of a Christian culture and his pagan sensuality, the pull of the 'old gods'. His *doppelgänger* is the Viking leader Guthrum

(Michael York), his sexual rival, who obeys the 'wisdom of the blood'. The presentation of their epic encounter eschews pageantry for a more realistic, bone-crunching clash; Alfred's cerebral text-book formations finally triumph against raw pagan vigour. James Clavell's neglected *The Last Valley* (1970), set in the Thirty Years War, starred Michael Caine as the captain of a band of mercenaries, an intelligent, perceptive man forced to be a hired killer: 'I was born in war. I have no country, no friends, no people. War is all the wealth I have.' His brief romantic sojourn in the valley merely postpones his inevitable death. Both these films were a significant attempt to rethink the figure of the action hero, but they wrenched the genre's conventions too far to be popular with audiences.

## The Imperial Adventurer

In contrast to the pre-war empire films with their gentleman heroes, Ealing made three films set in Australia – *The Overlanders* (1946), *Eureka Stockade* (1949) and *Bitter Springs* (1950) – that lauded the rugged toughness of the self-made man. All three starred the lanky Chips Rafferty, dubbed the 'Gary Cooper of Wagga Wagga'. The first two were scripted and directed by Harry Watt who conceived *The Overlanders* as a celebration of the qualities that make 'the Australian outback folk look the strong backbone of the country they are'.[9] Its epic story is the 'overlanding' of 100,000 cattle across 1,500 miles of the rugged, inhospitable Australian interior to prevent their capture by invading Japanese. Dan McAlpine (Rafferty) is the archetypal western hero: tall, laconic, tough, resourceful and indomitable, controlling unruly cattle, a querulous family, a garrulous, tipsy 'old un' and Jacky, the Aborigine scout, the stand-in for the tame 'injun' of American mythology.

Reviewers excused the slender and stereotypical characterisation in their haste to praise the sweeping visual style depicting the unfamiliar grandeur of northern Australia, scenery that could rival Hollywood. They commended these 'laudable attempts … to make the first outdoor films about the empire which will compete – for gunplay, muscle and excitement – with the best of American westerns'.[10] In the case of *The Overlanders* this critical enthusiasm was shared by popular taste. The film was, 'a consistent box-office success in Britain as an action picture whilst drawing specialist praise for its documentary virtues'.[11]

It proved to be a false dawn; the two subsequent films were unable to capitalise on this success. *Eureka Stockade*, the story of the mid-nineteenth-century struggle of the Ballarat gold-miners of New South Wales to achieve workers' rights and push a colonial government down the road to democracy, reduced Rafferty, the miner who becomes the settlement's first MP, to little more than a plaster saint. *Bitter Springs*, directed by Watt's assistant, Ralph Smart, returned to the formula of the epic journey but focused on inter-racial co-operation. At the turn of the century, Wally King (Rafferty), an ordinary sheep farmer, takes his family to a new home where he has to learn to live in harmony with the Aborigines. The cinematography of the journey was accomplished, but the conflict over the settlement at the Springs was clumsily handled and King is too sour and grudging to be an inspiring or charismatic hero. His leadership is undermined by the antics of Tommy Trinder, an ex-escapologist, who, with wild improbability, throws in his lot and that of his young son with King. Trinder's presence indicates a failure of nerve, or waning invention, and the incongruity of his music-hall style in this context was noted in almost every review.

Rank pursued the dream of competing with the Americans by using Jack Hawkins as the rugged hero in *The Adventurers* (1951), set in South Africa after the Boer War, and *The Seekers* (1954), set in nineteenth-century New Zealand. In the first he was miscast as a disaffected fortune hunter, but in the latter he plays Philip Wayne, a rugged but honest bosun, who turns his back on the corruption and class prejudices of England to make a life in the verdant antipodean spaces, 'a place where a man may breathe', and where an ordinary man of energy and muscle can forge a democratic settlement. It was another film in which the magnificent grandeur of unfamiliar scenery dominated. Wayne becomes corrupted by power and is even unfaithful to his saintly wife (Glynis Johns) with a Maori beauty. For this he has to suffer death in a purgatorial fire, leaving his legitimate son as the hope for an harmonious future.

In many ways these films continued the wartime 'drama of the common people', whose patriotic heroism was represented by adventurous colonial pioneers trying to create a community in hostile conditions. Although their racism is betrayed in the careless or patronising ways in which the indigenous peoples are represented, they attempt to align the white settlers with post-war anti-imperial sentiments by emphasising their democratic ambitions. They offered a 'safe' space where restless and dynamic working-class males could channel their energies into forging a classless society remote in time and space from existing social hierarchies.

However, as soon as the narrative was brought up to date, the hero became a middle-class 'eco-warrior'. Jack Hawkins's rubber planter menaced by communists in *The Planter's Wife* (1952) was his meritocratic naval officer transported to the colonies, conserving the crop for future generations. The hero of Harry Watt's *Where No Vultures Fly* (1951) was Bob Payton (Anthony Steel), a game park warden whose job is to preserve endangered species, not to calm unruly natives like his forebear District Commissioner Sanders. Payton is an insider, a 'white native', 'a third generation East African', who sees his duty as preserving the environment for future generations. The film's popularity – it was the highest grossing British film of its release year – may reflect the appeal of that message, but also the charm of its young star. After his success in *The Wooden Horse* (1950) where his powerful physique contrasted sharply with the pigeon-chests of his fellow POWs, Steel was dubbed the 'Wooden Dish' and marketed as Stewart Granger's successor, one who possessed, 'the virile build of an athlete, strongly attractive features and a touch of arrogance in his manner'.[12] *Where No Vultures Fly* deals quite swiftly with Payton's visionary scheme to create a game park, becoming preoccupied with his role as jungle adventurer, a familiar Hollywood type. At any moment this pipe-smoking family man is ready to leap aboard his jeep to ward off poachers or rescue some trapped animal, often photographed bare-chested in shots which linger on his muscular torso. His assistants, a group of black convicts he converts to conservation, remain the stereotype of biddable children/Man Fridays. He is their caring father, opposed to the corrupt white photographer-cum-poacher Mannering whose treatment of the natives and wildlife is blatantly exploitative. In their final 'showdown', Payton announces himself as a man of the future: 'You're out of date, Mannering. This is the new Africa and there's no place for you.'

The appeal of a film described as, '*King Solomon's Mines* nationalised by Sir Michael Balcon', was thought to reside for the most part in Steel's boyish charisma and youthful vigour: 'a young man who combines charm with muscle and dash'.[13] Steel's 'fan mail (mostly from women) is among the highest received by any British star'.[14] But in the sequel, *West of Zanzibar* (1954), Steel could not rescue a strained mixture of travelogue, wildlife documentary, jungle adventure and homily to racial harmony. This time critics sneered at Payton as a 'comic book character …

Buchaneering over Tanganyika', and wondered whether this, 'revival of the British pioneer type' would take with the new generation of cinema-goers.[15] *West of Zanzibar*'s failure at the box-office was a clear indication that it could not. Steel's image, for all its youthful athleticism, exuded the spirit of the public-school Corinthian, not the modern tough guy.

## The Contemporary Adventurer

The key action hero became the contemporary adventurer. By the mid-1950s adolescent taste rejected imperial or historical adventures, 'because they are felt to be unreal [audiences demand] guts, grimness and violence … in "authentic" (i.e. contemporary, "realistic") settings'.[16] Here again British producers were competing against Hollywood stars playing the tough, two-fisted modern professional whose archetype was Clark Gable.[17] Exotic locations, lushly photographed in CinemaScope, compensated for the sumptuous spectacle of the costume adventure. The Anglo-American Warwick Films, co-founded in 1952 by buccaneering producers Irving Allen and Albert Broccoli, and financed by Columbia, was highly successful with variations on this formula.[18] In the face of this competition, smaller British companies – Hammer, Anglo-Amalgamated, Tempean, Eros and the Danziger brothers (from 1954) – produced a budget version, using fading or second-drawer American leads, for the lower half of the ubiquitous double bill that they sold at a fixed price to the circuits. The second-feature market was saturated with pastiche images of the tough American action adventurer.

Rank, in a renewed attempt to capture an international audience, responded with a series of contemporary adventure films that used a similar range of male occupations and exotic locations, but with British leads.[19] After Anthony Steel failed to appeal in Betty Box's *Checkpoint* (1956), despite being cast as a glamorous racing driver in the Mille Miglia, his sky-blue overalls unbuttoned to the waist, Rank turned to younger actors who were more modern and classless. Michael Craig starred as rough and tumble First Officer Larry Ellis in *House of Secrets* (1956), a Cold War thriller. Commandeered by British intelligence as a temporary agent, Ellis is tough, gruff-voiced, resourceful, good with his fists and beloved by the obligatory night-club singer. Photographed with his shirt off on several occasions, he reveals a torso to rival Steel's. One critic thought him reminiscent of 'the younger Tyrone Power … He has a soft firm voice with a slight accent acquired during the six years of his schooling in Canada. Which is just what British films need for the American market.'[20] However, *House of Secrets* failed to take with audiences, despite 'having all the right ingredients'.[21] Clearly, cinemagoers preferred American stars in these roles.

This preference was encouraged by the muddle and confusion displayed by Rank. Several of its films, for instance *Passage Home* (1955), or the historical drama *Robbery Under Arms* (1957), had over-complex narratives, their stars adrift in roles which were incoherent, under-developed or ambiguous. Rank compounded the problem by using its young male stars inconsistently, therefore failing to build up coherent personae for audiences.[22] Craig was squandered as a dull second lead in *High Tide at Noon* (1957) and *Campbell's Kingdom* (1957), before a belated beefcake role as Rusty Miller, a Kenyan game warden, in *Nor the Moon by Night* (1958). Shorn of any residual imperial paternalism, Rusty's role simply allows him to rove freely among the big game baring his chest as often as possible in front of the admiring Belinda Lee. But the film was inept: Patrick McGoohan, who had attracted attention for his brooding, menacing villains in *Hell Drivers* (1957), *High Tide at Noon* and *The Gypsy and the Gentleman*, was wasted in a milk-sop role as Rusty's bookish brother. Another casualty was Tony Wright who had been profiled along with Craig as one of the very few British stars who could compete with Americans in the 'shirts off stakes'.[23] After *Seven Thunders* (1957), a wartime action drama where he played a muscular Cockney POW escapee in jeans and T-shirt, he was allowed to drift into second features when Rank resorted to American leads: Howard Keel in *Floods of Fear* (1958), Eddie Constantine in *S.O.S. Pacific* (1959).

## The Modern Tough Guy: Stanley Baker

The actor who did forge a consistent persona as the modern tough guy was Stanley Baker.[24] Baker had played brutal villains in MGM's *Knights of the Round Table* (Sir Mordred), Warwick's *Hell Below Zero*, and Rank's *Checkpoint* and *Campbell's Kingdom*, as well as psychotic sergeants in *Red Beret* (1953) and *A Hill in Korea* (1956). Commentators began to recognise the impact of his 'smouldering eyes, hatchet jaw and the look of a dozen demons hopping mad inside him … [He makes] the "jolly decent" heroes who try to look tough, just look SILLY.'[25] It took American McCarthyite exile Cyril Endfield to exploit his potential. Both *Hell Drivers* and *Sea Fury* (1958) concentrate on hard, brutal occupations – ballast

7. *Hell Drivers* – Stanley Baker, British tough guy (BFI Stills, Posters and Designs. By courtesy of Carlton International).

haulage and deep-sea rescue tugs – that require toughness just to survive. Endfield, whose model was the pre-war Warner Bros films, argued that there was, 'plenty of natural drama in the everyday jobs of men with physical contact with reality'.[26] In both, Baker is presented as a young man on the threshold of adult life who has to undergo a series of initiations into the brutal male culture from which he stands apart in courage, determination and sensitivity. His sensitivity comes from the need to exorcise past failures. Like his American counterparts he is given a 'remorseful secret', which leads to vulnerability and an insecurity about his role in the world, and some psychological depth. In *Hell Drivers* he plays an ex-con, Tom Yately, desperate to succeed in the rough world of ballast haulage where drivers are paid according to the number of trips they can make. For the first time in British culture, Baker plays a man who has to 'take it', taunted by the other drivers and violently brawling with the psychotic team leader Red (Patrick McGoohan). His only ally is the saintly Gino (Herbert Lom), another outsider. In *Sea Fury* Baker plays Abel Hewson, the son of an alcoholic miner, a drifter who has no option but to take on this 'rough, dirty work'. His competitiveness is coupled with an insecurity about his role in the world, needing the corroboration and love of a beautiful woman. In both films he takes her, reluctantly, away from the older man who befriends him. Baker's characters fulfilled precisely what Herbert Gans argues was the central need of British adolescents, a model of 'mobility aspiration ... an attractive, virile and ambitious hero, pursuing a combination of personal and social aspirations against a hostile environment ... seeking to establish his role and status in the adult world'.[27] The stress on individual merit leading to achievement and social advancement allowed upper-working-class audiences to experience pleasure through fantasies of empowerment and success and increased their self-reliance, self-confidence and opposition to state authority.[28] *Films and Filming* revealed that Baker's tough but vulnerable hero was sexually exciting for 'girls between the ages of 17 and 20'.[29]

Baker's officer hero, Captain Langford in *Yesterday's Enemy* (1959), is no gentleman. The film's producer, Michael Carreras, emphasised that death and fear were given 'their proper place', in a drama whose stark visual style, with no background music, romance or Technicolor, 'knocked the heroics out of war'. Peter Newman, who adapted his own play, thought the film an attack on the 'jolly romps' school and showed, 'the utter futility of war for victor, vanquished and victim alike'.[30] Langford's dilemma is that he feels he must break the Geneva Convention and kill civilians in order to obtain information that may save many lives. With similar ruthlessness he leaves the wounded behind in order that the fit may have a chance of getting through. Langford's men dislike him, the padre and the liberal war correspondent denounce him, but they all know he is their only chance of survival. Baker reflects these tensions in his performance. He alternates between muscular action hero, sweat pouring off him as he pounds his way through the steaming jungle, and a psychotic whose violence is explosive and dangerous; he has to be pulled back when he beats up a prisoner, crying, 'There's only one way to fight a war, any war, with gloves off', one of several near hysterical outbursts which reveal his stress and incipient breakdown.

Baker's violent man-on-the-edge became the dominant model for one version of the 1960s action hero, beginning with Columbia's extremely successful *The Guns of Navarone* (1961). It depicted what became the preferred group: a hand-picked commando unit, drawn from many races, chosen for their particular expertise, and detached from the routines of command, national loyalty or a cause.[31] These, 'pirates and cutthroats every one of them', including the best available assassin, Brown, the 'Butcher of Barcelona' (Baker), are led by Mallory (Gregory Peck), dedicated only to 'getting the job done' including executing spies if necessary: 'The only way to win a war is to be as nasty as the enemy.' In *Play Dirty* (1968), Michael Caine's Captain Douglas becomes brutalised by the gang of psychopaths he has to lead on a mission that is betrayed by the actions of a Machiavellian High Command. In *The Last Grenade* (1970), Baker played another key 1960s figure, the mercenary, Major Harry Grigsby, whose mission is one of revenge, tracking down his betrayer, another mercenary now working for the Chinese Red Guard. But the conflict is more pathological than ideological, a serious study in the action hero's degeneration into a psychotic.

## The Tough Debonair: James Bond

The figure which stood out against this trend was James Bond. In some ways Bond was a direct development of Warwick Films' earlier 'lounge-suited supermen' in *Interpol* (1957) or *The Man Inside* (1958). But in this case producer 'Cubby' Broccoli was convinced that Bond must be played by a British actor. The debonairs of the previous generation (including David Niven, Fleming's choice) were rejected as they 'lacked the degree of masculinity Bond demanded. To put it in the vernacular of our profession: Sean [Connery] had the balls for the part ... The whole point about having Sean in the role, with his strong physical magnetism and the overtones of a truck driver, was that it thrilled the women, but, more important, young men in the audience could feel there was a guy up there like them.'[32] Broccoli's assessment shows the strong continuities between Baker and Connery's rugged masculinity, and the latter's Edinburgh burr made the screen Bond classless rather than patrician.[33] His relationship with 'M' has an edge to it not present in the novels. Although Connery's Bond retained the easy, confident elan of the clubland hero, he is clearly not from that world. It was this paradoxical rugged elegance, insouciant but aggressively macho, that allowed Connery to project Bond's transitional status, incarnating both the unwavering patriotism of the traditional British gentleman hero and the guiltless sexual phil-andering of the international playboy who embodied the 'swinging' sixties.[34] Bond became, on both sides of the Atlantic, the 'swinging bachelor', a hero of consumption, refined, knowing, hedonistic and liberated.[35] His Aston Martin is the symbol of traditional excellence and the latest in technological wizardry. He is both a 'guy like them' and the projection of the male audience's aspirational fantasy of stylish and successful living.

As Kingsley Amis noted, Bond was also Byronic.[36] Connery's dark good looks, his thin, cruel mouth and calculating self-possession offered the Byronic male in contemporary garb; one whose sadism is directed against enemies of the state. The cruelty is lightened by the laconic, deadpan humour, those one-liners delivered with confident aplomb. The humour, as reviewers recognised, allows the audience to distance themselves from the palpable absurdities of the fantasy and participate in a familiar game.[37]

As commentators have detailed, the Bond films, starting with *Dr No* (1962), offered a package consisting of: star, action storyline, gadgetry, exotic locations, Ken Adam's modernist designs, music, logo and a parade of athletic 'Bond girls', changed for each film.[38] Adroit publicity and extensive merchandising made the annual release of the new Bond film a major media event. 'Bondmania' reached its height with the third film, *Goldfinger* (1964), when the distributors, United Artists, adopted a 'blanket release' strategy with 1,100 prints in worldwide circulation.[39] Connery was mobbed wherever he went on a scale that rivalled the popularity of the Beatles.[40] His Bond had become a modern folk hero with an instantly recognisable style and image. George Lazenby dented the series' popularity in *On Her Majesty's Secret Service* (1969), but when Connery was enticed back for *Diamonds are Forever* (1971), the momentum resumed.

As a modern folk hero, Bond spawned numerous imitators, including American ones. Rank revived the earlier clubland tough guy, Bulldog Drummond, in two films produced by Betty Box, *Deadlier Than the Male* (1966) and *Some Girls Do* (1969). But Richard Johnson lacked Connery's physique, athleticism and style. Tom Adams as Charles Vine in *Licensed to Kill* (1965) and *Where the Bullets Fly* (1966), was a bargain basement version, who played the role mainly for laughs.

## The Anti-Hero: Harry Palmer

Bond's only important rival as an action hero was Michael Caine's Harry Palmer, the name given to the insubordinate secret agent in the three film adaptations of Len Deighton's spy thrillers: *The Ipcress File* (1965), *Funeral in Berlin* (1967) and *Billion Dollar Brain* (1967). All were produced

8. *The Ipcress File* – Michael Caine as Harry Palmer, the insubordinate working-class anti-hero (BFI Stills, Posters and Designs. By courtesy of Carlton International).

by Harry Saltzman with Caine as, 'the anti-hero, someone people would identify with just as they fantasised with Bond'.[41] In the novels he is identified as a displaced 'scholarship boy', a figure from a provincial university, resentful about the privileges conferred by birth, class, a public-school education and the Old Boy network, who dissociates himself from the Establishment by his cynical humour.[42] The films pinpoint these attitudes in the tradition of the 'bolshie' Cockney working-class Other Ranker, previously located on the margins of the war films. One critic judged that Caine 'brings a dead-pan exactness to the part as a sort of wily NCO of life, resourceful, sensibly frightened at times, on the attack with women and implacably dumb-insolent towards officers and bosses'.[43] In *The Ipcress File*, he co-operates with his bosses, Colonel Ross (Guy Doleman) and Major Dalby (Nigel Green) because otherwise he would be back in detention for embezzling from the German army after the war. Palmer is imbued with traditional working-class certainties: bosses are vile, work awful and the only response is to look after Number One.

Palmer, like Bond, exhibits the 1960s concern with lifestyle. This Other Ranker is more sophisticated, discriminating and knowledgeable than his upper-class superiors. His cuisine and his taste in music identify Palmer as one of London's new bohemians, resourceful, intelligent and self-reliant, a 'cool' bachelor, at home in the metropolis.[44] He dresses, decorates and cooks to please himself, but practises his skills in love-making with the sexy Courtney (Sue Lloyd).[45] But Palmer is, in the end, a public servant whose unorthodoxies are tolerated because he is neces-sary. Although he recognises that his worth is measured entirely by his usefulness, in the final scene, having endured prolonged torture and attempted brainwashing, even he is surprised by the cynical callousness of the ruling classes: 'You used me as a decoy. I could have been killed or driven stark raving mad.' Ross tells him bluntly: 'That's what you're paid for.' It was this sense of betrayal that created the third great spy type, Le Carré's introspective heroes, discussed in Chapter 9.

*The Ipcress File*, with its topically cynical world of Establishment moles, double agents and ubiquitous betrayal, was a major success. Critics were reserved about Sidney Furie's over-ingenious 'eavesdropping' style of direction, but admired the film's freshness and contemporaneity, the 'current bachelor neatness' of Palmer's flat, and a working-class figure whose 'Cockney vowels' did not preclude an appreciation of Mozart and *champignons*.[46] The role established Caine as a major star and a new type whose attraction was defined by Penelope Gilliatt: 'Intransigence and opportunism are as central now to sex-appeal in English male acting as charm and height used to be. Make a crack, cheat the boss, expect nothing, go for the lot, and never commit murder except on expenses. The girls fall like skittles.'[47] Caine with his iconic black heavy-rimmed glasses was celebrated as a 'young meteor' in David Bailey's 'Box of Pin-ups'.[48] As a self-made Cockney, Caine was proud of his success, keen to play up to his celebrity, identifying himself as part of a new generation of meritocrats who refused to be self-deprecating.

*Funeral in Berlin*, with much more restrained direction by Guy Hamil-ton, retained the emphasis on the seedy minutiae of the espionage world and on betrayal. But in *Billion Dollar Brain*, Ken Russell's penchant for elaborate spectacle and exaggerated effects destroyed this milieu and reduced the impact of Caine's characterisation. After its modest performance, plans for a fourth film were abandoned.[49]

It was the Bond films that proved to be a lasting success. Bond's cultural roots were far deeper, combining the strengths of the debonair tradition, its charm and sex appeal, with the potency of the tough guy and the expertise of the trained professional. Bond therefore united the three central traditions of British masculine heroism to produce a modern folk hero. Bond's success restored a bruised and battered national pride, but as a part-playful fantasy that allowed the figure to be as harmoniously in tune with the 1960s as the Second World War officer hero was with the 1950s. I shall return to his changing image in Chapter 10.

# 5

# The Everyman

T he emergence of the ordinary man as the hero of the People's War was a key wartime development of masculinity; but, as has been shown, films that reconstructed the conflict concentrated on the middle-class officer, marginalising the role of the ordinary serviceman.[1] The emphasis of the action adventure films was on the hero's exceptional qualities, not his ordinariness. What did endure was the image of John Citizen as stoical paterfamilias and the boy-next-door. But this image had to undergo considerable mutation and reconstruction in order to remain relevant and acceptable. It was no longer enough for the Every-man to endure external events, to 'see it through'; peacetime stories had to become ones of transformation and change that also emphasised rootedness and traditional values.

## John Mills as Pip

The paradigm film was Cineguild's adaptation of Charles Dickens's *Great Expectations* (December 1946). Dickens's novel formed part of the nineteenth-century European *Bildungsroman*, the narrative of character formation and moral growth, in which the young man, from whose perspective the events are described, becomes an Everyman.[2] The moral growth of its hero Pip is the hard-won ability to recognise virtues of ordinariness; his desire for a better, more cultivated life has become confused with class status in what was Dickens's most sustained critique of the Victorian cult of the gentleman.[3] It was a story that provided a

9. *Great Expectations*. John Mills as Pip, 'pulling down the curtains and letting in the light': the Everyman on the threshold of a new world (BFI Stills, Posters and Designs. By courtesy of Carlton International).

clear continuation of the themes of the People's War and the casting of John Mills as Pip lent to the role his accumulated status as the English Everyman. Cineguild's adaptation installs Pip as the centre of the narrative by the voice-overs which promote identification and control the narration, and through the dramatic weight of his presence in virtually every scene. But Pip's 'normality' is also defined by the contrast with the menacing strangeness of the world he encounters. David Lean orchestrates John Bryan's forced perspective set designs and Guy Green's chiaroscuro cinematography to forge an English Expressionist style which renders Pip's world as terrifying and monstrous, populated by grotesque characters who threaten his well-being and sense of identity. Cineguild's status as one of Rank's privileged elite of Independent

Producers meant that Lean had exceptional resources with which to create a 'lavish spectacle' for austerity audiences.[4]

The adaptation employs the revised ending where Pip and Estella are reunited. This interpretation, illogically (Estella has been created to break men's hearts), but with satisfying romantic sentiment, allows Pip both to reject and possess the world of 'gentility'. It enables the film to celebrate the virtues of ordinary decency while allowing its symbolic incorporation into the more expansive world of the upper-middle-class. What is rejected is the petrified aristocratic ennui of Satis House. Its destruction, with Pip tearing down the curtains to let in the sunlight, has been interpreted persuasively as a revolt against the Victorian age as a time of 'oppression and fear' and the victory of a social democratic consensus.[5] For audiences recovering from the war, it offered a powerful image of moral growth and responsible social change. Pip achieves the rewards that are the right of every citizen. The combination of charismatic star, high production values and timely story made *Great Expectations* the second most successful film of 1947. As Pip, Mills won first place in the readers' polls of both the *Daily Mail* and *Picturegoer*. He was comfortably the most popular British male star, strongly liked by all groups of cinema-goers.[6]

## Stoical Ordinariness: Jack Warner and 'Son'

However, *Great Expectations* had no immediate successors and Mills was elevated to middle-class national icon with *Scott of the Antarctic*.[7] His place as Everyman was taken by Jack Warner as the stoical paterfamilias and his 'son' Jimmy Hanley, their images residues from the People's War. Warner's persona reached back further to Albert Chevalier's music-hall portraits of the respectable Cockney, 'the quieter, more sentimental coster who loved his family, and looked for peace with his friends'.[8] Warner first embodied the type as Corporal Horsfall in Ealing's *The Captive Heart* (1946), where he made the transition from variety comedian to straight acting. Horsfall is resilient and intensely patriotic, a loyal soldier and a good comrade, despite some grumbling. He initiates the singing of 'Roll Out the Barrel' which unites the POWs in their first act of defiance and solidarity. He is the loyal friend to Dai Evans (Mervyn Johns) and surrogate father to the errant but tractable Private Matthews (Jimmy Hanley), whom he schools out of a selfish, cocksure individual-ism into working for the team, sacrificing his own welfare for the good

10. *Holiday Camp* – Jack Warner as Joe Huggett, the stoical Everyman (BFI Stills, Posters and Designs. By courtesy of Carlton International).

of others. *The Captive Heart* was highly successful and Warner's eloquently understated reunion with his wife (Gladys Henson) was admired as 'masterly' in a film much praised for its 'restraint' and 'authenticity'.

*The Captive Heart* was clearly still a 'wartime' film which climaxes in the VE day celebrations, but Corporal Horsfall became Joe Huggett, the central character of Gainsborough's *Holiday Camp* (1947). The film offers another variegated community, booming after the war because reunited families were intent on celebrating a return to 'normality' by getting away to the seaside.[9] Shrewdly exploiting his scenes, Warner creates Joe Huggett as a middle-aged Everyman. Though he occasionally complains about the rather chaotic domesticity of his extended family and his best shoes which, 'draw my feet something terrible', Joe is basically good-natured and unflappable. Like Horsfall, he is nobody's fool, fly enough to rescue his son from the clutches of the card sharps and even to take them to the cleaners. A bracing sea breeze and cliff-top prospect even make him sentimental about the joys of a wife – Ethel (Kathleen Harrison) – who gives him what he wants, peaceful contentment with 'something plain about the home'. Warner's understated performance creates a solidly believable character who appears to be behaving quite naturally. Warner had, 'warmth, generosity, modesty and good humour ... and the unique ability, the quiet charisma, to project those qualities on screen'.[10]

The trade press identified the Huggetts as the 'sturdy hub' of a film that was 'novel and topical ... made explicitly for the ninepennies'.[11] Its success led to three further roles for Warner as Joe Huggett. The first, *Here Come the Huggetts* (1948), offered, 'Lively, Laughing, Loveable Huggetts ... Britain's very own family ... The Huggett family is like thousands of other families in Great Britain today, with the same problems, the same outlook, and the same amusements.'[12] The film's convincing roundedness of characterisation was largely attributable to the experienced scriptwriting of Mabel and Denis Constanduros whose sagas of a working-class family, the Buggins, begun in 1928, had gained renewed vigour as a highly successful wartime radio series.[13] *Here Come the Huggetts* concentrates on establishing the family's domestic mores and raises Joe from working-class bus driver to a more prosperous works foreman, living in suburban comfort with a semi-detached house, attached garage and small car. However, this milieu does not connote upward mobility or social pretensions, but the same set of traditional values and solid dependability, an all-purpose stratum of ordinary decency and 'respectability'.[14] Joe is conventional, even old-fashioned, in his habits, pottering around in a collarless shirt and pullover, feeding his chickens or mending something in his tiny workshop. The installation of a telephone fulfils his dream of modernity, a slight enhancement of his standard of living and domestic routines, not a major change.

Joe tries to patronise or bully his wife and three daughters, but the film continually unseats his attempt to play the strong, authoritarian Victorian patriarch; they usually get their own way in what amounts to a sensible 'rubbing along'. But unruly young women, as in *This Happy Breed*, remain the disruptive element. Joe's niece Di Hopkins (Diana Dors) is 'fast': Americanised and overtly sexual. Joe is embarrassed by this 'painted hussy' who embodies fears about a restless, superficial and selfish generation out for a good time. His own daughters are more tractable and sensible. The eldest, Jane (Jane Hylton), rejects the bohemian communist intellectual Harold Hinchley and marries ordinary sailor Jimmy, with Jimmy Hanley reprising his *Holiday Camp* role as the decent, cheery boy-next-door. The film ends with their wedding, thus underlining marriage and the family as the core values, an unbroken (despite the war) tradition of steadiness. This is mirrored by the royal wedding, which, for all the tribulations involved in turning out for the procession, rouses Joe and Ethel to a sentimental patriotism that emphasises their status as the national family. The Huggetts succeeded *This Happy Breed*'s the Gibbons as the screen's 'backbone of England', an image of a nation now united in modest contentment without the threat of war or mass unemployment, the post-war working-class ideal.[15]

*Vote for Huggett* (1949) launched Joe into public life, campaigning as a member of the Progressive (i.e. Labour) Party. His policies represent a commonsensical extension of the order and decency of his own household; in his eyes the small community of Strutham is 'like a family', and there must be give and take. But Joe's fight against local corruption affords him the opportunity to give the conniving and selfish middle classes their comeuppance. Straightforwardly telling the residents, 'there's a fiddle going on', Joe saves the day by commandeering dotty local gentry into donating part of their estate for his lido and park/pleasure garden, wholesome open-air recreation which embodies his sense of civic decency. However, the sprightly vigour and social democratic progressiveness of *Vote for Huggett* was not matched by *The Huggetts Abroad* (1949), which retreats into a conservative little Englandism where all foreigners are odd and there is no place like home, despite the queues and the rationing. Its meandering storyline collapses into a series of discrete episodes, indicative of the series' declining energy and its destiny as a radio 'soap', from 1953 to 1962.

The Huggetts' primary appeal was to suburban and provincial audiences. Their popularity was as the inheritors of the values of the People's War. With a Labour government in power there was no need to present ordinary people as poor and oppressed, or comic simpletons, but rather as the principal benefactors of a new egalitarianism. 'The Huggetts absolutely caught the spirit and feeling that existed after the war ... People didn't want more fairy stories; they wanted something in which they could recognise themselves.'[16] However, looking back on the series in 1950, one commentator thought the 'original streak of plebeian vulgarity' of *Holiday Camp* had got lost, becoming 'corseted' into a respectable lower-middle-class *métier*.[17] The later films certainly did not match the box-office success of *Holiday Camp*, which possibly indicated a cooling of interest on the part of the 'ninepennies'. It may also be the case that the appeal was to an older audience fraction, which continued to enjoy the radio series.

Warner's apotheosis came with his role as George Dixon in Ealing's *The Blue Lamp* (1950) where the paterfamilias became the idealised public servant. *The Blue Lamp*, made with the full support of the Metropolitan Police, was the first film to *centre* on the ordinary constable, both on and off duty. Its documentary qualities, with extensive location shooting and a detailed concentration on the routines of Paddington Green police station, creates an apparently uncontrived realism and authenticity. *The Blue Lamp* had strong continuities with Ealing's wartime films in depicting the caring and efficient all-male group, their camaraderie a blending of nations – 'Jock' Campbell, 'Taff' Hughes – and regions, with new recruit Andy Mitchell (Jimmy Hanley) up from Kent to join with the Londoners. There is no animosity between ranks or branches of the service, they form an idealised community, the village idyll transferred to London.

At the centre of this community is George Dixon, the dependable and knowledgeable local bobby nearing retirement after lengthy service. Dixon epitomises the cheery comradeship of the force, a member of the choir and the darts team whom he entertains with his apposite witticisms and mildly irreverent little ditties like 'All Correct'. At home he is the idealised paterfamilias enjoying tranquillity and quiet pleasures with his reliable wife (Gladys Henson), surrounded by his begonias and geraniums, the *rus in urbe* English idyll. The home only lacks a son to replace Bert, killed in the war, an important reminder of sacrifice and loss. That lack is supplied by his surrogate, Andy Mitchell, with Jimmy Hanley again performing the role of the eager and willing boy-next-door; the two actors locked into a mutual mirroring of the same stout and kindly virtues, a seamless continuity between youth and middle-age. It is Mitchell who has to bear the news of Dixon's death to his wife, a poignant martyrdom, whose shock waves are felt throughout the force.[18] As Dixon's replacement, Mitchell overpowers his killer Tom Riley. In the final scene he directs a man to Paddington station just as Dixon had done in the pre-credit sequence.

*The Blue Lamp*, lauded by the critics, was also the most popular British film of 1950. The film was exceptional in centring on the ordinary constable rather than the inspector, but Dixon reinforced existing popular conceptions of the police, what has been identified as an 'indulgent tradition' of representing the 'English Bobby' as, 'moderate and sensible: the epitome of English level-headedness'.[19] Dixon embodied that 'reliable, stout and kindly' ideal.[20]

Stanley Holloway, whose post-war film career partly shadowed

Warner's, played Arthur Pemberton, another paterfamilias-cum-local activist, in *Passport to Pimlico* (1949).[21] Pimlico is one of several Ealing communities that, transformed as part of Burgundia, exemplify the virtues of 'standing alone' and 'seeing it through' against a tyrannical state; actions which revived the core wartime myths of a unified co-operative solidarity.[22] This nostalgia marginalises Pemberton's imaginative scheme for the recreational use of the bomb site. The celebration banquet round his utopian civic dream, the new lido, is quickly soaked by a downpour which drives everyone back indoors into their own homes and mocks his desire for progressive change. As paterfamilias Henry Lord, a Cockney grocer living over his shop in the Boxes' *The Happy Family* (1952), Holloway has to defend his property against another set of overweening bureaucrats who wish to demolish the 'house of Lords' to make way for the Festival of Britain feeder road. The Lords, with their pet Belgian rabbit Winston, now celebrate a *defensive* lower-middle-class resilience. Conscious of having survived the Depression and the loss of a son in the war, Henry now sees the state as his enemy, but rejects the call for revolution from his communist son-in-law Cyril (George Cole). Instead, he raises his glass to, 'living quietly and being left alone', the Englishman in his castle ignoring the outside world.

This was a symptomatic image of the paterfamilias as a bastion against change, backward-looking, not facing the future and thus ripe for replacement as the idealised Everyman. As the cultural power of younger cinema-goers increased and enhanced prosperity made stoical restraint less desirable, the respectable lower-class paterfamilias became an increasingly marginal, residual construction. Warner's further 'Huggett' roles, *Those People Next Door* (1953) and *Home and Away* (1956), were second features. Warner's resurrection as PC Dixon from 1955 to 1976 was precisely for the older audience who stayed at home to watch the television. It was television 'soaps', beginning with the BBC's Grove Family (1954–57), that sustained this image of suburban respectability. There were two late flourishes, both adaptations of Bill Naughton's plays, *The Family Way* (1966) and *Spring and Port Wine* (1970). The latter's sexual politics were conventional, a plea for austere paterfamilias Rafe Crompton (James Mason) to leave his mental domain shaped by the hungry thirties and embrace a more relaxed present. But the Boultings' *The Family Way* took a fresh look at the sexuality of the archetypal northern patriarch, Ezra Fitton (John Mills). A man's man, fond of drinking beer and arm-wrestling, Ezra has never really taken to his

sensitive, book-reading son Arthur (Hywel Bennett). His deepest sus-
picions are aroused when word leaks out that Arthur's marriage to
Jenny (Hayley Mills) remains unconsummated. In defending her son,
Lucy Fitton (Marjorie Rhodes) reveals that Ezra's best friend, Billy
Stringfellow, accompanied them on their honeymoon to Blackpool.
Ezra's reaction reveals that his deepest emotional bonds were with the
man he was brought up with and worked with: 'Did you expect me to
leave him alone during holiday week just because I'd got wed to you?
... It takes a lifetime for a man to make a proper friend.' His most
cherished memories of that time are the early morning walks along the
seashore listening to his companion's appreciation of the beauties of
nature. What he has to acknowledge, ironically in an arm-wrestling
match, is that Arthur is Billy's child. As he sees Arthur off on his
delayed honeymoon he breaks down, his confusion and tears suggesting
the nebulous emotions he cannot control or understand.

## The Middle-class Boy-next-door

As the power of the paterfamilias waned, the interest shifted to the figure
of the boy-next-door, no longer simply a reproduction of the loved
father but a figure of mild rebelliousness, or at least some independence.
This reconstruction occurred first in the cycle of middle-class romantic
comedies that vied with war films as the most popular movies of the
mid-1950s. These comedies combined the appeal of slapstick with a
certain verbal wit derived from an earlier cycle of upper-class comedies
of manners; but now the characters were always young and the settings
much less luxurious. Indeed, their young couples were always very hard
up. They starred serious actors playing comedy rather than professional
funny men, hence the credibility of their characterisation.

ABPC's *Young Wives' Tale* (1950) and *Father's Doing Fine* (1952) were
transitional films that anticipated certain elements of the emergent
formation. They were adaptations of successful West End plays, as was
*For Better, For Worse* (1954), which had been running for over five years.
Dirk Bogarde's Tony Howard and his young wife Anne (Susan Stephen)
struggle to make a go of their marriage in the minute, sixteen by ten
foot, modern flat, which is all his slender income affords. Tony unhesitatingly insists that Anne has to give up her job when they marry
so that he is the sole breadwinner.[23] If the couple's roles are firmly
traditional, within the home they have an equal partnership with some

11. *Doctor in the House* – 1950s Bohemia, the student household: Donald Houston, Dirk Bogarde, Donald Sinden, Kenneth More and Suzanne Cloutier (BFI Stills, Posters and Designs. By courtesy of Carlton International).

role reversal: Anne is quite practical and commonsensical, Tony impractical, easily flustered and prone to panic. Symbolically the couple struggle to combine traditional Victoriana, her aunt's gift of a heavy mahogany wardrobe and sideboard, with the up-to-date: kitchen units, Hoover and Marvimix blender, all obtained on hire-purchase. Whatever the tribulations, they are determined to make it under their own steam, rejecting any help from her parents. Tony tells his father-in-law (Cecil Parker), 'There are hundreds of us in the same boat and they haven't got parents who can cough up £4.10s. at a moment's notice.' Their various domestic crises are overcome by youthful energy and optimism, the quality that most reviewers remarked upon.

However, it was Rank's cycle of films which gave the type a wide currency. Although John Gregson's Alan McKim in *Genevieve* (1953) was the first incarnation, it was Dirk Bogarde's performance as the personable young doctor, Simon Sparrow, in *Doctor in the House* (1954) that made a significant impact. Betty Box's experience of producing both the 'Huggett' cycle and *Miranda* (1948), by far the wittiest and most successful of that earlier cycle of upper-middle-class comedies, blended to create *Doctor in the House*. Its director, Gerald Thomas, saw the comedy as less quaint and whimsical than Ealing's variety, but with the emphasis on situation not farce, as in the 'Carry On' films.[24] This was achieved by screenwriter Nicholas Phipps's adept transformation of Richard Gordon's novel, which was little more than a collection of medical anecdotes, into a coherent narrative that charts the progress of four student doctors. Phipps's screenplay moves the story on at a brisk pace, allows a satisfying blend of verbal wit and slapstick, but above all creates four solid and believable central male characters. Perhaps the master-stroke was to have all four share a flat, creating what one might describe as a cosily bohemian environment, a rough and tumble student house-hold which offers a licensed space for rude high spirits, impromptu domesticities and unstuffy relationships. It was something new, different and obviously modern in British comedy.

Within the male quartet, Benskin (Donald Sinden) was the con-ventional womaniser; the asexual rugby hearty Taff Evans (Donald Houston) was the garrulous Welsh stereotype given a youthful gloss; Grimsdyke (Kenneth More) was, as has been argued, the modernised Edwardian. They serve as foils for Bogarde's contemporary middle-class Everyman. Bogarde possessed the looks and soft-spoken charm of the debonairs, but, like Kenneth More, he reconstructed the image into a more democratic figure. Simon is shy, diffident, vulnerable and anxious to do well. Unlike the debonairs, his masculine charm comes from naïvety rather than experience, an innocent and engagingly wide-eyed hero, exploring the mysteries of medicine and the fair sex. His sensitivity leads to acute reactions to the routines of hospital life: he faints in the operating theatre and hears the sea in his stethoscope. Simon was a figure which, within a fun-loving comic mode, offered an attractive presentation of male femininity.[25] Dressed in a sub-Coward red velvet jacket, he makes a hash of the whole encounter with a fashionable society woman, Isobel (Kay Kendall), in a comic parody of the sophisticated Man About Town. He takes flight from his landlady's sexually voracious daughter (Shirley Eaton), only to find himself on an impossible mission to seduce 'rigor mortis' (Joan Sims). But, true to his boy-next-door credentials, he falls in love with a pretty but sensible woman, Nurse Joy Gibson (Muriel Pavlow), his partner and helpmate. Joy links the world of work with domesticity. Like the patient wives of the 'serious' professional films, she admires Simon's basic dedication and aptitude as a student doctor. Their relationship is one of equals, a partnership, not a romantic fantasy, the officially approved middle-class ideal of the companionate marriage.[26]

*Doctor in the House* carefully retains a residue of the idealism of the doctor hero. Simon's first maternity case is treated without mockery and its successful outcome is an index of his professional competence. Dilys Powell memorably described the scene as a 'feeling space', where the sanctities of the medical profession can be unobtrusively shown.[27] As a modern, 'classless' doctor, Simon is at ease and relaxed in the company of the working-class mother, approachable and sympathetic rather than aloofly paternal. The handling of this scene in the film contrasts strongly with its equivalent in the novel which takes place in a foul tenement with a slattern mother and ends anti-climactically. However, that scene is the one overtly serious moment within a comic mode that deliberately punctures the pomposity and saintliness of the medical profession.[28] St Swithin's is dominated by Sir Lancelot Spratt, the blood and bones butcher surgeon from popular melodrama, given a splendidly roaring performance by James Robertson Justice: the paterfamilias as comic ogre. Although Sir Lancelot may be the quartet's scourge, he admires their youth and energy, particularly their enthusiastic competitiveness in defending the honour of St Swithins after the rugby victory. Sir Lancelot not only pays their fine like an indulgent father, but in the process he reminds the Dean of his own youthful peccadilloes.

It was the appeal of youth and optimism that was emphasised in one assessment of a film which 'has uprooted all records at the Odeon Leicester Square … What does this fantastic success signify? I suggest that a large part of the result is due to the buoyant youthfulness of the film. Here is freshness. Here is vitality.'[29] It became the most popular British picture of 1954. For reviewers, the film's light-heartedness, the refreshing way it gently debunked the medical profession, did not sacrifice the 'realism' and 'believability' of the characters: 'although the film is only a light-hearted frolic it has the ring of truth. These young hearties are real people.'[30] Dilys Powell saw the film's achievement as the successful representation of the 'well spoken young', rescued from the plethora of working-class spivs and delinquents.[31] Her comments help to identify Simon as a consensual middle-class image, one which, like the 'cadet', had been shorn of the anachronistic associations of the upper-middle-class 'young juvenile' of the previous generation. Bogarde became a major star, the 'idol of the Odeons'.

Rank executives had been very lukewarm about *Doctor in the House* and had ruthlessly streamlined the budget, but its success made them require a 'Doctor' film every two years, with Bogarde retained as Simon Sparrow.[32] Part of the attraction was the film's fundamental endorsement of wholesome monogamy and family values, an ideology that was more explicitly celebrated in a raft of films about newlyweds in which Rank placed its other young male stars. They played similar roles in films that were 'in good taste, and with sound moral standards'.[33] John Gregson starred in *Value for Money* (1955) and *True as a Turtle* (1957), dubbed by the critics a 'nautical *Genevieve*'. Donald Sinden starred in the sequel to *Miranda*, *Mad About Men* (1954). His hair was backcombed and lightened to make him look less rakish in a film whose sexual politics were much less *risqué* than the original, reinforcing conventional monogamy. Sinden was engagingly ineffectual but decent in *An Alligator Named Daisy* (1955), with enough good sense to reject his family's militarism, and the temptations of vulgar money, to wed his animal-loving girl-next-door (Jean Carson). As another middle-class newlywed, Pelham Butterworth in *Your Money or Your Wife* (1960), he had to dust and wash-up, an apron over his pin-striped suit, in order for the couple to survive financially. Michael Craig, Bogarde's replacement in *Doctor in Love* (1960), also starred in Betty Box's *Upstairs Downstairs* (1959), whose cast of eccentrics were used to hide the basic dullness of the central couple and the predictability of the plot. As a general's son in *No My Darling Daughter* (1961) he has a very mild flirtation with alternative values before plunging into a romance with cute tomboy Tansy (Juliet Mills), daughter of his father's business partner. Craig was an impecunious barrister in the final Box-Thomas contribution, *A Pair of Briefs* (1962). His misogyny crumbles in the face of the charms of his new colleague Frances (Mary Peach); but the comedy was leaden in Nicholas Phipps's weakest screenplay.

Anglo-Amalgamated made some rival films, produced by Betty Box's husband, Peter Rogers, and directed by Ralph Thomas's brother, Gerald. *Raising the Wind* (1961) was *Doctor in the House* set in a music academy. *The Iron Maiden* (1962) was another sub-*Genevieve* effort starring Michael Craig as an aircraft designer with a penchant for antiquated traction engines. Norman Hudis was taken off 'Carry On' duties to script two romantic comedies for Juliet Mills: *Twice Round the Daffodils* (1962) and *Nurse on Wheels* (1963). In both she falls in love with a soulful Ronald Lewis, playing Bogarde's role without the comedy. The former deserves some recognition as the obverse of *Carry on Nurse*, another study of anxious men in institutions, in this case a TB Sanatorium. Donald Sinden reprised his Benskin role as a lascivious RAF officer, and Donald Houston gave a fine performance as a macho Welsh miner who breaks down when he realises that he is in for more than 'observation'. However, the group settles down to some comradely male bonding in pursuit of the opposite sex culminating in the engagement of Everyman Bob White (Lewis) to Sister Catty (Mills).

These 'new men', the 'well-spoken young', were lovably flawed, moody, impractical, harassed, inclined to petulance and adolescent sulkiness, occasionally downright silly, rather than idealised and dashingly romantic. The comic mode licensed the weakness of these civilian counterparts to the war films' cadet, often played by the same actors, released from the burden of being heroic. The films open up a space, albeit a highly controlled one, in which women were allowed to be sharply critical of male behaviour, their irritating preoccupations and stubborn obsessions. They could also be the educator of the male. However, because these young men were basically decent, uninterested in wealth and conspicuous success, looking for a modest domestic contentment with a sensible woman, their desires were fulfilled. Lack of funds requires the couple to display the core values of respectability: thrift, sobriety, prudence, delayed gratification and self-help, all given a youthful gloss. The visual style, with its bright but cool colours, angular, clean lines and uncluttered compositions, encoded a bouncy optimism that signalled the end of austerity and the weakening of a rigid and stuffy middle-aged Victorian paternalism, beginning to lose its moral authority.

The huge success of *Genevieve* and *Doctor in the House* showed that, in the mid-1950s, these films had captured and helped shape a new mood. Both were word-of-mouth successes, which suggests that they attracted the middle-class 'occasional' cinema-goer in addition to the predominantly working-class 'habit' audience. Rank's 1955 preference survey clearly revealed that these films were enjoyed by the AB audience in very significant numbers with the DE fraction significantly underrepresented.[34] This middle-class audience further declined after 1954 and could no longer guarantee the success of the other films which have been briefly discussed, none of which was mentioned in *Kinematograph Weekly*'s yearly round-ups. Their production can only be ascribed to studio inertia, particularly Rank's refusal to recognise that the family audience was in decline. The continued success of the 'Doctor' series was probably caused by their unusually *risqué* and slapstick elements which would have had a strong populist appeal.[35] The casting of Leslie Phillips in the later films made the figure much more salacious.

## The Working-class Boy-next-door

The decline of the middle-class Everyman was partly due to the renewed competition from working-class figures, first the pop stars discussed in the next section and then in the early 1960s by the provincial boy-next-door, a placid version of the Angry Young Man. *A Kind of Loving* (1962) was a paean to ordinariness rather than anger and revolt. Its director, John Schlesinger, saw in Stan Barstow's novel 'a very true story about love. I thought it observed human beings and their emotions very beautifully. It wasn't exactly new.'[36] It did acknowledge that Vic (Alan Bates) has problems settling down and these are partly caused by the strength of his sexual desires for Ingrid (June Ritchie). These feelings could now be more openly acknowledged under John Trevelyan's liberal regime at the BBFC.[37] Vic is a more complex, rounded, sensitive and troubled figure than his predecessors, but much of his frustrations and animus can be channelled into that conventional figure of hate, the mother-in-law. The final scenes, which show the pair moving in to their own modest home, are quite optimistic.

It was sensitivity, complexity and a troubled sexuality that characterised these new working-class boys-next-door. Clive Donner's *Some People* (1962) moved away from the delinquency paradigm to offer a detailed and well-observed study of Johnnie (Ray Brooks), confused and unsettled about his job, his relationship with the middle-class Anne (Annika Wills) and with his rough-hewn father (Harry H. Corbett). The conflicts are resolved by Kenneth More in the service of the Duke of Edinburgh Award Scheme, which the film was designed to promote. David Hemmings, who played a supporting role in *Some People*, starred as the Everyman Dave Martin in *Live It Up* (1963). His confusions and longings become sublimated into forming a band with his mates. In *The Leather Boys* (1963) Everyman Reggie (Colin Campbell) finds a more thoughtful, sensitive and supportive companion in the homosexual Pete (Dudley Sutton) than in his coarse-grained wife Dot (Rita Tushingham). Although delicately handled, the film eventually settles into the established paradigm of heterosexual conformist and gay victim.[38] Campbell played a similar role in *Saturday Night Out* (1964), but in a straightforward story of heterosexual romance. Alan (Michael Crawford), in *Two Left Feet* (1963), has a confused and unsatisfactory liaison with the glamorous and experienced Eileen (Nyree Dawn Porter), before he settles down with sensible Beth (Julia Foster). His determination not to become a policeman like his father (Bernard Lee) is diluted when the paterfamilias delivers his sympathetic homily that offers an understanding of the problems and responsibilities of a generation that can choose its lifestyle.

Michael Crawford replayed this role in *The Knack ... and how to get it* (1965), but Richard Lester's film recognised that society was now more fluid and free-wheeling and the virtues of ordinariness were relentlessly dull unless played for comic effect and complemented by alternative images of masculinity: the lecherous Tolen (Ray Brooks), the classless modern cad, and the eccentric bohemian Tom (Donal Donnelly). Colin is more Fool than Everyman, but he wins through in the end. Clive Donner's exuberant *Here We Go Round the Mulberry Bush* (1967), based on Hunter Davies's witty novel, was also conscious of the social changes that were taking place. Its contemporary Everyman cycles round the parks and shopping precincts of Stevenage New Town. Jamie McGregor (Barry Evans) is a decent grammar-school lad trying to gain his A-levels, but confused about his social status and obsessed with losing his virginity, convinced the 'whole country's having it off' while he is the only one missing out. Donner's film is highly self-conscious, with its modish psychedelia, direct address to the camera, parodies of silent cinema and Swinging London, James Bond and Scandinavian sex films. It also glances backward to the New Wave when Jamie contrasts himself with the hero of *The Loneliness of the Long Distance Runner*. But he retains the boy-next-door's core decency, rejecting the 'liberated' sexuality of modern Mary (Judy Geeson) in favour of sensible Clare: 'That's the girl I'd like to marry. She seems a nice class of person.'

## The Pop Star as Boy-next-door

This construction of the working-class Everyman was overshadowed by a more important cultural development, the birth of the teenage pop star. Teenagers were the most visible beneficiaries of an expanding economy. Mark Abrams's widely used 1958 survey, which defined 'teen-agers' as the fifteen to twenty-five age group, estimated that their incomes had doubled since 1938 and that much of this 'discretionary spending power' was used to buy records and to see films.[39] As well as being male-dominated, 'the teenage market is almost entirely working class … not far short of 90 per cent of all teenage spending is conditioned by working class taste and values'.[40] Abrams concluded that in order to appeal to this market, entrepreneurs needed an understanding of American culture and its impact on working-class taste, characterised by its extreme volatility.[41] Britain's rock 'n' roll craze, fuelled by Elvis Presley's records and the release of *Rock Around the Clock* (1956), gave a clear indication of this new taste.

Anglo-Amalgamated led the way, releasing *The Tommy Steele Story*, the first British film deliberately targeted at a teenage audience, in June 1957, only eight months after Steele's first hit record. Producer Stuart Levy commented, 'We figure that if Americans could produce money-making movies about rock 'n' roll music, we had the necessary talent to do the same here. Steele, himself, has a tremendous following.'[42] *The Tommy Steele Story* was marketed as a, 'documentary about Britain's answer to Elvis' and 'The Sensational Success Story of Britain's Teenage Idol'. Norman Hudis's screenplay deployed the existing legend of Steele's rise to fame. Tommy Hicks is shown as an optimistic, directionless innocent who has a childlike delight in music and 'rhythm'; the film consistently links him to the 'natural' rhythms of Caribbean calypso. Back in London, unsure of his future, he plays to the bored patrons of a drab Soho coffee bar which he transforms into a world of uninhibited pleasure. At this moment he is 'discovered' by John Kennedy, another in a host of good-natured champions whose one desire seems to be to help him on. As a 'natural', Steele is at one with his audience. His supportive mum comments: 'You can give the young people the music they want. You're one of them and they understand you.' The film's slender storyline, its drab and rather rudimentary sets and pedestrian camerawork, serve only to heighten the vibrant energy of Steele's musical numbers. A representative critic commented, 'The quality of the film is that Tommy Steele, who dominates it, is a completely real person with an ability to project this reality with wholly unaffected ease.'[43] Reviewers sensed the emergence of an authentic, blond-quiffed folk hero, rising from the slums of Bermondsey, to show that success was possible for decent working-class youth.

Decency is the key quality manifested in the film and, as the voice and image of the new teenage culture, Steele was offered as the ordinary boy-next-door who loves his parents and is respectable, not rebellious. In a famous article Colin McInnes praised this 'honest and healthy' young man as a responsible role model: 'He is Pan, he is Puck, he is every nice girl's boy, every kid's favourite elder brother, every mother's cherished adolescent son.'[44] Steele was 'so much *nicer*' than Presley: '[h]is voice and cavortings are sensual, certainly, but in a strange way innocent, even pure.'[45] Steele was marketed as well-adjusted, happy and ordinary. In a magazine-style 'autobiography' he concluded: 'And as for you fans of mine who write and say what you like about me is the fact that I'm a pretty ordinary kid just like yourself [*sic*] – well, so I am. And that's the way I'm going to stay.'[46]

Herbert Wilcox was only one month slower out of the blocks, reconstructing Frankie Vaughan from old-fashioned crooner in top hat and tails, to rock icon in *These Dangerous Years* (1957). More overtly sensual than Steele, Vaughan was promoted as a British Brando, photographed in a leather jacket, cigarette dangling from the side of his mouth.[47] But this 'documentary', which foregrounded Vaughan's working-class Liverpudlian background, showed the rebel tamed. Vaughan plays Dave Wyman, leader of the gang from the 'Cassy', 'desolate backwater of Liverpool's prosperous river-front … an unsupervised world where boy is King'. As a product of that environment, Wyman, clad in leather jacket with sideburns and long wavy hair, appears to be the archetypal delinquent, which the film equates with his ability as a rock 'n' roll singer. But, like so many of Wilcox's films, it tries to have it both ways, celebrating Vaughan's raunchy sexual attractiveness in the rock 'n' roll numbers, but containing these within a highly conservative narrative which promoted traditional values. He is presented as the decent boy-next-door, steered along the right path by a surrogate father, the saintly battalion padre (George Baker). Wyman embraces the virtues of National Service army discipline as the route to a responsible and fulfilling manhood that is worthy of the memory of his father who won a DSO; he even chooses the army as a career. But the film's ostensible rejection of rock 'n' roll as a manifestation of delinquency proved to be no obstacle to Vaughan's fans, who mobbed him at the London première; Vaughan was voted Britain's 'Top Screen Singing Star' in *Picturegoer*'s 1958 poll. Subsequent publicity consistently emphasised Vaughan's ordinariness and his love of the home fireside.[48]

Terry Dene, who, before his nervous breakdown, was Tommy Steele's rival, starred in Butcher's *The Golden Disc* (1958).[49] It also used a documentary approach to educate its audience into the mysteries of the new youth culture. Another seedy and drab café with a middle-aged clientele is transformed into a swinging coffee bar complete with high swivel stools, circular counter, jukebox, Espresso machine, Art Deco lighting and mad-line drawings. Like Steele, Dene is presented as nondescript until energised by his performances. His check shirt, tight jeans and guitar announce an entertainer very different from the big-band crooners he replaces. The same girl who swooned and screamed at Denis Lotis at the beginning of the film sports her new 'Terry' T-shirt in the final shot to symbolise her change of allegiance. *The Golden Disc* did concede that there was a potentially aggressive record industry ready to swallow these raw talents, but determination and co-operative effort win the day.

The screen development of both Steele and Vaughan showed their incorporation into established patterns of entertainment and towards a broad acceptability. The driving force here was television. Pop stars' managers could not risk narrowing their artists' appeal and so alienating the family audience.[50] Vaughan's subsequent films – *Wonderful Things!* (1958), *The Lady is a Square* (1959) and *The Heart of a Man* (1959) – always present him as an outsider who becomes assimilated into everyday life. Wilcox borrowed devices from earlier films, the disguised butler in *The Lady is a Square* and the 'dream dance' sequence in *The Heart of a Man*, to effect the fantasy. However, audiences did not seem able to accept these manoeuvres and Vaughan reverted to a career in cabaret. Steele's film career was more successful. *The Duke Wore Jeans* (1958) was a well-worn Ruritanian make-believe in which Steele played both Cockney casual labourer Tommy Hudson and his aristocratic double, the Hon. Tony Whitecliffe. For Tommy, the solution to every problem is to 'be yourself', avoiding 'swank' and pretension of any kind. *Tommy the Toreador* (1959) was an even looser confection, a further development of Steele into a family entertainer with music-hall numbers such as 'Watch the Birdie', and sentimental ballads including 'Little White Bull', sung to an adoring group of children who could have been refugees from a Max Bygraves film. In *Light Up the Sky* (1960), he was the Everyman in khaki, endlessly cheerful, and he was the lovable orphan made good in *It's All Happening* (1963).

However, the pop star whose screen career best exemplified this desire to override generational, class and cultural differences in favour of broad acceptability was Cliff Richard. The singer was, 'very conscious that our careers depended upon the mums and dads and that we needed to appeal to them to get going'.[51] He represented a further stage in the manufacture of the anodyne teenage star: 'Before him, all pop singers sounded what they were, solidly working class. Cliff introduced something new, a bland ramble, completely classless.'[52] Cliff played the obligatory delinquent-who-reforms in his first film, *Serious Charge* (1959). *Expresso Bongo* (1959), Wolf Mankowitz's play which satirised the mythology of Steele's rise to fame, was drastically altered to accommodate Richard's wholesome, clean-living, boy-next-door image.[53]

Cliff was the quintessential decent young Everyman in three films – *The Young Ones* (1961), *Summer Holiday* (1962) and *Wonderful Life* (1964) – produced by Kenneth Harper and funded by ABPC. Each had screenplay and lyrics by Peter Myers and Ronald Cass, whose background was in West End revues. In order to avoid another 'rockumentary', especially about a star whose Hertfordshire upbringing was not susceptible to myth-making, they turned to the pre-war MGM musicals starring Mickey Rooney and Judy Garland.[54] In *The Young Ones* Cliff leads a group of teenagers fighting for the survival of their youth club against his property developer father (Robert Morley). Their brief music-hall revue shows the essential continuity of popular culture and the final number the fusion of generations in a celebration of the 'spirit of get up and go'. *Summer Holiday* was another popular hymn to youth and enterprise: their exploits in the London double-decker bus create a market for a new kind of holiday package. Sidney Furie's return as director for *Wonderful Life* meant a much more inventive and interesting visual style, including a clever pastiche history of cinema, but ended with another celebration of the blending of youth and experience. The liveliness of some of the numbers could not compensate for a feeble, hastily concocted storyline and the film's reception was very modest.

Both Michael Winner's *Play it Cool* (1962) and Michael Carreras's *What a Crazy World* (1963) tried to blend social comment with a celebration of decency, but this was clearest in the Beatles' debut film, *A Hard Day's Night* (1964), the second most popular film of that year. Its young director, Richard Lester, was optimistic about the possibilities for radical change in British society.[55] The Beatles' spontaneous actions and, particularly Lennon's, dry wit, have a certain irreverence whose freshness is set against a moribund older generation which fought the war but cannot accept further change. The stuffy businessman on the train to London is the first of those who get their comeuppance. Lester's kaleidoscopic visual style, with its hand-held camera, jump cuts, episodic narration and surreal humour, caught something of the freshness and iconoclasm of the early French New Wave films. The well-known expansiveness of the 'Can't Buy Me Love' number is a joyful defiance of petty rules and regulations. But the film also celebrates the virtues of the group's ordinariness and uncorrupted optimism. Liverpudlian Alun Owen's screenplay emphasises their provincial working-class authenticity in the face of an aggressively metropolitan publicity machine anxious to cash in on 'Beatlemania', incarnated by Kenneth Haigh's supercilious trendsetter who has a contempt for this new 'product'. *A Hard Day's Night* is therefore a transitional film, sharing the core values of the existing paradigm, but giving them a slightly harder edge.

For *Help!* (1965) Lester eventually turned to the more satirical and rococo writing of Charles Wood, whose screenplay constructs a film around rather than about the Beatles. The most effective joke is the first. The Beatles arrive at a very ordinary row of terraced houses with two biddies' cooing, 'Lovely lads and so natural ... And still the same as they was before they was'; but when they enter, the interior is open plan and palatial with a bizarre range of gadgets. Authentic ordinariness and their cult status are now completely incompatible and the sub-Bondian fantasy of the plot moves the action far way from ordinary life.

Only John Boorman's *Catch Us If You Can* developed this iconoclasm and is dealt with in Chapter 8; subsequent musicals returned to the boy-next-door paradigm but eschewed social realism in favour of free-wheeling fantasies. Anglo's *I've Gotta Horse* (1965), showed the pitfalls of putting on a show when its star, Billy Fury, is obsessed by his animal friends (dogs, race horses and a chimpanzee). The same company's *Three Hats for Lisa* (1965) offered Joe Brown as a grinning Bermondsey docker, Johnny Howjego, who initiates an Italian starlet with a penchant for British memorabilia into the delights of good old London Town assisted by Sid James as a singing cabbie. Paramount's *Half a Sixpence* (1967) opted for polished pastiche Edwardiana, a musical adaptation of Wells's *Kipps* especially designed for its star, Tommy Steele, that had already been a major Broadway and West End stage hit. As the orphan clerk whose windfall allows him entry into fashionable society, Arthur Kipps triumphantly rejects all the 'swank' and 'la-de-da' and becomes 'himself' by marrying an ordinary girl. Twenty years on Steele was the new Pip, whose 'great expectations' lead only to misery and who has to lose to win. *Mrs Brown You've Got a Lovely Daughter* (1968) offered a contemporary Pip. Herman (Peter Noone) has to reject fashionable London society, rediscover the virtues of his humble origins in Manchester and return to the plain and homely charms of his childhood sweetheart.

After the mid-1950s, there was no longer any room for the stoical paterfamilias. The Everyman became exclusively the boy-next-door, his image tailored to shifting social conditions and audience taste. These mutations tried to reconcile a desire for social betterment with stability and continuity. The Everyman needs to be understood in relation to the image of the delinquent, discussed in Chapter 7, and the rebel heroes of Chapter 8, which threatened the generational continuity of masculine values and social cohesion. Success never eradicates the Everyman's basic decency, though it may temporarily obscure it until he rediscovers the lasting charms of being ordinary.

# 6

# Fools and Rogues

After their significant decline during the war, the re-emergence of Fools and Rogues was a striking feature of post-war British cinema. The Fool, as a bumbling Everyman, exposes the arbitrariness of social regulations and masculine norms that were becoming either irrelevant or unattainable. The Fool always means well and tries harder than others, but his triumphs or tribulations say much about the possibilities of success. By contrast, the Rogue is best placed to adjust to rapidly changing social conditions and 'get away with it' against various regulations, restrictions and authoritarian institutions, notably the army and the health service, and lauds quick-witted opportunistic individualism at various social levels. The history of both types can best be understood through an analysis of the specific incarnations of particular stars. For reasons of clarity and economy I do not comment on television comedians – Benny Hill, Frankie Howerd, Morecambe and Wise, Stanley Baxter – whose films were a marginal adjunct to their television performances. The exceptions are Charlie Drake and Tony Hancock, whose films clearly extended their television personae.

## The Working-class Fool

During and after the war there was an increasingly vociferous attack by middle-class cinema-goers and middle-brow critics against the 'old-fashioned' comedy of music-hall stars.[1] The star who bucked this disdain was Sid Field. Like Formby, Field could 'suggest the dignity and pathos

12. *London Town* – Sid Field, camp Fool (BFI Stills, Posters and Designs. By courtesy of Carlton International).

of the ordinary man';[2] but he also commanded the interest of middle-class intellectuals through the sophisticated camp comedy of some of his repertoire.[3] His potential was wasted by Rank's *London Town* (1946), a clumsy and overblown attempt at a Hollywood-style musical comedy directed by Wesley Ruggles. This bid for the American market alienated home audiences. Both critics and the public enjoyed the individual sketches imported from *Piccadilly Hayride*, Field's successful West End show, but not the winsome plot, or the 'big' numbers.[4] The exquisite timing of the urbane interplay and sexual ambivalence of Field's sketches with Jerry Desmonde, particularly 'The Photographer', lie marooned between the leaden sentimentality of the scenes between Field and his young daughter (Petula Clark), or the cheesy grins of the Pearly Kings and Queens cavorting on 'Ampstead 'Eath. *London Town* was an expensive failure.

Three years lapsed before Field's second film for Rank, *Cardboard Cavalier* (1949). Field was given a more conventional role as the humble, harassed barrow-boy Sidcup Buttermeadow. But the film deployed the Puritan–Cavalier opposition incoherently and overemphasised the pathos of the 'little man', especially as the tongue-tied lover of Nell Gwynne (Margaret Lockwood). As before, the best scenes are those between Field and Jerry Desmonde as the starchy, self-regarding Colonel Lovelace. Sidcup flutters round him, awkward, innocent, vulnerable, anxious to please, but eventually pouting and sulky, wounded by the lack of faith in his abilities. Critics were savage about the film, which was another pronounced flop. There were no plans for further films when Field died suddenly in 1949.[5]

Field's successor was Norman Wisdom, whose incarnation of the little man was more sentimental. Rank signed Wisdom after his television Christmas Special had made him a household name.[6] Wisdom had started out in army concerts and on the variety circuit as a bizarre madcap, Dizzy-Wizzie. This modulated into the Successful Failure in a baggy dress suit with long drooping tails, and ended as the Gump whose peaked cap and ill-fitting suit evoked the most sympathy from audiences.[7] But Gump connoted both 'fool' and 'gumption', a combination of innocent stupidity and resourcefulness. The peaked cap signified gormlessness, but the Gump suit – the trousers too small, the jacket too tight, the tie askew and the shirt collar rumpled – signified a Chaplinesque aspiration towards gentility.[8] The key to Wisdom's screen success, beginning with *Trouble in Store* (1953), was the use of strong, coherent, believable narratives, rather than a loose collection of individual sketches. These stories allowed Wisdom to evolve the Gump into 'Norman', a less masochistic and madcap character, therefore more conventionally acceptable. The realist mode of Wisdom's films – which eschewed dream-sequences, fantasy or free-association – meant that all the gags were in character, with 'Norman' always established as a credible person with a plausible background. However, the director, John Paddy Carstairs, generated something of the break-neck pace of silent slapstick with a shot length under half the industry norm for this period.[9] Thus, without eradicating the energies of the Gump, the films work hard to offer a *contemporary* comic Everyman.

Field's foil, Jerry Desmonde, was used in several of the early films as

13. *Trouble in Store*: Norman Wisdom, the aspiring Gump, and Jerry
Desmonde (BFI Stills, Posters and Designs. By courtesy of
Carlton International).

a vainglorious, unscrupulous upper-class bully, the perfect opponent for
the indefatigable 'Norman'. In *Trouble in Store* as Augustus Freeman,
managing director of the high-class department store Burridges, Desmonde's grandiose plans are constantly thwarted by the innocent wiles  of
Wisdom, the store's 'boy', sticking up for himself. Much of the  enjoyable
tension comes from the carefully established realism of the settings and
the anarchic potential of the Gump. When happy or excited, Wisdom's
characteristic line of development is to abandon all restraint, collapsing
into hysterical, uncontrollable laughter. In one scene he competes with
the established window-dresser (a characteristically camp performance

by Michael Ward) to produce his own display. This becomes ever more extravagant and outrageous, his invention urged on by the street audience which has gathered to watch.[10]

However, 'Norman' is always more than the anarchic Gump; his persona encompasses a strong desire for acceptability and a viable social role. This is most strongly communicated through his romance with the sensible and kindly woman, the sweet, wholesome homebuilder, who discerns the loving and thoughtful qualities beneath his outward buffoonery. His yearning is expressed through the songs which are sentimental ballads performed straight, without any of Formby's knowing innuendo. As the proletarian chivalric knight, Norman becomes her saviour and protector. In *Trouble in Store* he rescues Sally Wilson (Lana Morris) from the clutches of the criminals in a spoof western shoot-out. With Freeman choking on his praise for the little man's heroism, Norman departs towards domestic bliss, Gump cap discarded. Although Wisdom was thirty-eight at the time, 'Norman' is presented, here as elsewhere in these films, as a young man in his mid-twenties, on the verge of the full adulthood that will be conferred by marriage.

Reviewers thought Wisdom's popularity would come more from the pathos of the little-boy-lost image and the appeal of a vulnerable boy-next-door rather than the slapstick; one described 'Norman' as a 'muffled Galahad', whose success shows that 'the meek inherit the earth and little men triumph over pompous authority, crooks and feminine indifference'.[11] *Picturegoer*'s three-way discussion between producer Maurice Cowan, Carstairs and Wisdom emphasised the pathos *and* the gumption. Carstairs argued that 'Norman' was, 'one of us … a loveable little fellow, simple and clean-living. He must never do a mean thing.' Cowan emphasised that he 'mustn't stand being trampled on'. Wisdom reiterated this point and contended that the figure invited mother love: 'Women, in particular will have a soft spot for him. They'd like to straighten his tie, or brush his hair for him.'[12] John Grierson identified *Trouble in Store* as a film which had finally caught up with an unruly popular taste, restoring the vigour of working-class cinema: 'I have seldom seen an audience more notably matching vitality with vitality, or saying so plainly "this is for us".' Grierson discerned that it combined the appeal of slapstick with an astute topicality: the enormous interest in shopping and consuming.[13] Certainly Wisdom's fans were overwhelmingly lower-class.[14]

The scale of Wisdom's success endeared him to Rank, which prized

'Norman' as a wholesome figure who appealed to the family audience, especially children; Wisdom's attempts to expand his range into more sophisticated and complex comedy were rejected. All twelve films through to *Press for Time* (1966) were released on Boxing Day to capture the holiday market. Each used the same narrative formula with 'Norman' placed back at the bottom of the heap where he renews his battles with pomposity, snobbery and prejudice. In the process he invades and overturns various bastions of respectability: the commuter train of *One Good Turn* (1954); the diplomatic service in *Man of the Moment* (1955); or the country mansion of *Up in the World* (1956). In the Harlequin tradition, his infectious good humour and determination to enjoy himself constitute a carnivalesque celebration of earthiness and infectious vulgarity, but always within the framework of his struggle to gain acceptability.

Wisdom's main rival was Charlie Drake, promoted by ABPC. Drake's first film, *Sands of the Desert* (1960) was a Wisdomesque mixture of slapstick and sentiment in which he triumphs over repeated humiliations through innocence and good endeavour. But *Petticoat Pirates* (1961), a direct counter to *The Bulldog Breed* (1960), began to exploit the disturbing distinctiveness of this strange homunculus, with his shrill, strangulated voice, and the raddled body of a 'battered Botticelli cherub'.[15] As a naval boilerman, the only male in a camp of Wrens, Drake is a more unruly and lubricious figure than 'Norman', with his roots in music hall, especially the character of Wee Georgie Wood. 'Charlie' has created his own madcap subterranean world complete with drinks bar and periscope, used to ogle the Wrens exercising in their gymnasium; he leers at the audience in complicity. The dull plot, in which the Wrens commandeer a battleship to prove their capabilities, is punctuated by Charlie's desperate attempts to prove himself. His nightmare of a court-martial, in which he plays both the prisoner and a range of accusers, is a disturbing sequence pervaded by fears that Charlie can never be conventionally acceptable. The ending, unlike the Wisdom films, offers not social integration, but the ambivalent image of Charlie marching along behind the new group of Wrens either in pursuit or longing to be one of them.

*The Cracksman* (1963) and *Mister Ten Per Cent* (1967) were more ambitious films in which Drake's little man fights against an uncomprehending and exploitative world. Their vision of society is much darker than that of the Wisdom films, with the accent not on the Fool's resilience but on his gullibility. The plot of *The Cracksman* is a succession of betrayals, by women and men, of Drake's innocent master locksmith Ernest Wright, 'the symbol of skill and integrity to the world'. Their disturbing pathos is not fully eradicated by his marriage to the beautiful Muriel (Nyree Dawn Porter), who turns out to have been on his side all along. In *Mister Ten Per Cent* Drake plays Percy Pointer, the construction worker with literary ambitions, silk cravat tied above his boiler suit, a version of the little man that gives full rein to his character's persistent yearning for culture and acceptance by the middle classes. He believes his ambitions are fulfilled when his sub-Coward romance *Oh My Lord* is put into production, only to find that it was because a theatre-owner needed to lose money and that the cast despise his efforts. When it turns into a hit farce, he tries to wreck the show dressed in a cape, but his 'phantom of the uproar' becomes a comic turn. After one performance he directly addresses a hushed and uncomfortable packed house asking, 'I wrote a play about the sadness of a man who cannot find love. Why do you find that funny?' The sympathetic Cathy (Wanda Ventham) saves the day by saying that it gives them pleasure; they are laughing with him, not at him. But it is a poised dramatic moment that encapsulates the age-old tragedy of the clown whose tears make the public laugh. Drake's little man was therefore a much more sombre creation than Wisdom's, and one whose pathos is quite disturbing.

## The Lower-middle-class Fool

Ealing's comedies concentrated on the lower-middle-class, 'ordinary people with the stray eccentric among them – films about day-dreamers, mild anarchists, little men who long to kick the boss in the teeth'.[16] As Holland in *The Lavender Hill Mob* (1951) Alec Guinness played the archetypal suburban worm turning. His resentments about his dull job and lack of promotion shape an imaginative and daring scheme. In the scene in the boarding-house barn, photographed in a pastiche Expressionist chiaroscuro, a Mephistophelean Holland suborns another archetypal lower-middle-class figure, Pendlebury (Stanley Holloway), a small manufacturer and artist *manqué*. Their Parisian excursion and the dénouement provide rich opportunities for controlled slapstick as the scheme starts to unravel.

In *Barnacle Bill* (1957), also scripted by T. E. B. Clarke, Guinness's William Ambrose is another innocent, a captain whose chronic sea-sickness means he can never leave land. He too is a 'mild anarchist'. As the new owner of a seaside pier he wrenches out the auditorium's outmoded seating to make a dance floor for the rock 'n' rollers. An exasperated and oleaginous mayor (Maurice Denham) splutters, 'You can't do this', only to be met with a firm, 'I have done it.' His transformation of the pier puts Sandcastle on the map and in the process he becomes the hero of imaginative middle-class enterprise which, in Ealing's universe, will always triumph over mean-minded and narrow bureaucracy.

In *The Man in the White Suit* (1951) this innocence has a darker side, reflecting the sensibility of the film's director, Alexander Mackendrick, whose films were always more abrasive than the usual Ealing output.[17] Its idealistic little man Sidney Stratton (Guinness) was a skit on the boffin, 'a comic picture of Disinterested Science'.[18] Stratton's surface naivety – the gauche graduate in his V-necked pullover with his shy boyish charm – hides a chilling self-absorption. His apparent idealism is based on a fundamental egotism which precludes sympathetic identification. Guinness was adept, as Kenneth Tynan noted, in portraying characters who were obsessives, guided by an *idée fixe* rather than a warm humanity.[19] His invention of the indestructible fibre is not to serve a real need, but the implementation of a formula which will prove his 'pure' reasoning to be correct. He cannot be bribed simply by money or sex, the methods used by the industrialists, as his real lust is for technology for its own sake, forged in a 'proper laboratory with really modern equipment and assistants of my own'. The white suit itself symbolises his ambivalence. It is at once a miracle of modern science, the garb of the modern-day 'knight in shining armour', as the admiring Daphne (Joan Greenwood) sees him, and the luminous clothing of an alien, a creature apart from the rest of humanity. The suit therefore functions as a parodic exaggeration of the keen-eyed inventor, the man in the white coat. In the final scenes he is enmeshed in a *noir* world where he is chased, harried and finally humiliated, surrounded by a baying mob as the suit disintegrates. This satisfies truculent Labour and greedy Capital but, in a final twist, the departing boffin cries, 'I see!', clearly undaunted by events, and regrouping his mental faculties.

Whereas Guinness's portrayals of the little man were shot through with egotism and calculation, George Cole's comic versions of the respectable suburbanite were more conventional. As the humble and timid bank clerk in Mario Zampi's *Laughter in Paradise*, he eventually succeeds through sheer fluke. Zampi's *Top Secret* (1952) was written especially to exploit Cole's mastery of facial expression, with a minimum of dialogue and a high proportion of slapstick.[20] As George Potts, humble government official and spare-time lavatory designer who becomes embroiled in Cold War rivalries, he succeeds through his resourcefulness under pressure. In *Will Any Gentleman … ?* (1953) Cole played another respectable humdrum bank clerk, Henry Sterling, Chaplinesque in his bowler hat and brush moustache, transformed by the Great Mendoza (Alan Badel) into a pleasure-loving lothario who terrorises his maid (Joan Sims) when he returns to the suburban stronghold. After this point Cole's parody of suburban decency, as in *The Green Man* (1956), could not compete with the 'domestic comedies' and Cole became the comic spiv of the St Trinian's films, discussed below.

The actor who developed and deepened the type was Tony Hancock, whose films extended his television construction of the shabby genteel suburban man, Anthony Aloysius St John Hancock, in crumpled suit, astrakhan collar, overlong black overcoat and Homburg hat, living at 23 Railway Cuttings, East Cheam, the rougher end of a polite neighbourhood. His expectations have been raised by Macmillan's 'soap-flake Arcadia', but his life continues to be one of drab mundaneness which leaves him feeling left out and resentful.[21] Hancock's self-deceiving little man is seeped in artistic pretension that always teeters on the edge of vulgarity. This was the basis of his first film, *The Rebel* (1961), where his bowler-hatted clerk escapes to Paris to fulfil his dreams as a Bohemian artist. That world turns out to be bogus and corrupt and his own success and acceptance within it, is based on a gross deception. Hancock's bewilderment and frustration, his rapidly changing moods, are registered by the quicksilver changes of expression that chase each other across his extraordinarily mobile face. Disillusioned and chastened, he returns to his former endeavours to sculpt 'Aphrodite at the Water Hole' modelled by his landlady, Mrs Cravatt (Irene Handl).

The critical and popular success of the film encouraged ABPC to sign Hancock for three more films.[22] Long-term scriptwriters Alan Galton and Ray Simpson were dropped for *The Punch and Judy Man* (1962), which suffers from repeated *longueurs*. However, Hancock's role as Wally Pinner, traditional entertainer in an age of television, gently fading amid the genteel decay of a seaside resort, was powerfully evocative of Britain's decline. Hancock, who disliked pathos, makes Pinner irascible and combative, for ever at odds with the stifling respectability which fulfils the dreams of refinement and acceptance nurtured by his wife Delia (Sylvia Syms). He takes symbolic revenge upon her through Mr Punch's mighty club. His rebelliousness comes to a head when he wrecks the gala evening designed to celebrate Piltdown's sixty glorious years. Unfortunately, Jeremy Summers's inexperienced direction builds the anarchy of the scene too quickly and some of its impact is lost. Hancock's artistic megalomania had tried the patience of ABPC executives and the film was poorly distributed without a West End première, losing money and causing further films to be abandoned.[23]

The other actor who developed the portrait of the middle-class little man was Peter Sellers, including two films for the Boultings: his comic union ideologue Fred Kite in *I'm All Right Jack* (1959), and his radical priest in *Heavens Above!* (1963) that I have discussed elsewhere.[24] His librarian John Lewis in Launder and Gilliat's highly successful *Only Two Can Play* (1962) captured the restless dissatisfaction and melancholy seediness of lower-middle-class provincial life in a way that rivalled Hancock, but the tone was lighter. Sellers's major contribution was to an internationalised British cinema in the 1960s through his creation of Inspector Clouseau, the parody of Sherlock Holmes and every other scientific detective. Sellers played the role five times, from *The Pink Panther* (1963) through to *The Revenge of the Pink Panther* (1978), in a series that was second only to Bond at the global box-office.[25] Clouseau is another little man, whose essential appeal, Sellers remarked, is that 'in all circumstances, whatever boob he'd made, the man must keep his dignity – which gave him a certain pathetic charm that the girls found seductive'.[26] Though endemically accident-prone, Clouseau retains his conception of himself as the world's finest detective and sage, greeting each situation with a jaunty aplomb that gave the character depth and humanity: 'You have high blood pressure? I had an aunt who suffered from high blood pressure. She was attended successfully by M. Auguste Boal of Nice.' He believes too, in his suave sophistication and virility as a lover, but his attempts to make love to his beautiful wife (Capuchine) in *The Pink Panther* are always frustrated by recalcitrant clothing, vindictive bedlinen and other impedimenta, part of producer-director-writer Blake Edwards's madcap world where every inanimate object is a potential trap: cars, showers, plugs, telephones, magnifying glasses, lamps, vacuum cleaners, doorbells, trolleys, even billiard cue racks. In *A Shot in the Dark* (1964), Clouseau is equipped with an effective foil, Herbert Lom's irascible Commissioner Dreyfus. *The Return of the Pink Panther* (1975) added Cato the Chinese house-boy (Burt Kwouk), always primed to test his master's reflexes in ever more Byzantine sadomasochistic ambushes. Clouseau's strangulated French accent with its baroque pronunciations reached epic proportions: 'Ave yew gurt a lee-sense fur yewr munkay?' Though a commercial formula, Sellers's Clouseau was a marvellously inventive satire of middle-class pretensions and, as such, a major contribution to a more free-wheeling British culture.

## The Upper-class Fool: The 'Silly-Ass'

The Silly-Ass had been an important inter-war type. P. G. Wodehouse's Bertie Wooster was the literary template;[27] Ralph Lynn was the screen incarnation in adaptations of Ben Travers's Aldwych farces. Its currency lapsed during the war when there was little space for parodic gentle-manliness. David Tomlinson played revivals of the type in *All for Mary* (1955) and *Three Men in a Boat* (1956). In his three service comedies, *Carry on Admiral* (1957), *Up the Creek* (1958) and *Further Up the Creek* (1958), he played an incompetent eager beaver, lurching from disaster to disaster. Tomlinson's romantic chivalry contrasted with Leslie Phillips's incarnation, twitching that rakish moustache in his endless pursuit of women. Phillips played endearingly indolent noodle officers in *The Night We Dropped a Clanger* (1959), *Watch Your Stern!* (1960) and *The Navy Lark* (1959) where he reprised his radio role as the dunderheaded Sub-Lieutenant Pouter. Whenever he is required to take action Pouter is consistently surprised and bewildered; his tag lines, 'I say' and 'Oh lumme!', became national catchphrases.[28] In the POW comedy *Very Important Person* (1961), Phillips had a well-tailored role as Jimmy Cooper, insouciant but dim. He was partnered by Bonzo Baines, played by Jeremy Lloyd, whose gangling awkwardness and vacant expression typecast him for a succession of silly-ass roles in the 1960s.[29]

The Boultings' use of the type was much more pointed. Terry-Thomas's Cadogan de Vere Carlton-Browne, incompetent head of Miscellaneous Territories, in *Carlton-Browne of the FO* (1959) or his Major Hitchcock in *Private's Progress* (1956) and *I'm All Right Jack* (1959), constantly bemoaning the 'absolute shower' of idlers who can 'break into a muck sweat just by standing still', were still amiable buffoons, but their incompetence exposed the woeful inadequacies of the Old Guard in the face of an acquisitive society in which everyone is on the make. But the Boultings' key creation was Stanley Windrush (Ian Carmichael), the idealistic innocent, hopelessly adrift in a changing society for which he is ill equipped as the 'last true dim gentleman'. Carmichael who, like Tomlinson and Phillips, trained as a song and dance juvenile in West End revues, gave finely judged performances that never allowed his character to be merely a buffoon. Stanley was essentially a parody version of the cadet, no longer the maturing hero but the hapless dupe of 'Uncle Bertie'/Major Tracepurcel (Dennis Price) and his working-class familiar, Stanley Cox (Richard Attenborough), in *Private's Progess*. The pair are an unholy class alliance of corrupt entrepreneurs for whom 'war is a time of opportunity'. In the contemporary *I'm All Right Jack*, Stanley becomes the focus of forces he cannot control or understand: a victimised worker eliciting a display of mass solidarity, a rallying point for conservative elements who, like his Aunt Dolly, applaud the 'officer who does not mutiny', and a media celebrity whose protests are silenced. This modern Candide is not even allowed the solace of a rural retreat, but must run headlong from pursuing Bacchantes. Stanley's failure is symbolic of moral breakdown and the redundancy of the gentlemanly ideal. The popularity of both films suggests that the Boultings captured a mood of cynicism about British society.

## The Proletarian Rogue

The proletarian Rogue, as in Trinder's wartime Jack-the-Lad, was nearly always Cockney because of the capital's labour tradition of casualised entrepreneurialism that favoured the irregular opportunist and fostered a tradition of competitive individualism, where a bit of sly fiddling is just 'doing the business'.[30] 'Fiddling', underworld cant for living just within the limits of the law, had come into general use during the second half of the Second World War as a way of circumventing rationing and other restrictions; it had no connotations of guilt.[31] The post-war 'fiddler' was represented as the spiv. Unlike his criminal counterpart dealt with in the next chapter, the comic spiv was a kind of folk hero: 'The word "spiv" had tolerant and humorous overtones … In Britain the black market seems to have been a genuinely popular institution for bending the rules without breaking the system.'[32] This comic spiv was thus a lovable rogue, affectionately caricatured in Sid Field's Slasher Green, the 'lad from the Elephant and Castle' in his zoot suit, one example of what had become a radio and music-hall cliché.[33] Without harming anybody, the Rogue annoyed or frustrated, or simply circumvented, those unsympathetic authority figures who try to curb his activities. His style and activities were represented as a licensed anti-authoritarianism, providing an outlet for working-class petty entrepreneurs with brains and energy but limited opportunities.

British producers' prejudices against the vulgarities of music-hall comedy left this appealing figure to small production companies such as Advance with the two Hal Monty comedies *Bless 'Em All* (March 1949) and *Skimpy in the Navy* (November 1949). Monty plays his music-hall character, Skimpy, a fly Cockney, chirpy and priapic, accompanied by his two sidekicks, Jack Milroy and Max Bygraves. Monty's modest popularity was eclipsed by 'your old china' Ronald Shiner, who, with his huge beaked nose, slits for eyes, convex body and screeching, squawking voice, was not only a parrot in human form – as symbolised in his last film, *The Night We Got the Bird* (1960) – but also a modern version of Mr Punch, an aggressive trickster who always refuses to accept authority. Shiner's screen apprenticeship as the Cockney Rogue had been served in the later Formby films before he starred in *Worm's Eye View* (1951), produced by the minute Byron Films. The huge success of this low-budget second feature was another case of the cinema catching up with popular taste. R. F. Delderfield's play about a quintet of RAF men billeted at a boarding-house on the Lancashire coast during the war had become a West End institution, running continuously for six years from December 1945. It combined well-worn jokes, stock comic situations and stereotyped characters – including an avaricious, prying landlady and her henpecked husband – with the topicality of service life. Shiner repeated his stage role as Private Porter – 'a sharp, aggressively confident cockney – pert and hard-bitten'[34] – who spends his war engaged in various fiddles. He rejects the egalitarian idealism of the communist Taffy because he can work the system to his advantage: 'If this is what you blokes call capitalism it's okay by me. Why? Because I know me way rahnd it, that's why.' Porter's rebellion against propriety and virtue was 'the upsurge of the age – the eternal barrow-boy triumphing over the lesser mortals'.[35] His energetic resourcefulness was the admirable cleverness, not only of Cockneys, but of the working-class in general.

Byron made a hasty follow-up by adapting another stage hit, *Reluctant Heroes* (1951), an early National Service comedy first performed in September 1950. Shiner played the bullying, energetic Cockney Sergeant Bell, the old sweat, always one jump ahead of his recruits, the public school and 'varsity' man Michael Tone (Derek Farr) and the gormless

14. *Reluctant Heroes*: Ronald Shiner as the Rogue – 'I know me way rahnd' (BFI Stills, Posters and Designs).

Blackpudlian, Horace Gregory (Brian Rix). The trade press noted the appeal of the deep familiarity of the jokes and situations here given a topical gloss, in what proved to be another major success.[36]

Shiner continued to play the same street-wise Cockney throughout the decade, but his subsequent films were often stale or uneven vehicles for his talents. *Little Big Shot* (1952), in which he played a caricature spiv-gangster, was debilitated by 'artless gags' and 'devoid of real wit'.[37] His first film for Rank, *Up to His Neck* (1954), directed by John Paddy Carstairs, was a remake of Jack Hulbert's *Jack Ahoy!* (1934). It had some inventiveness and a strong role for Shiner as the stranded sailor who becomes king of a South Sea island. In Remus's *Dry Rot* (1956), another Whitehall farce, he played a crooked Cockney bookie, Alf Tubbe, complete with bow-tie, flash waistcoat, trilby and mock-genteel elocution. But neither recaptured the success of his earlier films. After *Not Wanted on Voyage* (1957), another remake, Shiner went into supporting roles.

This was an example of declining star charisma, not the popularity of the type. Shiner was displaced by younger and more energetic versions of the working-class artful dodger. George Cole provided a cartoon version as Flash Harry in the St Trinian's films: pencil moustache, sideboards, zoot suit, cravat and rolling gait. As the series 'progressed', his Cockney patter became ever more rococo. But the services continued to be the main target for the Rogue's fiddles and dodges. Byron combined with Hammer to produce *Up the Creek* (April 1958) and *Further Up the Creek* (October 1958), both directed and co-written by Val Guest. In the first, Peter Sellers played the Shiner role, a fly chief petty officer whose fiddles have transformed a mothballed cruiser into a vital ingredient in the local economy. In the sequel, Frankie Howerd played the role with his usual air of exasperated righteousness as he dragooned credulous tourists into taking Mediterranean cruises courtesy of an uncomprehending navy. However, it followed too hard on the heels of the original to be successful. It was also a crowded market: a television spin-off, *I Only Arsked!*, was released in November 1958 with Michael Medwin as the clever Cockney, Corporal Springer, full of manic energy and always one jump ahead. Bernard Bresslaw played the simpleton.

Anglo-Amalgamated's *On the Fiddle* (1961), adapted from another Delderfield service comedy set during the war, was a more sustained attempt to reinvigorate the type. Alfred Lynch's Horace Pope, 'Pompey', a Cockney wide-boy, having carelessly allowed himself to be enlisted, goes about making the RAF work for him as the go-getting entrepreneur. In a marvellously energetic performance by Lynch, every new situation becomes the opportunity for an imaginative dodge, assisted by the muscular simpleton Pedlar (Sean Connery). Horace has a simple philosophy: 'It's only honest if you make money out of it. Everyone's on the fiddle.' Nobody is really abused by his schemes which generally have the effect, in the grand tradition of working-class comedians, of allowing ordinary people to have a better time. The real enemies are kill-joy brass hats and inept regulations. It was a return to the war, but Horace was clearly a contemporary Rogue played by a new star who had, 'take[n] the trouble to create a real character not just a caricature'.[38]

However, *On the Fiddle* was not conspicuously successful, indicating the exhaustion of the service comedy cycle; Launder and Gilliat's *Joey Boy* (1965), with Harry H. Corbett, was residual. The emergent type of Rogue was the business 'fixer', a natural extension, as Attenborough's Sidney Cox had shown in *I'm All Right Jack*. Laurence Harvey's Johnny

Jackson, smooth-talking, louchely smart, incessantly active and playing every new social trend for what it is worth in *Expresso Bongo* (1959), was the first, followed by Ian Hendry's rather seedy version in *Live Now – Pay Later* (1962) and *This is My Street* (1963). *Nothing but the Best* (1963) was the key film. Frederick Raphael's screenplay abandoned social realism and sober moralising for comic fantasy, openly parodying *Room at the Top*. Jimmy Brewster (Alan Bates) is the working-class lad on the make who befriends seedy, disgraced gentleman Charlie Prince, played by Denholm Elliott, the actor who went on to specialise in such roles. Beginning Jimmy's sentimental education in the bar of the Young Pretender, Charlie coaches his apt pupil in the manners, mores, clothes and attitudes of the contemporary successful 'man at the top', all smart one-liners, outward style and 'contacts'. Jimmy is a forger, not, like Charlie, of cheques, but of a whole identity. He gradually takes over his *doppelgänger*, finally strangling Charlie with his old school tie and marrying his sister Ann (Millicent Martin). Jimmy suffers from none of Joe Lampton's scruples. He makes love to an older woman, his landlady, as a cynical ploy to buy her silence and returns to his roots merely to despatch his parents to Australia so that his humble origins will pose no impediment to his marriage with the boss's daughter. Ann, too, is no virginal innocent, but a sharp-witted woman who enjoys the high life. Jimmy's charm, in Bates's charismatic performance, comes from his open and engaging frankness. He does not despise those at 'at the top' but reproduces their own ruthlessness in getting what he wants.

The heartless professional-on-the-make recurred as Ian Hendry's journalist in Val Guest's *The Beauty Jungle* (1964); Laurence Harvey's advertising executive in *Darling* ... (1965); Anton Rogers's chameleon entrepreneur in the Boultings' *Rotten to the Core* (1965); Warren Mitchell's insurance supervisor in *All the Way Up* (1970); and Peter Cook's business efficiency expert in *The Rise and Rise of Michael Rimmer* (1970) whose takeover of a ramshackle opinion poll organisation is but one stage in his eventual ascent to a presidency. By this point the type darkened into a destructive anti-hero: Nicol Williamson in *The Reckoning* (1970), and Roger Moore in the Dearden-Relph *The Man Who Haunted Himself* (1970), where the businessman is split between his ethical and predatory selves.

While these Rogues were a comment on the venal morals of affluence, the other working-class Rogue was the sexual adventurer, determined not to miss out on the permissive society. The paradigm film was *Tom Jones* (1963) which Alexander Walker judged a 'watershed', redirecting British cinema from social realism to more light-hearted fantasy, a quality it shares with *Nothing but the Best*.[39] Woodfall's energetic adaptation of Fielding's novel found in this eighteenth-century bawdy picaresque epic, a palimpsest for 'swinging London'. It circumvented Victorian respectability and had 'an exhilarating effect on audiences'.[40] The visual style was expansive, innovative, joky and knowing. The ambiguous social status of Tom (Albert Finney), the foundling, makes him the free-wheeling innocent, generous and loyal, whose creed is 'Tomorrow do thy worst for I have lived today'. His behaviour is spontaneously sensual and non-conformist as the narrator insists. In Finney's words, he behaves 'naturally – that is, doing whatever is natural for him to do at a given moment'.[41] United Artists' promotion of the film was blatantly erotic, including one poster that showed Finney surrounded by women in various stages of undress with the caption: 'The Whole World Loves Tom Jones'.

*Tom Jones* inspired a number of historical romps – including *The Amorous Adventures of Moll Flanders* (1965) and *Lock Up Your Daughters* (1969) – but its true successor was *Alfie* (1966) with Michael Caine as the Cockney 'natural man', knowing and sharply contemporary. Caine and director Lewis Gilbert decided that the overt and stagy direct address of *Tom Jones* needed to be modified by bringing 'the camera in very close and have me speak not to an audience, but to a close confidant'; the increased intimacy fitted the realistic setting.[42] Alfie's confidences come, as if naturally, in mid-scene when he comments on his state of mind or the peculiar obsessions of his latest 'bird'. Although, as Walker noted, Alfie was, 'a recognizable pretender to middle-class status in his flannels and navy blazer with its Services badge on the breast pocket (the perfect notation mark of male solidarity allied to spivish vanity)', he is not after executive status but the working-class dictum of 'looking after Number One', a cushy lifestyle spiced with varied sexual pleasures.[43] Bill Naughton's adaptation of his own play retains its moralising framework, but audiences were quite capable of blocking out the moralising; young males were able to identify conspiratorially with this Jack-the-Lad whose promiscuity coincided with Caine's own star persona and reported lifestyle. Paramount's publicity proclaimed, 'Michael Caine *is* Alfie'. Commentators saw Alfie as a stage on from Harry Palmer, more self-admiring and confident, 'the sort of man once thought totally un-English but now being fished out of the proletarian pond where Englishness never flourished ... a Latin-style tom, in fact'.[44]

## The Middle-class Rogue

If the working-class Rogue was intent on grasping the opportunities his brains and guile created, the middle-class Rogue was determined not to have his status eroded and to prosper behind his veneer of respectability. The figure was first incarnated by Alastair Sim whose appearance and precise Edinburgh diction suggested an avuncularity and gravitas which belied his cunning opportunism. Sim found his *métier* as the man on the qui vive, constantly sailing close to the wind, punctilious and proper on the surface, but really a careerist wheeler-dealer. In *The Happiest Days of Your Life* (1950) as Wetherby Pond, headmaster of a boys' school, his nimble intelligence, pawky wit and egotism are stretched to the limit in devising stratagems to prevent parents or governors discovering the nightmare arrival of the 'monstrous regiment', a relocated girls' school led by their combative headmistress Margaret Rutherford. Any whiff of scandal could wreck his cherished dreams of promotion to a decent headship. When the governors inquire why the boys are practising needlecraft, and on crêpe de chine underwear, Pond replies, 'Lucky to get it. Lucky indeed.' When they finally rumble his deception and demand an explanation, he replies crossly, 'Can't you see I'm trying to think of one?' As with all Sim's characters, Pond is essentially a loner, making only temporary alliances, often chortling to himself at the cleverness and dexterity of his own scheming. Sim's marvellously expressive face is able to register swiftly moving changes as his character oscillates between fear, greed, admiration and suspicion. Like the working-class Rogue, he has complete self-confidence, protected by mock outrage, always certain that he has a perfect right to do what he is doing.

As Deniston Russell, ex-major, now pseudonymous pulp crime writer, slumming it amid the lurid sensationalism of sub-Spillane sex and violence, Sim's role in *Laughter in Paradise* (1951) was the same enticing mixture of surface respectability and seedy opportunism – for which he is ever apologetic but unrepentant – as he ducks the matrimonial clutches of Elizabeth Robson (Joyce Grenfell). In *The Belles of St Trinian's* (1954), the first of Launder and Gilliat's series of films derived from Ronald Searle's creations, he played the type in drag. His mirror-image was Cecil Parker, whose forte was rogue top brass: Air Vice Marshal Bertram Buckpasser in *The Night We Dropped a Clanger* (1959), Commander Stanton in *The Navy Lark* (1959) and General Fitzadam in *The Amorous Prawn* (1962). He played Sim's role in *The Pure Hell of St Trinian's* (1960), as

'Professor' Canford, a bogus educator who looks like a Mississippi gambler. Parker, like Sim, often expressed a self-admiring delight as the Rogue, hitching up his body, raising his shoulders, putting his head to one side and laughing softly to himself.

Sim and Parker were too old to engage in any philandering which they left to a younger man, the cad or bounder, who combined roguery with the youthful vigour of the playboy. The uniform of the type was as fixed as that of the spiv: loud check jacket, cravat or old school tie, flat cap worn at a rakish angle, moustache, and hearty 'Oh, good show' banter, usually delivered from a seated position behind the wheel of an open-topped sports car. Rex Harrison's upper-class 'rotter' in *The Rake's Progress* (1945) exercised a fascination for both sexes. For women he retained a louche charm even in his duplicities; while men gained, 'a great deal of vicarious pleasure out of seeing him get away with it'.[45] Excluding Kenneth More's version, Harrison's successor was the flamboyant Terry-Thomas. His cad/rotter was a populist version of upper-class dandified elegance, self-consciously aware of his immaculate attire and its precise accoutrements; a cigarette holder added that touch of rakish cosmopolitan sophistication.[46] His rich, fruity voice and famous gap-toothed smile completed the Rogue version of the Man About Town, engaged in endless schemes to disguise his lack of funds. Women were the usual target, always sized up for their bank balance as well as their figures. In *Blue Murder at St Trinian's* (1957), he played another residue of the war, Captain Carlton-Rickitts, proprietor of the Dreadnought Motor Traction Company in Wantage. As an undischarged bankrupt trying to keep up appearances, he is the only man desperate enough to take the girls on their invasion of Europe. His lust for the sixth formers and foreign beauties is displaced by his seduction of Sergeant Gates (Joyce Grenfell), a task he performs with alacrity once he hears of her expectations upon the death of an aged aunt. 'Call me Romney', he whispers, as they dance a slow foxtrot in a Florentine night club.

In Mario Zampi's *The Naked Truth* (1957) and *Too Many Crooks* (1959), Terry-Thomas played womanising and tax-dodging businessmen, with secrets to hide and wives to deceive, always looking for a quick fix. As Raymond Delauney in *School for Scoundrels* (1960), he attempts to impress Janette Scott with his sporting prowess, supercharged sports car, gourmet knowledge and general *savoir faire*. As Major Albert Rayne in Rank's *Make Mine Mink* (1960), he formed part of an eccentric 'gang' of fur thieves in a bid to recapture the pleasures of wartime, the only period in his life which had been exciting, satisfying and meant something. The pathos deepens the characterisation and there is a rich irony in a figure whose manhood is restored through joining a woman's group.

After this Terry-Thomas degenerated into a cartoon version in Paramount's two bloated mid-Atlantic comedies *Those Magnificent Men in Their Flying Machines* (1965) and *Monte Carlo or Bust* (1968). But the gentleman Rogue's most characteristic guise, as an ex-officer, the comic equivalent of the maladjusted servicemen explored in Chapter 9, was given definitive treatment in Allied Film Makers' *The League of Gentlemen* (1960). Bryan Forbes's clever adaptation of John Boland's satirical novel neatly inverts Jack Hawkins's distinguished line of morally unimpeachable officers in the role of ex-Lieutenant-Colonel Norman Hyde. In the opening shots his emergence, late at night, from a manhole dressed in a dinner jacket, provides a brilliant Gothic metaphor for these 'underground' men who periodically rise up to prey on the decent Jekylls of society. As his Number 1, ex-Major Race, Nigel Patrick plays another of his smooth and raffish debonairs who have hit hard times. Race and the remainder of Hyde's band of 'crack recruits' are distinguished by their opportunism, not integrity. Unable to adjust to peacetime society, their resurrection of the 'good old days' of army discipline is a welcome escape from the drab and unfulfilling second-rateness of their civilian lives. Each seems far happier in the company of men than of women, who are scorned, resented, preyed upon or loathed; the film is shot through with misogynist comments about female sexuality, the counterpart to this strong homosocial bonding. In sum they symbolise an officer class gone rotten, but the film is equally cynical about lawful society which is either stupid or self-serving. Captured after the failure of their precision raid, Race advises Hyde to cash in by flogging his memoirs to the Sunday papers: 'there's always an angle'. Hyde can become a media celebrity – the last refuge of scoundrels. *The League of Gentlemen* was very popular.[47] Like the Boultings' films, it used a comic type to explore the resentments of the middle-classes in an egalitarian society where their status has been hopelessly undermined.

## Fools and Rogues: The 'Carry On' Films

The 'Carry On' films are a special category as they used multiple leads and represent the most successful and long-running British comedy series.[48] If the series is notable for its sexism, it is also characterised by its relentless exposure of masculine egotism and incompetence. Its notorious vulgarity was, at least initially, an anti-puritanical bloody-mindedness, a celebration of lower-class resistance to refinement and rules; an insistence on a legitimate preoccupation with sexuality, physicality and the pursuit of pleasure.[49] Its ensemble style had its roots in music hall, but here the actors were not comedy stars, but relative unknowns whose personae could be developed through the series itself.[50] This evolution was controlled by Peter Rogers and Gerald Thomas, who produced and directed every film, and by the use of only two scriptwriters, Norman Hudis for the first six and Talbot Rothwell for the remaining twenty-three. The screenplays – with the exception of *Carry On Sergeant* (1958), adapted from another Delderfield service farce *Bull Boys* – were generated in-house as the key instrument of control.[51] Once the shooting stage had been reached the actors were never allowed to improvise. Both writers deployed the basic comic strategies of slapstick and innuendo, but Hudis's screenplays were carefully constructed situation comedies with believable characters in straightforward, rather sentimental narratives set in familiar institutions: the army, hospitals, education and the police. Hudis argued that: 'Much of the humour in a Carry On was anticipated by the audience, not because the jokes and routines were old, but because the general subject matter was so very familiar ... the immediate warm, intimate range of people's everyday experiences.'[52] By contrast, the real strengths of Rothwell, a fervent admirer of Max Miller, came through generic parody that facilitated more extravagant, anarchic situations and characterisation, ribald puns and bawdy innuendo: "'I've got it." "Well you didn't get it off me."' From *Carry On Jack* (1963), the series used an 'A' certificate for greater licence. Beginning as a particular niche within Anglo-Amalgamated's portfolio of popular genres, Rank took over the series in 1966, an indication of its willingness to depart from 'family entertainment' in the hope of financial gain.

The staple type of the series was the Fool. In the early films the accident-prone comic Everyman is Kenneth Connor, who played similar roles in *Watch Your Stern!* (1960), also by Rogers and Thomas, *What a Carve Up!* (1961) and *Nearly a Nasty Accident* (1961). In *Sergeant* he played the hypochondriacal weakling Horace Strong, his head stuffed full of amateur psychological jargon. Strong is a neurotic version of the beleaguered 'little man', always despised by authority and eternally in flight from strong and determined women; here they are the virago, Hattie Jacques's formidable medical officer, and the predatory husband-seeker, Nora (Dora Bryan). Some of the best comedy is generated through his transformation into a parody of the macho action man, striding around the compound and sweeping the amazed Nora off her feet. Strong focuses the film's concern with the taxing demands of conventional heroic masculinity, the need to be capable and cool in a crisis. His subsequent roles were variations on this theme, most notably Hengist Pod in *Carry On Cleo* (1964), the dull-witted, henpecked British slave who becomes Caesar's champion. He seems to have been less favoured in the later films, where he tended to be replaced by Peter Butterworth, still the little man, but more sly and self-regarding, and far less innocent (always the core of Connor's performance) which fitted better with the series' increasing salaciousness.

There was a second variant of the Everyman, still an accident-prone simpleton, but closer to the conventional romantic action hero. In *Sergeant* it was Bob Monkhouse, in *Jack* (1963) Bernard Cribbins as Midshipman Albert Poop-Decker, the parody of Hornblower, and Roy Castle in *Khyber* (1968). Jim Dale was used most frequently as Bertram Oliphant West, the debonair adventurer, in *Follow That Camel* (1967), Marshal P. Knutt in *Cowboy* (1965), also as a hapless version of Dr Kildare/ Simon Sparrow in *Doctor* (1967) and *Again Doctor* (1969). Although his incompetence, gullibility and naive chivalry with women generate considerable slapstick, his main functions were to shoulder the burden of the plot and to provide a foil for the more eccentric characters.

One of these was the third variation of the Fool, the 'gay fool'. The obvious embodiment is Charles Hawtrey. In *Sergeant*, his Peter Golightly was an extravagant parody of the eager beaver cadet – innocent, child-like, in a world of his own – as an effeminate sissy, fluttering and twirling, fussing and fretting; unable to perform the usual manly tasks: 'So sorry. I'm all thumbs today.' He was initially complemented by Kenneth Williams. In *Constable* (1959), Williams and Hawtrey perform a camp duet together within the main narrative as constables in drag on undercover work to catch shoplifters. This was extended in *Teacher* (1960) where they are competing English and Music masters squabbling over who has artistic pre-eminence in the Shakespearean production. At the end they embrace during the communal joy at the headmaster's decision to remain, only for Williams to be slapped by Hawtrey for exceeding the bounds. As Margaret Anderson argues, this construction was full of

ambiguity and contradiction.[53] Both actors' performances are characterised by very abrupt changes of register, moving between upper- and
working-class idiom as well as hetero- and homosexual allusions and
innuendo. Both are offered as incongruous objects of female desire, in
deliberate defiance of audience knowledge about their sexual preferences.
The lasciviousness and heterosexual potency of Hawtrey's whimsical,
camp child-innocents were often played up, as in *Henry* (1970) or *Jungle*
(1970). The cleverest example comes in *Doctor* where he plays Mr Barren,
who has to be coaxed and nursed through the traumas of a sympathetic
pregnancy by his wife. Williams's Randy Lal, the Khasi of Kalibar, in
*Khyber*, follows this pattern, but he is often pursued by a virago (Hattie
Jacques) as in *Doctor* or *Camping* (1969). This deliberately exaggerated
theatricality meant that the subversion of male heterosexuality was safely
distanced from audiences.

In the generic parodies, Williams had a more important role. His
effeminacy, narcissism, hysteria, refinement and pettiness could be
incorporated into a complex and original development of a very traditional type, the self-regarding, vainglorious boaster. Its cultural roots go
back at least to *commedia dell'arte*'s braggart captain, whose 'character was
best delineated not so much by physical traits as by his pretentiousness
and indigence, which always amused the poorer classes in particular'.[54]
It was a type that encouraged Williams's histrionic mannerisms to take
wing, especially those wildly flaring nostrils and the prodigal vocal
cadences, as he schemed, lied and cheated. In *Cleo* his Julius Caesar
indulges in Churchillian rhetoric in front of the Senate, only to cower
under his bed at the slightest hint of danger. His strutting, bellowing
Prussian Commandant Burger complete with monocle in *Follow That
Camel* does nothing but bluster. Perhaps his best role came as Citizen
Camembert, the 'big cheese', in *Don't Lose Your Head* (1966), where his
refined taste as a connoisseur who delights in possessing an aristocratic
château is always at odds with his role in the revolution. His desire to
capture the Black Fingernail is outweighed by his neurotic fastidiousness
about damage to the furniture. Here, as in all Williams's roles, there are
the inevitable and tell-tale lapses into vulgarity that mark him as truly
'common'.

The complement to these fools and braggarts was the wily, quick-
witted Rogue incarnated by Sid James. James had developed a reputation
as the 'Prince of the Wide Boys' through a series of film roles playing
unscrupulous but warm-hearted entrepreneurs like Sid Gibson in *Make*

*Mine a Million* (1959). He had become a household name as the fly vulgarian in *Hancock's Half Hour*, whose character combined earthy realism with opportunism. His early 'Carry On' roles emphasise the former quality. In *Cabby* there is a certain pathos to his increasingly desperate desire to maintain cab-driving 'as the last male stronghold' against the onslaught of 'Glam Cabs'. In *Cruising* (1962) he could still celebrate his rise to the rank of captain despite his humble origins and proletarian accent. But the later Rothwell scripts exaggerate his character into the scheming chancer, dedicated to avoiding work, with the exaggeratedly lecherous laugh, combining Rogue with leading man. Part of the joke was that, however elevated his rank or sumptuous his costume – Regency buck, Roman commander, imperial governor, English monarch – James behaved like a contemporary street-wise Cockney. After *Cruising*, where he is pursued by the predatory Dilys Laye, he becomes the pursuer, completely confident about his own manly charms. Like all the Carry On males, he refuses to tolerate old, ugly or uppity women, but is permanently on heat for attractive young ones. But even in *Henry* (1970), the most extended variation upon this theme, for all his energies and scheming, James rarely 'gets it'. By then, the contrast between his ardent pursuit of Barbara Windsor and his increasingly raddled body was starting to assume epic proportions.

The Fool's gullibility and innocence show a nostalgia for a better world. The Rogue's energy and adaptability were a way of coping with a changed and changing post-war world. For the working-class fly wide boy this could be openly acknowledged, whereas the middle-class opportunist was slightly shame-faced. Once the impact of the war and National Service began to wane, an obsession with service comedy and war relics was replaced by the newly affluent and sexually adventurous opportunists of the 1960s. The 'Carry Ons' had their own momentum and rituals which could deploy Fools and Rogues in a variety of guises, but even the gargantuan energies of this series were declining by the early 1970s when a new cycle of sex comedies replaced innuendo with far greater explicitness.

# 7

# Criminals: Spivs, Delinquents and Gangsters

As I have argued elsewhere, post-war British culture, unlike American or French, offered a limited cultural space to representations of the 'city boy', the urban criminal.[1] The censors were hostile, as were the critics. Many of the films discussed in this chapter have low or oppositional cultural status, produced either by small companies with one eye on the American market, or by iconoclastic film-makers. However, some proved to have marked popularity indicating that, particularly in the immediate post-war period, the criminal gave a recognisable shape to fears about wartime dislocation and the growth of crime and violence which had spilled over into the 'austerity' period when there were chronic shortages of consumer goods.[2] More generally, as Robert Warshow argued in 1948, the urban criminal is both fascinating and fearful, 'what we want to be and what we are afraid we may become', the ultimate embodiment of a ruthless 'terrible daring' that struggles for success. In his punishment and fall he becomes a modern tragic hero.[3] In a British context the criminal was a creature of the secret, nocturnal London of the imagination, the mythologised metropolitan *demi-monde* of Soho, the 'square mile of vice', or the East End. It was a city at once sharply contemporary, and also Gothic, deriving from Dickens, and Thompson's 'city of dreadful night'. In the late 1950s and 1960s, two other periods of rapid change and moral anxiety, the criminal recurred, but in a more realistic setting.

There were three main criminal types. The first was the petty criminal, the spiv or wide-boy, flashily dressed with cheap ostentation, whose violence is often random and uncalculated. This type's deployment was limited because of British culture's more sustained and profound investment in the second type, the delinquent, dark twin of the boy-next-door, the product of broken wartime homes and absent fathers. Although the distinction between spiv and gangster was often blurred, I use the latter term to designate a third type, a thoroughly professional criminal who acts with assurance and calculated brutality. The two types are often contrasted in the same film. Where the spiv is incorrigibly loquacious with his smart patter, the gangster is laconic, preserving an enigmatic quality that links him to the Byronic male. A fourth type, the maladjusted veteran, is dealt with in Chapter 9. All three criminal types are overtly narcissistic, signifying both conspicuous consumption and a moral degeneracy.[4] The criminal occupies a homosocial culture and his relationships with women are typically fraught, often violent.

## The Spiv

The template for the spiv had been drawn, as I have shown, by Stewart Granger in *Waterloo Road*, a serio-comic creation. His post-war successor was Nigel Patrick's Bar Gorman in Edmond T. Greville's Expressionist thriller *Noose* (1948). Gorman incarnates the popular stereotype: gaudy bow-tie, loud, double-breasted suit (the jacket with wide lapels, cinched-in waist and padded shoulders), a camel-hair coat, a soft trilby worn at a rakish angle, all completed by a pencil moustache twitching over rapid, stage Cockney patter. Gorman is a fixer, the go-between for the Soho gangster Sugiani. But he is, in many ways, a sympathetic figure opposed to extremes of violence, a family man who commands some admiration as a nimble dodger. He displays the type's desperate bid for *significance*, an ex-dishwasher longing to be somebody, who cannot resist grabbing his desk nameplate as he tries to make his getaway. 'I wish I'd been one of the world's workers like you,' he tells his friend Nelly, who weeps at his fall. Patrick's performance was appreciated by reviewers: 'He is the spiv par excellence, in every step of his gait, every shrug of his well-padded shoulders, every manner of speech. He is a joy every moment he is on the screen.'[5]

Gorman was still a serio-comic figure. It took the combination of American and French talent and experience to render the type as fully tragic: Richard Widmark's Harry Fabian in Twentieth Century-Fox's *Night and the City* (1950), director Jules Dassin's last film before his blacklisting. Fabian is an 'artist without art', a small-time fixer who longs for that 'big break' which will give him the lifestyle and admiration he craves. But the London he moves in takes its colouring from the 1938 source novel, Gerald Kersh's macabre, Expressionist *roman noir* with its powerful Dickensian echoes. Max Greene's chiaroscuro photography translates this into a claustrophobic, paranoid city populated by predatory grotesques including Fabian's boss, Phil Nosseross (Francis L. Sullivan), huge and bloated in his misshapen suit behind the barred slats of a cocoon-like office, presiding over his night club and the disintegration of his marriage like some mournful maggot. For all Fabian's sexual charm, his immense, neurotic energy and knowledge of the city's hidden recesses, he gets hopelessly out of his depth. In the memorable closing scenes he pounds along claustrophobic alleyways, or across the bombed rubble round St Paul's, trying to elude the thugs of the gangster Kristo (Herbert Lom) whom he has crossed. The back-lighting and wide-angle photography make the buildings loom over him, reflecting his own delirium and broken dreams, while shafts of light attack his hunched and sweating figure trapped in doorways. 'I just wanna be somebody … I was so close to being on top … so close,' he murmurs to his fellow outcast Molly, who watches the inevitable fall of the overreacher, neck broken, pitched into the fog-bound Thames. His is an existential tragedy, 'the archetypal modern man, running in terror through a dark city'.[6]

*Night and the City* was perhaps too bleak to be popular and was dismissed by critics as ersatz Hollywood. It had no major successors, only the occasional second feature: Dermot Walsh in *The Frightened Man* (1952) and Sydney Tafler in Ken Hughes's *Wide Boy* (1952). Tafler's Benny Merce – 'a real Charing Cross Road boy. Talks rather smooth' – had the familiar long drape jacket and flashy tie, and the film evokes with compassion and conviction his seedy, shabby world of drab cafés and grimy bedsits, where the opportunity for blackmail becomes a chance of escape into a better life. But once armed with a gun, Merce is out of his depth and falls to his death in a desperate attempt to escape the police, convinced that his girlfriend has betrayed him.

There was another flurry of interest in the spiv in the late 1950s, after the publication of the Wolfenden Report in 1957 had made the business of prostitution topical. But *The Flesh is Weak* (1957) and *The Shakedown* (1960), both with screenplays by Leigh Vance, make the figure more violent, vicious and Italianate, as does Patrick Alexander's *Passport to Shame* (1959), thereby distancing the type from audience sympathies. Vance's screenplay for *Piccadilly Third Stop* (1960) was more compassionate to the home-grown version, Dominic Colpoys-Owen (Terence Morgan), a man caught between classes, aping the accent and lifestyle of the Mayfair set, but an outsider – in the first scene he gatecrashes a society wedding – who is deeply resentful of their wealth and privilege. The film is pervaded by a strong sense of social decay and dissolution in which Dominic, another artist *manqué*, is desperate to escape the round of petty fixing at the behest of two gangsters, the well-bred Edward (Dennis Price) and the American tough guy Joe Preedy (John Crawford). Dominic shares with the Italianate spivs an almost pathological loathing of women, expressed in his ruthless exploitation of the ambassador's daughter (Yoko Tani). Wolf Rilla's fluid and imaginative use of a *noir* visual repertoire lends an atmosphere of brooding fatalism to Dominic's fall, thrashing around in the tunnels of the Underground.

This more inward exploration of the type found its most compelling expression in Ken Hughes's *The Small World of Sammy Lee* (1963), based on his television play in which Anthony Newley had also starred. Hughes's extensive location shooting transforms Soho from a mythical *demi-monde* into a seedy quotidian actuality. Newley's wide-boy is the sad side of Laurence Harvey's pushy entrepreneur in *Expresso Bongo*, making a meagre living as compere in a third-rate strip club. Small-time, solitary, at odds with his life – a Jewish upbringing that demands responsible business success and a stable marriage like his downtrodden elder brother (Warren Mitchell) – Sammy occupies, 'a world that he flirts with, but he doesn't belong to, this world of pimps, prostitutes and layabouts. Because of this loneliness, this need for affection, there springs an impulse for self-destruction.'[7] That impulse takes the form of reckless gambling that creates a desperate struggle to gather together enough money to stave off a beating by his creditors. In the five hours that remain, he pleads, cajoles, wheedles and smarms his ways towards salvation, scuttling through the crowded streets in a continuous hustle. In the process he becomes increasingly criminalised, losing his precarious grip on his identity. His final bolt for Victoria Coach Station and the bus to Bradford to join the homebuilding Patsy (Julia Foster), culminates in his one decent gesture: not to involve her and take his battering on the back-lit waste ground.

The sense of rootlessness that pervades this film pushes the type towards the alienated young men analysed in the next chapter. By this point the cultural function of the spiv had declined. He was essentially an anti-austerity figure. In an era of increasing prosperity and social fluidity, it was not daring that was needed but the brazen front exemplified by Alan Bates in *Nothing but the Best* or Michael Caine in *Alfie*.

## The Delinquent

Within the general anxiety about the increase in crime, juveniles were singled out for special concern.[8] Although it had a topical urgency, the representation of the young 'delinquent' formed part of a longer tradition of authoritarian ideas about the vulnerability of lower-class youth to modernity: mass culture, the disorientation of city life and rapid social change.[9] The construction of the delinquent reaches further back, not only to the 'original hooligans' of the 1890s but beyond to earlier urban predators, the garrotters of the mid-Victorian period, and the 'unruly apprentices' – the 'Roaring Boys', idle, violent and profligate – of the seventeenth century.[10] These figures are all historical variations of a 'law and order myth' which requires convenient scapegoats that objectify social ills.

Initially, the delinquent was represented as a 'baby-faced' spiv/gangster, first recognisable in John Gilling's *The Black Memory* (1947). Johnnie Fletcher (Michael Medwin) is a young, cocky, flashily dressed, street-wise know-it-all, unreachable by education, parental guidance or control of any kind. He speaks in an Americanised underworld argot: 'The dicks know me in this part of town. They've got their glimmers on me already.' Although Johnnie claims to be toughly amoral – 'I'm one of the lucky guys. I ain't got a soul' – when cornered he panics, draws a gun and is killed like the American gangster he replicates. This low-budget second feature had little impact; it was Richard Attenborough as Pinkie Brown in the Boultings' *Brighton Rock*, released four months later, who caught the public's attention. Graham Greene's Pinkie, 'a character possessed by evil', was rendered by Attenborough as the 'Little Caesar' of pre-war American gangster films, exhibiting the cruelty, misogyny and repressed homosexuality that were aspects of that type as Pinkie struggles to retain control over his disintegrating gang and combat the threat of foreign mobsters. His hatred of the mother figure, Ida, is exceeded only by his loathing of his loving wife Rose. But within those well-established conventions, Attenborough gave a powerful performance as a lonely psychotic, capable of finding fulfilment only in cruelty or violence.

*Brighton Rock*'s preface carefully distanced the events as a product of the inter-war Brighton, 'of dark alleyways and festering slums … now happily no more'. But the meticulously detailed shabby and seedy interiors and the extensive location shooting made reviewers unsure whether it was a genre film or a quasi-documentary about the post-war delinquent. This ambiguity was also clearly present in Launder and Gilliat's *London Belongs to Me* (1948), despite another supposedly pre-war setting. Attenborough's Percy Boon, though sharing Pinkie's craving for style and significance, is more the younger version of the spiv than the American gangster who overreaches himself and commits manslaughter. The film contained several memorable close-ups where Attenborough's face is shown glistening with sweat, contorted by uncontrolled panic.

Gainsborough's *Boys in Brown* (1949) was the first film to concentrate coherently on delinquency rather than under-age gangsterism. It established what became the paradigm, the contrast of the 'decent lad gone astray', whose problems can be explained sociologically and who can be recuperated through a surrogate father, with the unredeemable 'criminal type'. Here, Attenborough's Jackie Knowles and Jimmy Hanley's Bill Foster, victims of a deprived background and absent fathers, have drifted into petty crime through boredom and restlessness. Both respond well to the avuncular paternalism of the borstal governor played by Jack Warner. But reviewers were particularly struck by the character of the renegade, Rawlins (Dirk Bogarde), whose intelligent subversions of the system are given considerable narrative space, creating a certain ambiguity and possible sympathy. In the end, the film opts for repudiation as he breaks down into hysterical sobbing in an attempt to avoid punishment. In its failure to explain Rawlins, *Boys in Brown* exemplifies a central confusion in post-war British films about the delinquent: the slippage between a social explanation and an individualised pathology.[11]

Bogarde's most celebrated incarnation of the type came in Dearden and Relph's *The Blue Lamp* (1950). Its opening voice-over draws confidently on what were, by then, well established official discourses that offered a coherent explanation of a distinct generational group of the young working-class, 'broken and demoralised by war … [who] lack the code, experience and self-discipline of the professional thief, which sets them as a class apart, all the more dangerous for their immaturity'. As the embodiment of these 'restless and ill-adjusted youngsters', Bogarde's

Tom Riley is a lean, marauding loner living on nervous energy and in love with sensation as he does the rounds of milk bars, amusement arcades and billiard halls accompanied by a jazz score which emphasises the connection between instability and modernity. His seedy bed-sit, by the intrusive railway line, is bare and functional except for some tatty Hollywood pin-ups. This milieu lends him a sense of impermanence which contrasts strongly with the warm rootedness of the Dixon home. Riley is never 'at home', he is in a constant state of agitation and Gordon Dines's *noir* cinematography uses chiaroscuro lighting, tight framing and low-angle shots to create an atmosphere of unstable volatility.[12] Riley tells his blonde girlfriend Diana (Peggy Evans), another casualty of wartime dislocation, that feeling scared is what life is all about: 'It's a kind of excitement ... makes you think quicker ... Afterwards you feel terrific.' At this point he runs his hand along the phallic revolver (like his avatar, the American gangster), to underline the connection between sex and violence. He shoots PC Dixon in a moment of near-hysterical panic after which the 'legitimate' underworld joins forces with the security services, the police and the public to effect his capture at the White City dog-track, a fantasy resurrection of wartime unity. He is actually disarmed by Dixon's surrogate son Andy Mitchell (Jimmy Hanley).

Reviewers endorsed the film's structure of values, seeing Riley and his mate Spud as a 'pair of young toughs, vicious products of the indiscipline and violence released in times of war'.[13] However, it is possible that the film's huge success was the product of contradictory allegiances. For older audiences, as has been argued, Warner was an important icon and the film's depiction of the triumph of decency, law and order was deeply reassuring. However, for a young audience, Bogarde's good looks and the vibrant eroticism of his performance offered an 'illicit' fascination, as evidenced by *Picturegoer*'s readers.[14] Bogarde played a series of 'running man' roles – *Blackmailed* (1951), *Hunted* (1952), *The Gentle Gunman* (1952) and *Desperate Moment* (1953) – where his sensitivity is played up, a 'cadet' with the capacity for violence.[15] *Films and Filming*, unusually sympathetic, thought Bogarde's good looks 'made out of the spiv, the deserter and the petty thug creatures of mystery and fascination'.[16]

However, most British producers, especially Dearden and Relph, embraced a law and order paradigm that pathologised the delinquent. When they returned to the subject with *I Believe in You* (1952), the Riley character, Jordie Bennett (Laurence Harvey) – stylish, cool, calculating, sexually predatory and associated with the debauched *noir* milieu of the youth club with its pulsating jukebox – is marginalised. Instead the film concentrates on the decent, good-natured Charlie-Hooker (Harry Fowler), dressed in a nondescript zip-up jacket. Where Jordie remains opaque, Charlie's aggressive and abusive behaviour is carefully explained as provoked by the death of his father in the war and his resentment at his stepfather. Once he is 'believed in' by his surrogate father, he turns his back on drink, sex and violence for the path of a steady job and matrimony to Norma (Joan Collins), no longer enamoured of Jordie. But the film's poor performance indicates that it was the subversive version that audiences enjoyed.

These tensions are played out in Daniel Angel's low-budget *Cosh Boy* (1953) which exhibits an obvious fascination with youth culture as an absorbing, sexy spectacle at the same time as repudiating it. James Kenney completely dominates the film as gang leader Roy Walsh, stylishly groomed, arrogant and erotic; a young man determined, 'to be a big shot and not work me guts out either'. The hapless Joan Collins succumbs to his charismatic glamour, becomes pregnant and dies. The anti-social behaviour of the 'cosh boy' is traced to the same causes: the loss of a father in the war linked to a soft and weak-willed mother who fails to recognise, let alone control, her son's behaviour. The crude 'solution' becomes his stepfather's belt, generously applied, in which the police collude. The trade press recognised Kenney's appeal,[17] but *Cosh Boy* received generally hostile reviews. One judged that the film, 'at this time when the country is still agitated by the sordid consequences of the Craig and Bentley case … exploits rather than discourages juvenile delinquency'.[18] Some local authorities panicked and banned the film which scuppered its box-office chances.[19]

The furore surrounding *Cosh Boy* showed the importance of the figure. As the war receded, the delinquent replaced the spiv (and the maladjusted veteran) as a 'concealed metaphor' for fears about the long-term effects of wartime dislocation, social change, lack of community cohesion and the breakdown of traditional values, particularly among the working classes.[20] These discourses worked together to create a figure who is 'on trial' for his lifestyle and values, not simply his actions. In various guises – 'Cosh Boy', 'Teddy Boy', 'Beat' – the delinquent formed a convenient, highly visible, folk devil.[21] He lacked an authoritative male role model, exactly the advantage which the boy-next-door and the cadet enjoyed.

15. *Violent Playground* – David McCallum: 'Go, Johnny, go!' (BFI Stills, Posters and Designs. By courtesy of Carlton International).

This lack was to be supplied by a caring professional who represents the moral and social authority, and the loving concern, that the young man needs. British producers' repeated emphasis on the need for some form of correction or punishment, or even retribution, as a 'solution' to the problem of delinquency, must be seen in relation to the ideological work of the British Board of Film Censors which was determined to take up the role of caring moral guardian for potentially susceptible, 'young and immature', cinema audiences in the context of 'the present widespread concern about the increase in juvenile crime'.[22] Films about the delinquent were required to have strongly presented 'compensating moral values' and a happy ending. Some projects which were more sympathetic towards young offenders failed to get made.[23]

When Dearden and Relph returned to the figure in *Violent Playground* (1958), they did try to renegotiate the type by making estate gang leader Johnny Murphy (David McCallum) more sympathetic and dropping the figure of the reformable boy-next-door. The choice of McCallum was important. With his 'blond hair, lean looks and slight stature', he had been touted as 'Britain's James Dean' since his appearance as an East

End youth, in check shirt and denim jeans, in Clive Donner's *Secret Place* (1957).[24] Dean was a major star for British audiences as 'the defeated teenager: sensitive, incoherent, rebellious, moody, grave, the victim of adult misunderstanding'.[25] Johnny is up-to-date and attractive, no longer dressed as the young spiv but in the Italian 'Toni Boy' style – tieless check shirt and casual jacket – 'the first time in the history of masculine clothing that a fashion originated other than at the top of the social scale'.[26] Johnny is also given psychological depth. His exploits as the notorious 'firefly' re-enact his moment of triumph and importance when he rescued the twins from a blazing building. His sensitivity, isolation and exclusion from the world of wealth and privilege are all sympathetically shown as he strives, like Dean, to understand himself and his place in the world. His relationship to Sergeant Truman, the reconstructed father figure, as has been shown, is characterised by its instability and ambiguity. Their rapport is shattered when Johnny leaps into his provocative jive routine, which expresses, in the film's eyes, a bewildering sexual ambivalence, an alien, unfathomable culture. In the final scenes, he reverts to the machine-gun-toting hysteric, another juvenile Hollywood gangster. Like Jordie Bennett and Tom Riley, Johnny lies outside the Dearden-Relph consensus.

Edmond T. Greville's *Beat Girl* (1960), though preoccupied with female flesh, was prepared to go further in its sympathetic treatment of youth culture, represented by another 'British James Dean', Dave (Adam Faith), leader of the Soho 'Beatnik crowd'.[27] Dave does not remember his father and recalls the horror of a war spent in an underground shelter, 'where we lived like a bunch of scared rats ... When it was over I played on the bomb site, down in the cellar with the rats.' Like his upper-middle-class friend Tony (Peter McEnery) who rejects the values of his war hero father, Dave's alienation is sympathetically portrayed; it is passive and cerebral rather than violent and threatening. When a group of Teds smash up his car he remarks, 'fighting's for squares'. When the 'Beat girl', Gillian Hills, is restored to her family, the last word is with Dave who muses sardonically, 'Funny, only squares know where to go.' Inconsistently, and within a sleazy framework, *Beat Girl* used a new pop icon to question establishment values, but Beat was never an important British youth movement.[28]

If *Beat Girl*, like *Sammy Lee*, was pushing towards understanding the type as alienated rather than criminal, contemporaneous films reveal a continued confusion or conservatism. *No Trees in the Street* (1959), together with *And Women Shall Weep* (1960), reverted to the earlier stereotype of the neurotic baby-faced gangster. In the former Melvyn Hayes played a particularly diminutive Little Caesar, machine-gun-wielding and hysterical. David McCallum's return to the type in *Jungle Street* (1961) was not as James Dean, but as a petty spiv who kills an old man and is eventually dragged away screaming by the police. Johnny Briggs's Frank Morley in *The Wind of Change* (1961) added a vicious and pathological racism to the delinquent's sins. *These Dangerous Years* (1957) and Eros's *Serious Charge* (1959), as has been noted, tried to square the circle by using the appeal of the rock 'n' roll star as the reformable delinquent, but the latter's vicious local gang leader, played by Andrew Ray, was the conventional stereotype. This showed that things were just as bad in the new towns (in this case Stevenage) as in inner-city suburbs. Butcher's *Rag Doll* (1961) with accomplished direction by Lance Comfort and a sharp screenplay by Brock Williams, still reproduced the type with the sexy and glamorous Jess Conrad as Joe Shane, the failed pop singer turned petty criminal who crawls to his death in a field.

After this point the energy and urgency drain out of these films, marking the exhaustion of the type. Dearden and Relph's final delinquency film, *A Place to Go* (1963) based on Michael Fisher's novel *Bethnal Green*, was feebly old-fashioned as the *Monthly Film Bulletin* pointed out. *Mix Me a Person* with Adam Faith and Sidney Furie's *The Boys*, both released in August 1962, were tedious and over-long courtroom dramas about misunderstood youth. There was no need to protest so much. A vigorous youth culture was now firmly established which could be celebrated, not excused.

## The Gangster

The gangster occurs infrequently in British cinema and often as ersatz Hollywood, including Renown's notorious *No Orchids for Miss Blandish* (1948). More frequently, the gangster was xenophobically pathologised as a foreign mobster: 'Knucksie' Sugiani (Joseph Calleia) in *Noose*, Colleoni (Charles Goldner) in *Brighton Rock*.[29] Herbert Lom's early career was spent playing variations of this type from *Appointment with Crime* (1946) through to *Frightened City* (1961). British National's *Appointment with Crime* was the first post-war film to offer a vernacular version, William Hartnell's Leo Martin, a tough professional thief intent on revenge. The original screenplay by director John Harlow was clearly designed to allow the actor to build on his admired role as the ordinary man turned revenger in the studio's *Murder in Reverse* (1945). Hartnell's dominating performance in *Appointment with Crime* is a masterpiece of tight, concentrated ruthlessness encased in a close-fitting, zipped-up leather jacket which seems the only way he can contain his seething energies. His speech is terse, clipped and delivered with a malevolent sneer of the thin mouth under that sharp nose. His behaviour towards others, including the dance-hall hostess he befriends, is entirely ruthless, though he has the revenger's sense of malign justice. His capture, screaming about his damaged wrists trapped in a train window, is a moment of awe and wonder.

This accomplished film, despite lacking a West End showcase, did well, 'record breaking its way round the provinces'.[30] One reviewer identified it as 'a genuine attempt at the popular level to create a hard-bitten English counterpart to the Hollywood gangster legend'.[31] Another thought Hartnell should be developed 'into a British Cagney or Bogart. He has every quality of toughness to commend him.'[32] Indeed, Hartnell, born illegitimate in the slums of south Pancras, was a British 'city boy', surviving and succeeding in a competitive world.[33] But British National lacked the resources to promote him and he slipped into supporting roles.

Martin was really a tough version of the spiv and although there were one or two other Anglo-Cagneys – Bill Rowbotham [Owen] in *Dancing with Crime* (1947), or the fallen boxer played by Terence de Marney in *No Way Back* (1949) – the dominant early post-war version of the British gangster was the inverted Man About Town. In *Dancing with Crime*, the tall, elegant Barry K. Barnes played the type with a thin-mouthed reptilian viciousness. This portrait was taken much further by Griffith Jones as Narcy in Warner-British's *They Made Me a Fugitive* (1947). Screenwriter Noel Langley's creation of Narcy, not in the source novel, combined realism with the macabre, admirably complemented by Caval-canti's Expressionist direction. Narcy is both a product of wartime dislocation – 'not even a respectable crook, just cheap, rotten, after the war trash' – and also a Gothic villain, an East End version of the cruel, sexy aristocrats of the Gainsborough costume melodramas. In the role, Griffith Jones could use his debonair good looks to produce a restrained and chilling menace. Narcy will deal in anything including drugs, is prepared to beat up and torture women and have potential informers murdered. His style and elegance – the monogrammed shirts, cravats, silk scarves, dressing gown and cigarette-holder – betray the type's self-absorption and corruption even as they signify success: 'I built this business up from nothing.'[34] However, it is precisely his nervousness about real 'class' that makes him seek out the disaffected ex-RAF officer Clem Morgan (Trevor Howard) analysed in Chapter 9: 'Not that I ain't got it but he was born into it.' He must have the style, and the woman, which Clem possesses. Indeed, he cannot co-exist with Clem, that contemptible 'noorotic … amerchoor' with his well-bred scruples. Their struggle to the death, round the lurid neon letters of the Valhalla Funeral Parlour, is inevitable. As a Gothic villain without a soul, Narcy is unrepentant, even *in extremis*.

*Sight and Sound*'s reviewer was flustered by Narcy, whom he thought much more than 'merely a copy of the American gangster-model … the atmosphere of London's underworld is all too plausibly conveyed'.[35] Another, who quite clearly perceived Narcy's links with Mason's 'wicked gentlemen', was also strident in his condemnation.[36] Clearly, a raw nerve had been rubbed. They were right to be alarmed. *Picturegoer*'s readers found Narcy fascinating and highly erotic, confirming popular female taste for 'unspeakable' men.[37]

Although Jones reprised his performance in *Good Time Girl* (1948), as the Brighton gangster Danny Martin, smooth, smart and menacing – 'I'm a rough boy. Or didn'cha know?' – it was not the central role in an overcrowded film and Jones was allowed to drift into second features. Much the same happened to Maxwell Reed, who *Picturegoer* claimed was 'irresistible' to female fans because he 'presents a quality of sinister brooding that will send the most delightful cold shivers tingling down the[ir] spines'.[38] As Felix Fenton in British Lion's *Night Beat* (1948), who has spent a profitable war acquiring a Soho night club very cheaply, Reed incarnated the narcissistic gangster, dressed in a dark tuxedo with a carnation and a rakishly draped upper pocket handkerchief. At the same time Reed's sheer size, that huge, hulking muscularity, gives Fenton a strong sense of menace, often imaginatively emphasised by his positioning in narrow doorways. His all-white flat above the club – a mecca of vulgar classicism with its erotic statuary – represents both his decadence and his own assertion that he has escaped his sordid and depressing working-class upbringing. His relationship with Julie (Anne Crawford) has flashes of tenderness, and his death at the hands of the vengeful *femme fatale* Jacqueline is a moment of pathos.

The key film was *The Third Man* (1949), imbued with a strong sense of dissolution and decadence in the war's aftermath, contrasting a pre-war Vienna of 'Strauss music, its glamour and easy charm' with the divided post-war city rife with corruption. The body fished out of the Danube merely shows that 'amateurs can't stay the course like professionals'. Carol Reed employs Robert Krasker's Expressionist cinematography, with its pervasive use of back-lighting coupled with the famous tilt, to create a nightmare city of looming shadows and lost souls. As a man perfectly adjusted to a fallen world, a creature of the city's divisions and its labyrinthine underworld, Harry Lime (Orson Welles) symbolically disappears into the underground sewers like a modern Phantom of the Opera. He exudes a charismatic, old-world charm, coupled with a ruthless modern cynicism. Lime is the corrupt *doppelgänger* of his boyhood friend Holly Martins (Joseph Cotten), a slow-witted Everyman – 'honest, sober, sensible' – plunged into a nightmare.[39] Their bond is intensified by the 'shared' woman, the stateless Anna (Alida Valli). In the famous scene on the Prater wheel, a Mephistophelean Harry gives Holly an education into a post-war sensibility where there are no heroes and the only sensible course is to despise and exploit 'ant-like' humanity. Lime claims to have cultural history on his side. The aristocratic bravura of the Borgias led to the Renaissance, mundane decency to the cuckoo clock. Harry's death, by Holly's hand, after the famous chase sequence in the sewers, rids the city of a corrupt gangster, but in the process kills his own more imaginative, daring and creative self. Harry is indeed everything Holly feared he might become and secretly desired. The downbeat ending, in which Anna walks away from Harry's grave right past the waiting Holly, maintains this ambivalence.

The anxieties of the war's aftermath gave rise to several notable British gangsters, but the figure is remarkable by its absence in the 1950s, with the honourable exceptions of Ken Hughes's 'trilogy' all released in 1955: *Confession* with Sydney Chaplin as the tough gangster-on-the-run; *Joe Macbeth*, which tries to elevate the type by making Paul Douglas a Shakespearean tragic hero; and *The Brain Machine*, which creates an evocative underworld of West End tenements and seedy Soho night clubs. Maxwell Reed gives a moving performance as a brain-damaged gangster, wrestling with his destiny but moving inexorably towards his doom. Towards the end of the decade the type returned, inhabiting a more realistic environment, inspired by the aesthetic of the New Wave films, as a more ordinary figure whose individual villainy is being replaced by organised crime.[40] Johnny Mansell (George Baker) in Renown's *Tread*

*Softly Stranger* (1958) was a hybrid figure, both the older-style suave villain and the muscular tough guy. The darkly menacing Michael Craig in Independent Artists' *Payroll* (1961) was more desperate and brutal. In both films the move north, to 'Rawborough' and Newcastle respectively, imbued the criminal with the same macho virility as the 'Angries'. Both gangsters have a weakness for a well-turned calf, to their cost.

Anglo-Amalgamated's *The Criminal* (1960) and *The Frightened City* (1961) were set in London and were more explicitly preoccupied with this change from old-fashioned individualism to a ruthless form of anonymous organisation. In the latter, Sean Connery imbues his old-style cat burglar with the rugged, charismatic athleticism that was to win him the Bond role. But Leigh Vance's screenplay sentimentalises his role as the foolhardy reformable young villain. By contrast, Joseph Losey's *The Criminal* (1960) was a sustained attempt to rethink the figure, using a Brechtian critical realism to explore the causes and consequences of crime and the kind of men it breeds.[41] Johnny Bannion (Stanley Baker) was based on the notorious Soho criminal Alfred Dimes who acted as a consultant on the film. Losey saw in Dimes a man capable of 'violence of unbelievable brutality', but also 'a certain kind of compassion'; a man whose potential creativity was shackled by the rigid machismo of the 'hard man'.[42] In Baker he had an actor who, as I have shown, was pioneering a new kind of British tough guy, no longer the inverted gentleman.

*The Criminal* depicts a man whose true environment is the enclosed and brutal homosocial environment of the prison, a primitive culture where Bannion feels secure and utterly self-confident. Once outside that world, his cool machismo is vulnerable, restless in the modish, pre-'swinging sixties' luxury of his West End flat, furnished for him by his former associate Mike Carter (Sam Wanamaker), the new Transatlantic 'organisation man'. He is also undecided about his affair with Suzanne (Margit Saad), which releases a tender, romantic side to his nature that he finds difficult to acknowledge and which leads to his rearrest. In his contradictions and confusions, Bannion is a man whose hour has come, meeting his inevitable death in a wintry field, the mute starkness of which is the culmination of Krasker's harsh, bleak, alienating visual style, a world away from the romantic Expressionism of his work for Reed. Bannion's death has a terrifying grandeur and also a sense of insignificance, displayed in the final extreme high-angle shot where Carter, cradling Bannion tenderly in his arms, dumps him unceremoniously on the frozen ground when he fails to reveal the money's location. In Losey's Brechtian logic, Bannion is fascinating, compelling and ultimately unimportant, except to those foolish enough, in Cleo Laine's plangent song, to love a 'thieving boy' .

*The Criminal*'s *fin-de-siècle* pessimism found favour with left-wing critical elites, but was too uncompromising for popular taste. The same fate befell *Nowhere to Go* (1958), director Seth Holt and Kenneth Tynan's adaptation of Donald Mackenzie's deadpan thriller. Paul Gregory, played by the glacially handsome American George Nader, is Bannion's symbolic replacement, without depth or identity beyond his own cool, slick professionalism. He moves stealthily through a world of space and silence, broken only by the intermittent jazz score. Paul Beeson's cinematography strips away any lingering Gothic overtones to create a harsh, alienated world. Long shots and slow pans often show empty, yawning spaces; doorways frame further spaces which stretch into the distance. In this deracinated society Gregory appears as a representative figure, unknowable even to his close associate Victor Sloane (Bernard Lee).[43] Both men are motivated solely by greed and eventually destroy each other. As the wounded Gregory drives to his death in the wintry emptiness of the Brecon countryside, the camera moves in on those cold eyes closing as he falls from the lorry's cab into a remote field to the bewildered gaze of a farm hand. His death points no moral to adorn the tale and the only regret is felt by the bored upper-class socialite, Bridget Howard (Maggie Smith), who has fallen in love with him.

Holt thought *Nowhere to Go* at least two years ahead of its time.[44] In retrospect it can be seen, more directly than *The Criminal*, to anticipate the typical 1960s cool professional whose story can take an heroic or anti-heroic form. The development of the criminal anti-hero was delayed by the plethora of international spy thrillers and caper films funded by Hollywood majors that replaced the home-grown crime thrillers from *circa* 1963 onwards.[45] Gregory's heir was Michael Caine in *Get Carter* (1970). Director Mike Hodges used Wolfgang Suschitsky, the cinematographer for *The Small World of Sammy Lee*, to create a realistic Newcastle as a degenerate society predicated on graft, corruption and ubiquitous pornography.[46] The elliptical editing keeps the sharply observed details flowing as London gangster Jack Carter (Caine) returns to his childhood home to avenge his brother's death. Caine's characteristic downbeat register needs only a slight inflection to convey fathomless menace, completed by laconic black humour. Carter has the classic gangster's fastidious narcissism and a chilling self-possession as he pursues his quest for 'justice', whose strict code deals out to sleazy villains, like Eric Paice (Ian Hendry), the punishment that fits their crimes. Armoured by vengeance, Carter has no sentimentality towards women who are used for sex, humiliated, bullied and killed, a critique of a man who cannot form loving relationships.[47] He has the melancholy of the Jacobean revenger-hero at the corruption of innocence, weeping when he sees his niece, possibly daughter, forced to perform in a blue movie.[48] His self-containment is therefore not the absence of feeling, but an icy control keeping in check raging emotions that occasionally threaten to overwhelm him. He too is a doomed figure whose hour has passed. His sudden death, from a long-range bullet fired by an anonymous assassin, completes the tragic pattern eloquent in its starkness.

*Get Carter* was a critical but not commercial success.[49] Its knowing self-referentiality – Carter reads *Farewell My Lovely* as he journeys north – and complex clues, have endeared it to *cinéastes*. Equally significant was another film that has acquired cult status, *Performance* (1971), shot during the summer of 1968, but whose release was delayed for over two years by anxious Warner executives.[50] *Performance* shares *Get Carter*'s sense of city corruption, a sleazy London of bent businessmen, oleaginous lawyers and pornographic film-makers, but the main interest of writer and co-director Donald Cammell was in the confrontation and exchange between the criminal underworld and a counter-cultural 'underground' dominated by hallucinogenic drugs and baronial rock stars. As a member of the 'Chelsea set', Cammell had access to both worlds.[51]

*Performance*'s East End hard man Chas Devlin (James Fox) is the muscle for Harry Flowers (Johnny Shannon), a screen version of Ronnie, one of the notorious Kray twins. Chas, 'The Lone Ranger', turns his beatings, notably of the chauffeur, into artistic performances, taking a sadistic pleasure in the precise, controlled gradation of violence and relishing his own gallows wit. Fox is another underworld dandy whose immaculately groomed appearance and obsessive tidiness betray his narcissism and complacent self-possession: 'I know who I am.' But it is precisely this certainty about his sexuality and identity that the film undermines. His overheated antagonism with his boyhood friend Joey Maddocks (Anthony Valentine) betrays a fear of the homosexual elements in their relationship, and his triumphant killing of Maddocks after the latter has stripped and beaten him is his undoing with the organisation. He becomes a liability, 'an ignorant boy, an out-of-date boy'.

Unconsciously he seeks out his opposite who is already waiting for him, Turner (Mick Jagger) the rock star who has lost his 'demon', the 'madness' necessary to perform successfully. He never ventures outside his house in Notting Hill, a psychedelic mausoleum stuffed with Arabian exotica and rebel icons designed by Christopher Gibbs, another member of the Chelsea set.[52] Turner's dark locks, unnatural pallor, long thin fingers, fear of daylight and mirrors mark him as a modern vampire, androgynously sexual in his fluid *ménage à trois*. Like Dracula, he awaits the arrival of the victim who will revive his powers. On the run and at their mercy, Chas, confused by drugs, is powerless to resist the ways in which Turner and Pherber (Anita Pallenberg) progressively undermine his macho identity. 'Have you never had a female thought?' questions Pherber as she holds a mirror so that her breast appears on his chest. Chas's despairing cry that he is 'normal', 'all man', is the last gasp of his old self. When he implores their help in obtaining a passport photograph to get abroad, Pherber and Turner reconstruct his identity. The spiv/ gangster image is replaced by a hippie incarnation with ruffled shirt, velvet suit and long-haired wig. Settling into this new 'alternative' self, Chas relaxes, his love-making with the androgyne Lucy (Michèle Breton) is amused, tolerant, affectionate; the opposite of his sadomasochistic sexual 'performance' with the model Lorraine in the opening shots.

In the process his hard male energy has transferred to Turner who recovers his demon as an East End gang leader singing the electrifying 'Memo to Turner', a moment when the audience glimpses Jagger's 'true' performance abilities and their disturbing basis in power and violence. If Chas now dreams of the mystical expanses of Persia, Turner seems intent on corporate takeovers. But the scene is also Dionysiac, the gangsters shedding their clothes in an ecstatic display which leaves them exhausted and possibly transformed. In the final scenes the identities of Chas and Turner have become interchangeable. Both have entered a surreal, unrestrained, Nietzschean space where 'all is permitted'. The film's baroque, allusive style allows this fantasy to play itself out in an ambiguous allegory.[53]

*Performance*'s fundamental re-examination of the gangster, through a counter-cultural reappropriation, was welcomed by young Londoners when the film was finally released.[54] It marked a further stage in British culture's fluctuating embrace of the criminal, so often presented as a figure of fear and repulsion. But, like so many of these films, it lacked a strong generic context in which similar films could be produced. The cultural history of this type is therefore characterised by short bursts of activity, quiescence and the occasional important film, not a sustained development.

# 8

# Rebel Males

I n post-war British culture rebel males are those whose dress, behaviour, conduct, attitudes and values are at odds with the dominant
middle-class ideology. They are often sexually transgressive, and they
contest class barriers and undermine masculine norms. Some of this
transgressive potential, as I have shown, was channelled through versions
of the Rogue and the criminal. The other key rebel figures were the
Byronic archetype, and the Angry Young Man, which was a product of
social changes that challenged middle-class norms. This transmuted, in
the more fluid cultural patterns of the 1960s, into the Alienated Young
Man, vulnerable, disillusioned and unsure of his identity and direction
in life.

## The Byronic Male

Gainsborough's revival of the Byronic male was one of the most notable
wartime cultural interventions. However, when Sydney Box took control
of the studio in 1946 there was a shift to contemporary subjects and a
concern for historical accuracy rather than Gothic 'excess'.[1] *The Bad
Lord Byron* (1949) was hamstrung by nit-picking period detail and a
laborious 'debate' about the meaning of his life. Dennis Price's performance as Byron substituted a foppish *ennui* for romantic mysteriousness.
The rebel version was channelled in a disparate group of films that
centred on an angry, dispossessed young man, aggressive and sexy, whose
passions know no bounds: *White Cradle Inn* (1947) and *A Man About the*

*House* (1947); *Blanche Fury* (1948), *The Mark of Cain* (1948), *So Evil My Love* (1948), all adapted from novels by Joseph Shearing; and *Kind Hearts and Coronets* (1949). The most successful was Cineguild's *Blanche Fury*, a deft combination of a sophisticated visual style (using the same design team as in *Great Expectations*) with the pace and brio of the Gainsborough costume films. As in his swashbuckling roles, Stewart Granger combines a muscular athleticism with a Mediterranean sensuality in his portrayal of Philip Thorn, the bastard son of Adam Fury's 'romantic adventure' with an Italian woman. Clare Hall's new owners, who have taken the Fury name, are mean-minded and repellent, whereas Thorn is the charismatic Byronic male pursuing his true destiny, 'decided long ago before I was born'. As the dispossessed anti-hero, Thorn has an intense moral ambivalence that commands both sympathy for his cause and revulsion at the utter ruthlessness with which he pursues it. His strength, dynamism and sense of purpose sexually arouse the other outsider, the strong, independent governess Blanche (Valerie Hobson), chafing under her 'enforced' marriage to Lawrence Fury. She colludes in his murder of the adult Furys, but the murder of the young daughter which makes Thorn whole – 'Today I am myself' – is also the point where Blanche revolts, convinced of her own irrelevance. In an ambiguous ending she gets Thorn executed for murder, but dies giving birth to their son who will inherit the estate.

Ealing's one construction of the type was *Kind Hearts and Coronets* (1949), adapted from Roy Horniman's Edwardian black comedy, *Israel Rank*. It was a product of the dissident sensibilities of writer-director Robert Hamer rather than the studio. Louis Mazzini (Dennis Price) is another young, hybrid outsider, condemned to lower-middle-class suburbia by his mother's 'disgraceful' marriage to an Italian street singer; a situation which, for Mazzini, merely underlines the hypocrisy and injustice of the English class system. With inexorable logic he uses the palpable weaknesses of his victims – the aristocratic D'Ascoynes, all played by Alec Guinness – to provide the means for their own downfall and his concomitant rise towards his inheritance. Mazzini is much more intelligent, masterful and sexually attractive than his social superiors, qualities which he uses to seduce both the lustful Sibella (Joan Greenwood) and the prim Edith (Valerie Hobson). The film's erotic charge was too potent for Balcon who toned it down by re-editing the trial scene.[2] The ending is again ambiguous: Mazzini may even escape punishment. Leaving the revelatory memoirs on the table of his cell is either the criminal mastermind's fatal slip, or a remediable forgetfulness. However, although the film was critically admired and has subsequently acquired a high valuation, there is no evidence that it was well liked. The problem lay in the detached, precise and unemotional tone with which Mazzini narrates his exploits which precludes identification. The emotional involvement of melodrama could not be replaced, for popular taste, by wit.[3]

*Blanche Fury* and *Kind Hearts and Coronets* were isolated films. Cine-guild's energies went elsewhere and Hamer's career at Ealing was stymied by Balcon's intransigence.[4] The type occurred as the tragic artist-dandy in films that attempted a high cultural engagement with European romanticism: *Corridor of Mirrors* (1948) starring Eric Portman, Thorold Dickinson's *The Queen of Spades* (1949) and The Archers' *The Red Shoes* (1948), the last two both starring Anton Walbrook. All displayed an inventive but allusive visual style that was 'more for the connoisseur than the ninepennies'.[5] The Archers' *Black Narcissus* (1947) and *Gone to Earth* (1950) offered a more populist version starring David Farrar, chosen by Powell because of his 'dark and saturnine good looks' and, 'the kind of physical appeal which is rare among British actors'.[6] In *Black Narcissus*, Farrar's Mr Dean, the Indian general's local agent, is a cynical outsider who has tried to unfasten himself from any conventional moorings, the Englishman who has 'gone native'. He takes delight in using his sexual attractiveness to torment and mock the nuns. Farrar's provocative masculine presence is emphasised at every turn, in his laughter, his singing, his unbuttoned shirts or revealing shorts and in his taunts about local girl Kanchi (Jean Simmons): 'Are you sure there's no question you're dying to ask me?' The subtle but overpowering eroticism of the Palace of Women, brilliantly created by Alfred Junge's sets, finds its outlet in Dean who becomes the object of the guilty and suppressed sexual longings of Sister Clodagh (Deborah Kerr) and Sister Ruth (Kathleen Byron).

However, although Dean's arrogance, braggart self-assurance and dissipation – at one point we see him feeding grapes to his pet monkey, like a latter-day Earl of Rochester – are all stressed, Pressburger's screenplay makes Dean more ambivalent than in the novel, less sure of himself. This gradually prepares the audience for the concluding scenes in which *he* becomes the longing, desiring figure. His rejection of Sister Ruth, who invades the masculine domain of his bungalow in her mad, headlong flight, borders on the hysterical. It is an outburst of such intensity that it reveals the strength of his feelings for Sister Clodagh, reinforced by the red light which falls across his face at this point. The film's penultimate shot is a close-up of Dean, gazing longingly at her departing figure. The beating rain signifies not merely the accuracy of his scoffing prediction of their failure, but also his own forlorn and hopeless desire, which has overthrown his bachelor self-possession. *Black Narcissus* was a marked box-office success. Like *Blanche Fury*, it combined the passionate eroticism of melodrama with an imaginative visual style.

By contrast, *Gone to Earth*, adapted from Mary Webb's novel, was greeted as ridiculously old-fashioned melodrama.[7] Farrar's fine perform-ance as Squire Reddin, powerful, cruel but also intensely vulnerable, held no interest: 'a refugee from the Lyceum'; 'right out of an old melodrama'; 'the villain of East Lynne'; 'The Shropshire Cad'; 'he should have been called Jasper'; 'the same old bounder'.[8] This wonderful film, mangled by Selznick the American co-producer as *The Wild Heart*, died the death and the currency of the Byronic male lapsed, shouldered out by the war films and domestic comedies. Farrar's English aristocrat, faking his own suicide and not averse to beating his black servants in ABPC's *Duel in the Jungle* (1954), and Stewart Granger's chillingly amoral murderer in *Footsteps in the Fog* (1955), were isolated examples of the type.

## Byronic Revival: Hammer's Dracula

As I have shown, Hammer's Baron Frankenstein was a Byronic figure, the true successor to Gainsborough's sexy Gothic aristocrats. Once more a small pragmatic studio, looking for commercial success, saw the potential of an erotic licence not available to films set in contemporary Britain. Hammer followed *The Curse of Frankenstein* with the even more successful *Dracula* (1958).[9] The Transylvanian Count, the most notorious of Romanticism's 'Fatal Men', was another popular archetype capable of endless mutation.[10] The power of the vampire myth, as Franco Moretti observes, comes from the identity of fear and desire.[11] The director, Terence Fisher, felt his contribution to the myth was to heighten the sexuality, the 'charm of evil'.[12] In Christopher Lee he had an actor fully capable of realising this charismatic eroticism. Lee's height, dark 'foreign-looking' complexion and 'cold expression' – qualities that had often led to his being cast as a villain rather than a leading man – created a Byronic figure of power and mystery. Lee's Count is handsome, arrogant and sadistic; often shown in long takes that emphasise his strength and grace of movement, his crimson-lined cloak swirling. As the object of fear and desire who invades the bourgeois family, Dracula not only seduces the young and innocent niece – Lucy (Carol Marsh) – but the wife, Mina Holmwood (Melissa Stribling), who secretes Dracula's coffin in the wine cellar. These encounters are presented with a delicate but arousing sensuality where the beauty of the sets and colour cinematography belied the strict economy of the production. This finesse, including the avoidance of any clumsy metamorphoses, helped Lee evoke terror and pathos as a being simply obeying its own implacable nature, 'a romantic and tragic figure'.[13] This ambivalence is retained even in his brilliantly executed death which fills an audience with 'awe and horror … Both repels and rouses … exploit[ing] the ambiguities of repulsion and curiosity'.[14]

Lee's bulging postbag confirmed his status as Mason's heir. *Picturegoer* profiled this 'Horror Heart-Throb' with the 'tombstone voice … which gives the girls goosepimples', and saw the romantic loneliness of his creation as the key to female cinema-goers' sympathetic interest.[15] This romanticism was crucial. Tempean's *Blood of the Vampire* (1958), in which a portly Donald Wolfit played the figure as an evil butcher, was not popular.[16]

Like Frankenstein, the Dracula cycle was one of the mainstays of Hammer's production schedule, but here too the films vary in the potency and inventiveness with which the vampire is used. The most compelling was *Taste the Blood of Dracula* (1970), in which Dracula acts as the catalyst which 'liberates' a younger generation to overthrow their hypocritical and corrupt bourgeois fathers. The final two films, *Dracula A.D. 72* (1972) and *The Satanic Rites of Dracula* (1973), have been vilified for translating the tale into a contemporary setting. But the new team, scriptwriter Don Houghton and director Alan Gibson, returned to the basis of the myth, reviving Peter Cushing as Van Helsing, an adversary of stature and depth who understands the power of evil. In *The Satanic Rites* Dracula is a modern anti-hero, the property developer, but also, as in the legend, the bringer of plague whose purpose is nothing less than universal destruction. His instruments are no longer susceptible females but a corrupt elite of politicians, scientists and the military. The use of a hawthorn bush to trap Dracula, puncturing his hands and wreathing his forehead in a crown of thorns, is a powerful image of the anti-Christ.

However, audiences might be forgiven for thinking the Count was metamorphosing into another Bond villain.[17] By this point Hammer's Dracula films were also competing breathlessly with its own new development. *Countess Dracula* (1971) and Tudor Gates's 'Karnstein trilogy' – *The Vampire Lovers* (1970), *Lust for a Vampire* (1971) and *Twins of Evil* (1971), based on Le Fanu's lesbian vampire Carmilla – were more shocking, scandalous and erotic than anything the 'Dracula' films could construct; women led the way into worlds of forbidden pleasure that left males, even undead ones, redundant.

## The Angry Young Man

The Angry Young Man was one of the most widely discussed cultural phenomena of the 1950s, forming a new social group, the 'unclassed'.[18] In the popular imagination they became Britain's 'rebels without a cause', a specifically post-war generation in revolt against a vaguely defined 'Establishment'.[19] Penelope Houston summarised the type: 'A young man in a provincial lodging, precariously poised between working-class origins and professional future, openly derisive of the "system", the Establishment, taking out his frustrations in buccaneering talk and a raw social and political awareness.'[20] Vilified by the traditional intelligentsia, the Angry Young Man was embraced by a left-liberal critical fraction, anxious to champion 'the rebellious non-hero of the 1950s', as the way forward for a moribund culture.[21] The BBFC's new secretary, John Trevelyan, sanctioned the Angry Young Man films as responsible adult entertainment.[22]

The Angry Young Man's forerunner was the 'scholarship boy', represented by David Fenwick (Michael Redgrave) in *The Stars Look Down* (1939). Richard Hoggart characterised that type as one of the 'uprooted and the anxious', at the friction point of two cultures, at home in neither. The scholarship boy was unable to believe in a public role, exhibiting a 'deep sense of being lost, without purpose and with the will sapped'; he possessed a submerged idealism but a pervasive indecisiveness.[23] As the opportunities for higher education increased after the war, the scholarship boy became an increasingly important figure, whose characteristics were reconstructed as the Angry Young Man, a tougher and more aggressive version. The Angries' toughness represented a traditional northern working-class culture that David Storey defined as a raw, physical world of machines and labour as opposed to the, 'poetic' cultivation of the South associated 'with femininity, with a woman's sensibility and responsibility. The North–South dichotomy became a masculine–feminine one.'[24]

The Angry Young Man was a troubling figure for a conservative British film industry. Rank, reluctant to show films on its circuits that were a strident challenge to family values, rejected the attempts of its contract star Dirk Bogarde to get *Room at the Top* produced.[25] It was left to independent producers to adapt the celebrated texts. The Boultings' *Lucky Jim* (1957) was generally regarded as having missed the point of Amis's novel. The distinctive figure of Jim Dixon, the lower-middle-class invader of academe, was, as played by Ian Carmichael, too readily assimilated into the twins' existing comic world of fools and knaves. Tony Richardson and John Osborne at the newly formed Woodfall Films were the key figures. Richardson argued: 'It is absolutely vital to get into British films the same sort of impact and sense of life that what you can loosely call the Angry Young Man cult has had in the theatre and literary worlds.'[26] But their first attempt, an adaptation of Osborne's *Look Back in Anger*, was hamstrung when the distributors, Warner Bros, stipulated that its contract star, Richard Burton, play Jimmy Porter.[27] Burton can convey Jimmy's rasping verbal assaults on the atrophied Edwardian imperialism of the upper-middle-class, the hypocrisy of the lower-middle-classes, the inanities of the well-made play and the venality of the Sunday papers. He also manages to emote a fear and fascination with his wife's devouring reptilian sexuality, a vision that conflates castration anxieties with a symbolic incorporation into the great maw of the middle-classes. But, as commentators noted, Burton, then thirty-five, looked too old to create convincingly the other key aspect of Jimmy, his vulnerability and inchoate struggle to find an identity.[28] And, for a cinema-going audience, Jimmy's essentially cerebral, intellectualised dissidence – epitomising the 'non-U intelligentsia' – that had so impressed audiences at the Royal Court, held little interest.

For film audiences, Joe Lampton was *the* Angry Young Man in *Room at the Top* (1959), adapted from John Braine's novel. Joe's transition from literary to cinematic anti-hero was aided by the film's aggressive marketing as a 'savage story of lust and ambition', the caption hovering above a sensual picture of its stars, Simone Signoret and Laurence Harvey. Braine judged Joe a clear-eyed portrayal of upward mobility and the desire to succeed: 'Most ambitious working-class boys want to get the hell out of the working class. That was the simple truth that had never been stated before'.[29] His ruthlessness was predicated on the existence of a welfare state where 'the young man on the make has to be a bit tougher and learn how to fiddle more cleverly'.[30] That ruthlessness is accentuated in Neil Paterson's adaptation, as its elision of the novel's retrospective first-person narration makes Joe Lampton (Harvey) more predatory, less self-questioning. Unlike the biddable boy-next-door Charlie Soames (Donald Houston), whose expectations are encompassed by the 'house down town, the second hand Austin and a wife to match', Joe's ambitions take the shape of millionaire industrialist's daughter Susan Brown (Heather Sears), 'the girl with the Riviera tan and the Lagonda'. For Joe, newly exhumed from the squalor of Dufton to the open spaces of Warnley, this is his right: 'Things have changed since the war. If I want her, I'll have her.' The war has radicalised Joe. It smashed his home, killed his parents, and trained him during his time as a POW not to escape, the privilege of the officer class, but in the skills he needs to get on in peacetime. Joe's ruthlessness is made less unpleasant by the obnoxious snobbery of the upper class, the withering contempt of Susan's mother, the 'lady of the manor', and the contemptuous braying of ex-Squadron Leader Jack Wales, a much nastier character than in the novel.

The adaptation retains Braine's deep and central ambivalence about Joe's attitudes and the price of his success, mostly conveyed through his relationship with Alice Aisgill (Signoret). As her husband George (Allan Cuthbertson) is merely a callous philanderer, the affair can be sympathetically presented. Their sexual encounters, though unusually frank, are handled with sensitivity and restraint by director Jack Clayton. The lyrical rural idyll of the four days in Dorset is perhaps the most powerful section of the film, informed by a Lawrentian sensibility which opposes sexual fulfilment to materialism. The rich and varied spaces of the rooms in which he and Alice make love and the sensual intimacy of their scenes together are contrasted with Joe's caricatured seduction of Susan in the boat house and the frigid yawning spaces that characterise the Brown mansion. Signoret's justly admired performance makes her rejection and subsequent death poignant and Joe's achievement of success becomes all the more empty. He ends as a tragic figure, crying in the honeymoon limousine for a love that can never be his.

Joe Lampton's popular rival was Alan Sillitoe's Arthur Seaton (Albert Finney) in Woodfall's *Saturday Night and Sunday Morning* (1960). Unlike his predecessors, Arthur is neither uneasy about his class position, nor resentful about his lack of success. His confidence and rebelliousness come from a secure sense of an unbridgeably divided society in which the role of the working-class bloke is to avoid being 'ground down' by the bosses and to take his pleasure while he can: 'What I want is a good time. All the rest is propaganda.' Arthur is a 'fighting cock', conscious of his youthful energies, his virility and his independence. He is uninterested in upward mobility or promotion, those are for the likes of prematurely middle-aged and biddable workers like Jack (Bryan Pringle) whom Arthur has cuckolded. He also rejects the new consumerism; it is his father's generation whose quiescence has been bought by television.

The first half of the film celebrates Arthur's physical pleasures through its concentration on Finney's robust body working, washing, dressing to go out, drinking, fishing, fighting, running, making love. He is consistently contrasted with the weak or hunched bodies of his fellow workers or his diminutive mate Bert (Norman Rossington). In everything he does there is a sensual delight in his own strength and tough masculinity. Even when he tumbles down the stairs of the pub, or is 'bested' by the two squaddies set on him by Jack, he takes a distinct pride in the bravado that got him into those situations. In bed with Brenda he shows, in a way that was distinctive and innovative, an admiration for her body and pleasure in his own roused passion.

The second 'half' of the film is darker. In the scenes with Brenda which follow her pregnancy, Arthur is now unsure and diffident, holding his body as though it were a burden to him, uncertain how to act and what to say. Even though Brenda's rejection for a younger woman does not accumulate the tragic weight that Alice's has in *Room at the Top*, it acts as a powerful counter to Arthur's assurance. His relationship with Doreen (Shirley Anne Field) is more circumscribed and his impending marriage less emotionally fulfilling. Her dreams are completed by the anticipation of a new semi-detached. Arthur, moody, truculent, but distinctly uncertain, throws a stone at this utopian prospect. According to Sillitoe, this gesture is an act of continued rebellion with Arthur softened but unbowed.[31] Director Karel Reisz thought it was an impotent and futile gesture in the face of Arthur's inevitable conformity.[32]

The film's reception suggested that it was Arthur's rebellious energy rather than his eventual conformity that had most impact. Isabel Quigly emphasised his '*bounce*, the youthful bumptiousness of a new class that begins (between bouts of despair at the *status quo*) to stretch and feel its muscles'.[33] Critics felt that the twenty-two-year-old Salford-born Finney, whose persona was unformed, was exactly right for the part. 'His Arthur Seaton comes entirely alive in time and place.'[34] Unlike Burton and more than Harvey, Finney could convincingly embody working-class energy and resilience. Producer Harry Saltzman was convinced he had become a genuine working-class hero with whom young males identified completely.[35] Finney's Arthur was marketed as 'a convention-smashing, working-class Don Juan', whose rebellion 'comes from living louder and faster than anyone else'. As with *Room at the Top*, *Saturday Night* was judged to have a broad appeal: 'to class cinemas (for the quality of its production) and to industrial halls for its identifiable truth about working-class life'.[36]

Arthur's energies went into Finney's next great creation, Tom Jones, the sexual adventurer. However, the drift of the Angry Young Man movement was into a more pronounced alienation. In *The Loneliness of the Long Distance Runner* (1962), Sillitoe adapted and enlarged his own short story to remodel the image of the delinquent, converting what I have shown was a pathologised type into an engaging rebel, a paradigm shift that went beyond Clive Donner's *Some People*, Sidney Furie's *The Boys* or Betty Box's *The Wild and the Willing*, released at almost the same time. Colin Smith (Tom Courtenay) is a petty thief, but his behaviour is offered as an understandable rejection of a society that offers lifelong workers like his dying father virtually nothing. 'I don't like the idea of slaving my guts out so that the bosses can get all the profits. It seems all wrong to me. My old man says the workers should get the profits. But I don't know where to start.' That last sentence is important, as the screenplay is careful to present Colin's unfocused rebellion as another inchoate struggle to work things out for himself, rather than becoming a mouthpiece for Marxist dogma. Sillitoe argued that his story was about being yourself and refusing to have an identity imposed on you from whatever quarter.[37]

Tony Richardson's direction attempts to realise this struggle through a more sustained attempt at first-person narration than *Saturday Night*, encouraging sympathetic identification with the protagonist whose consciousness we inhabit. The lyrical moments during his early-morning runs with their subjective camerawork, offer precisely the sense of space, freedom and self-sufficiency that Colin lacks in the rest of his life and that he could enjoy only briefly in the interlude in Skegness with Audrey. It connects Colin to the tradition of bloody-minded proletarian heroes of the 1930s, heroes of novels rather than films.[38] It is his folk memory of that inheritance – 'All I know is that you've got to run' – that sustains Colin's integrity against the new consumerism and the seductiveness of being the borstal governor's 'blue-eyed boy'. The ironies here are rather heavy-handed – the beating up of the rejected favourite Stacey as the boys sing 'Jerusalem'; the depiction of affluence as an extended advertisement – but they do underline Colin's wisdom in rejecting what is offered, since both are based on exploitation. In the working-class Courtenay the film had a new kind of star, very different from the charismatic Finney: flat-voiced, gracelessly awkward, with plain, pinched, perpetually worried features. Colin's wholesale rejection of society modulated into a reconstruction of the 'uprooted and the anxious' scholarship boy to form a new type, that, in the absence of a convenient label, I shall call the Alienated Young Man.

## The Alienated Young Man

As I have shown, part of the energies of the Angry Young Man go into the figure of the Rogue; *Nothing but the Best* remade *Room at the Top* as the triumph of the adaptable chameleon. The Alienated Young Man is the vehicle for the negative energies of the Angries which make them dissatisfied with any form of success. Lindsay Anderson's *This Sporting Life* (1963) offered a bleak and tragic version of the Angry Young Man. Richard Harris's titanic but thwarted Arthur Machin is closer to Stanley Baker's tough guys, but without their ability to succeed. In *Room at the Top*'s dark sequel, *Life at the Top* (1965), Joe's attempts to break free of his provincial roots are wrecked by the indifference of the metropolis and its media professionals. The type was central to Michael Winner's early films with their disillusioned, obsessive anti-heroes 'who dream of an alternative life' that they cannot achieve.[39] In *West 11* (1963), adapted from twenty-year-old Laura del Rivo's first novel, the central character Joe Beckett (Alfred Lynch) is 'a young man without roots or purpose who feels detached from life … [one of] the aimless, drifting, living-for-kicks population of London's bed-sitter belt'.[40] Winner's generally spare and restrained direction is complemented by Otto Heller's bleakly beautiful monochrome location photography that used a minimum of artificial lighting to capture the feel of the area. Joe's alienation is offered as the existential dilemma of an, 'emotional leper. I don't feel anything … I don't belong anywhere.' He is surrounded by similarly unstable, deracinated characters, including his girlfriend Ilsa (Kathleen

Breck), desperate to be a successful model. Joe falls prey to a malcontent from the previous generation, Captain Richard Dyce (Eric Portman), a maladjusted veteran anxious to maintain his faded gentility by crime. As a corrupt father figure, he suborns Joe into attempting to murder Dyce's wealthy aunt which he claims will restore Joe's manhood and self-belief. Joe's fumbled attempt, shown in a mixture of impersonal aerial long shots and disorientating close-ups, retains audience sympathy. In a sentimental conclusion, a chastened Ilsa will wait for him.

Winner's *The System* (1964) and *I'll Never Forget What's 'Is Name* (1967) were a diptych, based on original screenplays by Peter Draper, in which the central character moves from the provinces to London.[41] Draper attempted to describe the frustrations and anxieties young people experienced, 'trying to shape their own shaky morality' in an affluent, exploitative society that showed the bankruptcy of official values.[42] In the Devonshire seaside resort of 'Roxham', a group of smartly dressed young men operate the 'system', a series of scams to part the 'grockles' (holidaymakers) from their money. Their leader is Stephen Taylor – 'Tinker' – (Oliver Reed), an outsider who has stayed on. His success as snapshot photographer and 'seaside Don Juan' gives little satisfaction. He contemptuously rejects his suburban conquests as narrow-minded and unambitious, 'a three-ply bungalow with four square yards to mow every Saturday'; but falls in love with Nicola (Jane Merrow), the girl in the Buick Riviera, for whom he is a just a holiday romance, abandoned for a modelling contract in Rome. Although Tinker is briefly energised by resentment at her braying male friends, as a class warrior he makes a poor showing. He cannot cope with a woman as rootless and selfish as himself who has far greater confidence and self-possession. Unable to return to his male group which is in the process of breaking up, his only recourse is to dream of the opportunities represented by London.

In *I'll Never Forget What's 'Is Name* that success has been achieved. Reed plays Andrew Quint, one of the 'young meteors', a top London advertising executive in his early thirties, with a fashionable home, wife and two mistresses, but still unstable and unsatisfied. Directing with more confidence, Winner uses a huge number of camera set-ups to achieve an unsettling, staccato rhythm or rather dissonance, that mirrors the surges and reversals of Quint's restless, kaleidoscopic life. Despite the grand gesture of strolling into work with an axe and chopping his desk to pieces with which the film begins, Quint's opting out is flawed. His attempt to return to his former life, as assistant editor of a small literary magazine with his Cambridge chum Nicholas, produces only further disillusionment. Revisiting his past – school reunion, old Cambridge tutor – Quint realises its contemptible venality. His more satisfying relationship with a working-class girl, Georgina (Carol White), is ended when she is killed in a car crash, the fault of a drunken, maudlin Nicholas who has sold out to Jonathan Lute (Orson Welles), Quint's former employer. Quint's final commercial, which he thinks makes a great statement of bitter, socially conscious opposition, wins an award in a competition rigged by Lute. He ends as he began, working for Lute's main competitor and back with his wife Louise (Wendy Craig), who tells him: 'What a long way to go to cross the street.' Both films use Oliver Reed very effectively. He projects a sense of barely contained physical energy and anger that can never find its occasion, becoming a powerless Byronic anti-hero, whose distant gaze suggests that nothing really satisfies or truly engages him and who has nowhere to go.

Winner argued that *I'll Never Forget What's 'Is Name* 'dealt with themes ahead of its time. In 1967, no-one was opting out; no-one was going back to the simple life. It was a get-another-car society, totally.'[43] But five months earlier, Antonioni's *Blow-Up* (1967) had its 'young meteor' fashion photographer Thomas (David Hemmings) actually disappear. The alienated hero had also been visible in John Boorman's *Catch Us if You Can* (1965) whose sympathetic producer David Deutsch allowed Boorman to ignore the demands of the production company, Anglo-Amalgamated, for another paean to exuberant youth. The film opens with a celebration of the wacky new Bohemia of the group, the Dave Clark Five, shot in a sub-Lester kaleidoscopic montage. But the style of the early scenes is abruptly abandoned in favour of a fluidly photographed journey westwards made by a disillusioned Steve (Dave Clark) and Dinah (Barbara Ferris) the 'Meat Girl', symbol of an aggressive advertising campaign, whom he has 'liberated'. Boorman wanted the journey to be the pair's 'coming to terms with the English soil and landscape and customs'.[44] This becomes a complex process of understanding and rejection of the changing, incoherent England that they encounter: a hippie commune on Salisbury Plain that is crushed by the army; a corrupt and predatory couple amid the old-fashioned Bohemia of Georgian Bath; the fake ranch of ex-Stepney youth leader Louis. Steve, saturnine and wary, rejects all these lifestyles; Dinah, more trusting and accepting, flirts with them. In the end their *Ultima Thule*, a small island off the Devon coast, is chimerical, linked to the mainland at low tide and already occupied by her boss, who has orchestrated their capture expertly to achieve maximum publicity. Dinah returns to that world, Steve to the arms of his comrades-in-pop who have followed on his heels in their Mini Moke.

These tentative moves towards discovering an alternative lifestyle were the theme of Karel Reisz's *Morgan – A Suitable Case for Treatment* (1966), adapted from his own influential television play by David Mercer. It explored a schizophrenic protagonist, idealistic but unable to believe in the possibility of meaningful social action.[45] Morgan Delt (David Warner), a struggling artist, is marooned between the Marxist certainties of his parents' generation – 'He wanted to shoot the royal family, abolish marriage and put everybody who'd been to public school in a chain gang. Yes, he was a hidealist, your dad was' – and the vacuous, middle-class affluence of his beautiful ex-wife Leonie, now engaged to a fashionable antiques dealer. Like his 'Angry' predecessors, Morgan still suffers from the 'perils of hypergamy'.[46] His rebellion is incoherent, fanciful, part playful, acting out jejune Hollywood fantasies of rugged potency. Morgan is a man incapable of violence and the stress falls on his romantic vulnerability and need to be loved: 'I'm frightened,' he confesses to Leonie as he waits for the inevitable ending to their idyllic interlude in the Welsh mountains. Warner's gangling presence, his soulful eyes and boyish looks, create a Holy Fool unable to cope with a hostile world whose revolt can be linked to the then fashionable Laingian philosophy that insanity is the only valid response to a repressive familial and state structure. Morgan's marriage cannot be remedied, nor can the disintegrating society it exemplifies. In one of the film's most memorable images, Morgan lies in the battered remains of his gorilla suit on waste ground adjoining Battersea power station fantasising about his own execution. The final scene offers consolation if not a solution: when Leonie visits him in the mental home she coyly admits that she is pregnant with his child and he shapes the flower-bed into a floral hammer and sickle that neatly conflates Marx with a hippie counter-culture.

*Morgan* was highly successful, indicating that a popular space had finally opened up for the Alienated Young Man. One reviewer thought it was indeed *Look Back in Anger* ten years on: 'But *Morgan* represents a development: now that we live under Wilsonism, the man's search for "good, brave causes" has become a deeper, less extrovert, more guilt-ridden acceptance of ever making socialism … a sombre and more desperate direction.'[47] Peter Watkin's *Privilege* (1969), with a screenplay by Johnny Speight, recast this as a nightmare in which the alienated young pop idol Steve Shorter (Paul Jones) is simply a tool of a totalitarian British state. Rank found the film offensive and it received limited release.[48]

The most celebrated rebel hero was Mick Travis (Malcolm McDowell) in Lindsay Anderson's *If …* (1969). Anderson used the public school as a metaphor for a moribund, brutal and corrupt English culture run by masters who are perverts, eccentrics or nonentities. The headmaster (Peter Jeffrey) is a platitudinous moderniser who gives the sixth form lessons in business management. *If …* employed a loosely Brechtian schema in eight 'chapters' – including unsignalled switches from black and white to colour, realism to fantasy – to engender a critical response, drawing on the middle-class dissident tradition, Romanticism and European art cinema.[49] In Travis the film offers an instantly recognisable inverted image of the action hero – narcissistic, arrogant, macho – who can lead the revolt against a decaying despotism. Anderson thought he was 'a hero in the good, honourable, old-fashioned sense of the word'.[50] Together with Wallace (Richard Warwick) and Knightly (David Wood), his revolt escalates from growing a moustache, drinking gin and smoking, to stealing a motorbike, firing at the cadet corps and finally machine-gunning the assembly of staff, dignitaries and parents at Founder's Day. They were sexual rebels too, as shown in the fantasy of Travis's spontaneous and unrestrained love-making with the working-class girl at the café and the delicate lyricism of Knightly's affair with the younger pupil Bobby Phillips. *If …* 's rebels were, simultaneously, the demolishers of treasured symbols of English patrician culture and generalised apostles of sexual and social revolt to whom 'violence and revolution are the only pure acts'. This universality ensured the film's unanticipated success both in Britain and abroad.[51] In McDowell it had another charismatic anti-hero who, like Finney, could be identified with his role.

Rebels in this period are young men who feel they are not getting their fair share. Initially this revolt had to be conducted in costume, but there is a direct line from Stewart Granger's Philip Thorn to the Angry Young Man. Both are conscious of their talents and attempt to move between classes. Although the impact of the Angry Young Man was significant, it was short-lived; by the time the figure reached the screen, the working-class was undergoing a period of rapid change and realignment within an increasingly affluent consumer culture. The energies of the type bifurcated, either into the adaptability of the Rogue, or into the ennui and torpor of the Alienated Young Man. *If* ... renewed the rebel's energies by reinscribing the figure as an anarchic insider which could be universalised. The figure that does not fit this paradigm is Dracula. As with Mason's 'wicked gentlemen', the rebel aristocrat erupts at unpredictable moments, a 'return of the repressed', invading a restrained middle-class hegemony with erotic excess. I return to this point in the next chapter and the conclusion.

$$\boxed{9}$$

# Damaged Men

The films analysed in this chapter explore varieties of male social and psychic disorder. These men have little mastery over their emotions, their bodies, their sexuality and their identities. They act violently, often murderously, under compulsions that are irrational and often inexplicable. The interest in the representation of confused and disordered male identities was influenced powerfully by the rise of a popular Freudianism, centrally Freud's conception of the struggle of the Ego and the Id involving the 'return of the repressed'. This appropriated discourse must be read not as a universal truth, but *historically* as a specific example of the deployment of predominantly Gothic conventions, one that provided an apparently scientific explanation for sexual and psychological disorder.[1]

These damaged men can be analysed as two inter-related types. The first, which dominated the immediate post-war period, was the maladjusted veteran whose war service had caused psychological damage and/or social dysfunction. The second, the schizophrenic, was more obviously generic. It was archetypal rather than social, forming part of British cinema's post-war investment in Gothic horror. It too was spawned by war trauma, but developed into a more wide-ranging concern with the instabilities of masculine identity.

## War Trauma and the Maladjusted Veteran

The Second World War, like other extended conflicts, had profound psychological effects upon its combatants, often making their reintegration into civilian society problematic.[2] Expert medical opinion, from as early as 1941, had drawn explicit attention to the severe problems of readjustment which males returning from active service might face. Numerous articles in *The Lancet*, the *British Medical Journal* and *The Practitioner* highlighted potential psychological problems: 'The war with all its wreckage will present us with a heavy increase in neurotic disability.'[3] This discourse was popularised by handbooks like *Living Together Again* that identified 'tell-tale signs' of psychological maladjustment: long periods of silence and depression, nightmares, sleepwalking and aggressive outbursts, fits of rage and moodiness necessitating long solitary walks.[4] The ex-serviceman, bereft of the comradeship which had sustained him, was thought to lack confidence and feel alienated, 'surrounded by a jostling and often hostile world which is blind to his new values and to his maturity'; his wife or loved one would become, 'a ghost and a stranger'.[5] The veteran was 'inwardly a very different man, tougher, more experienced, more demanding and prey to disillusionment', constantly feeling 'there is an unbridgeable gap between them and the people who have not shared their war experiences'.[6] Mass-Observation noted a pervasive 'fear of purposelessness ... Unable to feel assured of their future as members of a purposeful community, many are thinking in terms of private adventurism or escape, so accentuating the potential conflict between wartime co-operation and post-war selfishness.'[7]

The government recognised that the abrupt conclusion to hostilities exacerbated these problems as nearly seven million moved rapidly from the forces to civilian occupations.[8] An MoI documentary, *A Soldier Comes Home* (April 1945), with a screenplay by Dylan Thomas, focused on the difficulties a working-class soldier experienced in readjusting to civilian life after his experiences in the Far East. It offered understanding and toleration from loved ones as the solution. Although the level of official concern was part of a welfarist interventionism that extended to all aspects of the veteran's life, including rehabilitation centres and psychological outreach, the preoccupation with these 'difficult', 'damaged' men – who had disturbing similarities to the 'shell-shocked' victims of the First World War – began to shape a myth of the war as a traumatising experience. The 'small army' of deserters, thought to number around 15,000, formed a highly visible social group.[9]

Korda's *Perfect Strangers* (1945) and Ealing's *The Captive Heart* (1946), with their transformed and reinvigorated debonair heroes, were products of the wartime structure of feelings and proved to be aberrations. The main line of development came from Eric Portman's Captain Ellis in *Great Day*, already analysed. He was the paradigm for subsequent representations that centred on ambivalent, sensitive, tortured and tormented male protagonists engaged in a moral struggle within their own natures, who are plunged into neurotic self-doubts and a crisis of sexual and social identity.[10] As the cycle of films developed there was a shift from the damaged Everyman to the psychotic and the criminal with a greater capacity for violence. In an episode of Ealing's *Train of Events* (1949), demobbed soldier Philip Martin (Peter Finch) appals himself by his capacity for uncontrollable violence after being 'well trained to kill ... six years of war toughened me', and murders his faithless wife.[11]

## The Damaged Everyman

A varied group of films made by a range of production companies in the immediate post-war period offered the damaged Everyman – Butcher's *I'll Turn to You* (1946), Gainsborough's *The Years Between* (1946), Ealing's *Frieda* (1947), Merton Park's *The Fool and the Princess* (1948), Two Cities' *The October Man* (1947), London Films' *Mine Own Executioner* (1947), The Archers' *The Small Back Room* (1948), Constellation's *The Small Voice* (1948), Wilcox's *Elizabeth of Ladymead* (1949), Renown's *The Glass Mountain* (1949), George King's *Forbidden* (1949) and Vic's *Something Money Can't Buy* (1951) – showing the importance of the type. Gainsborough's *The Years Between* (1946), adapted from Daphne Du Maurier's successful play, was announced as 'the most topical film ever made'. It had the courage to broach the difficult issues of male displacement and sexual uncertainty arising out of women's increased independence during prolonged absence.[12] Colonel Wentworth (Michael Redgrave) has spent almost the entire war reported killed as a cover for his intelligence activities. His wife Diana (Valerie Hobson), kept ignorant of this deception, has become accustomed to running the estate and has taken her husband's place as the local Member of Parliament. Wentworth cannot accept the independent woman his wife has become; as a war hero he feels entitled to have everything return to the *status quo ante* – 'I want the wife and home I left behind' – and to resume his sex's traditional role of running things. This displacement activates Wentworth's worst nightmares and in his confusion and disappointment he starts to become feminised, ordering the servants to replace household objects they have not in fact moved and constantly fussing about domestic order, like a caricature of the neurotic housewife. His male self-assurance lapses into sexual craving and a petulant infantilism. He is tormented by his son's close emotional ties with their neighbour, who was about to marry Diana, and his own estrangement from the boy. Wentworth's bewilderment and crisis of identity as husband, father and legislator contrast with Diana's confidence. Both her newly forged socialist feminist agenda and her patience, resilience and phlegmatic strength in the face of her husband's scorn are presented as wholly admirable.

In the play Diana abandons her socialism and the exhausted marriage is sustained only by Wentworth's decision to accept a government post that will take him abroad; it is the son Robin on whom vague hopes for a different and better future rest. The film, with heroic implausibility, uses Nanny (Flora Robson) as a saintly mediator, exhorting her employers not to 'lose the peace', but to set an example to other families and nations by living harmoniously. This is symbolised in the final shot of the Wentworths smiling at each other from opposite sides of the House of Commons. Critics were revealingly divided as to whether Wentworth was sympathetic or not. One called him 'one of the most unlovable heroes in contemporary fiction'.[13] Another, exasperated by the unflurried perfections of Diana, empathised with a man, 'physically worn out, mentally on the edge', and admired Redgrave's performance which 'sharply conveys the exhaustion and sardonic disillusion of the colonel'.[14]

*Frieda* extended Dearden and Relph's earlier *The Captive Heart* by exploring the longer-term problems of the returned POW. Although resoundingly middle-class, Flight Lieutenant Robert Dawson (David Farrar) was offered as a representative Everyman, the 'average Allied serviceman' returning to the heart of middle England, Denfield.[15] His German wife Frieda (Mai Zetterling) is symbolic of the war's legacy, inducing in Robert a confusing mixture of shame, responsibility and guilt which trammel his feelings towards the home and the people he has always known, especially Judy (Glynis Johns), widow of his dead brother Alan, whom he would have married. Coupled with Frieda he remains the pariah, the outsider, as strongly marked as the other town veteran Jim Merrick whose face has been hideously scarred from the blow of a Nazi prison guard. *Frieda* deploys a *noir* chiaroscuro to render Robert as a divided figure, half in shadow, half in light. The choice of Farrar, who went on to play the tortured Sammy Rice in The Archers'

*The Small Back Room* (1948), carries with it the suggestion of possible violence lying beneath the conventional restraint and good manners. His fight with Frieda's unrepentant brother releases this murderous energy. In attempting to strangle Richard, he is clearly trying to exorcise Frieda, as he has just been goaded into seeing both Frieda and Richard as one, a dark deformity which will recur in his children. Afterwards he becomes that terrifying figure from German Expressionist cinema, the somnambulist, his body trudging forward, his mind possessed by dark forces which he cannot control. In parallel, Frieda moves inexorably towards the weir. In Ronald Millar's play, Frieda pulls back from this impulse, but her decision not to marry Robert and return to Germany is irrevocable. The film opts for a more romanticised and reconciliatory solution as Robert rescues Frieda from her suicidal plunge.

Producer-writer Eric Ambler's original screenplay for *The October Man* drew on his experience of producing government short documentaries to prepare servicemen for demobilisation.[16] It plunges John Mills, the quintessential decent Everyman, into an existential crisis. Jim Ackland (Mills), a nervous, mild-mannered industrial chemist, is attempting to rebuild his life after a bus crash from which he emerged physically unscathed but mentally unbalanced, deeming himself responsible for the death of a friend's young daughter who was accompanying him on the journey. During a year's subsequent hospitalisation he has twice attempted to commit suicide. This scenario, with its burden of guilt for the destruction of an innocent life, would certainly have been read as a metaphor for post-war traumatic stress.[17] Jim's gradual, faltering attempts to get back into society take place in a suburban boarding-house, whose decaying middle-class gentlefolk are united by their hostility to outsiders, quite prepared to believe that Jim is capable of the murder of fashion model Molly Newman (Kay Walsh). Roy Ward Baker's subtle direction uses *noir* lighting and unbalanced, cluttered compositions to create a pervasive tense claustrophobia in which the gentle, introspective Jim, in his damaged state, begins to believe he could indeed be Molly's murderer, acting out his repressed desires for a 'loose' woman who had tried to seduce him, even though his conscious mind tells him that he was elsewhere. He cannot pinpoint the causes of his neurosis, confessing to his girlfriend Jenny Carden (Joan Greenwood) that there is 'something in my mind, a sort of fear, as if it's dangerous to stay alive'. To her pleas that he trust the police he replies, 'perhaps they couldn't hang me, but they could make me wish they could'. Once again the film holds back from tragedy, Jim eventually pulls himself together and resists the urge to plunge in front of the oncoming express.

There was some critical carping about the contrived endings of these films, which seemed to defy the narrative logic, but their popularity may indicate the wisdom of sugaring the pill. They explored the problems of the returning veteran, but within a comforting framework of ultimate reassimilation. By contrast, *Mine Own Executioner*'s more extreme version of the type and its bleak conclusion proved less successful, though its integrity was admired by reviewers. Nigel Balchin's adaptation of his own novel was a detailed and knowledgeable depiction of the schizophrenic, a virtual textbook case of combat neurosis. Adam Lucian (Kieron Moore) is a pilot who has developed murderous psychopathic tendencies after being shot down in flames near Rangoon and spending nearly a year in a Japanese POW camp. Under treatment by lay psychologist Felix Milne (Burgess Meredith), he obsessively relives the traumatising experience in dreams (in waking life it is blocked), coupled with constant irritability, aggression and violence. In his drug-induced flashback (rendered as point-of-view subjective camera shots) he confesses to having broken under torture and to harbouring a racist loathing of his captors. His supreme moment was killing one of the camp guards by clubbing him over the head as he escaped. Blending social realism with a tempered Gothic register, Lucian becomes another somnambulist for whom wartime guilt and violent misogyny have become hideously entwined. He acts out the murderous impulses barely contained by Robert Dawson and dreamt of by Jim Ackland. In the film's most powerful scene, he sees the figure of his wife metamorphosing into the camp guard and shoots her, before wandering off to commit suicide.

In *The Small Voice* (1948), a modestly budgeted but stylish thriller produced by Anthony Havelock-Allan, Murray Byrne (James Donald), a playwright crippled by brutal Nazi interrogators, has become a misanthropic war wreck. His one pleasure is to torment his wife Eleanor (Valerie Hobson), whose loyalty and affection are interpreted as pity. Like Sammy Rice in *The Small Back Room*, Byrne is symbolically impotent and his relationship about to collapse. His *doppelgänger* turns up in the form of Boke (Harold [*sic*] Keel), a tough convict on the run after having attacked an army officer with a knife, who has the charismatic sexual energy Byrne lacks. Boke is a walking critique of Byrne's ideas that criminality is caused by circumstances; Boke's father was a concert violinist who offered his son every opportunity. Their rivalry is given a claustrophobic intensity as the Byrnes are imprisoned in their own home, shot in *noir* visual style by Monty Berman with chiaroscuro lighting, low-angles and cramped, off-centre compositions. The sexual rivalry intensifies the struggle between the two males whose deepening relationship anticipates *Performance* in its complex psychic exchange. In their final confrontation Boke is a willing victim, allowing Byrne to recover his manhood by shooting him. Several critics, including Lindsay Anderson, recognised the depth of this film.[18]

By around 1950 the topical urgency of the type was waning, and its representation became less frequent, especially as the war film revived. Ivan Foxwell's *The Intruder* (1953) glued the two together. Robin Maugham adapted his own successful novel whose working-class Everyman was offered as representative of 'the disillusionment which men and women in the Fighting Forces were experiencing on their return home'.[19] Ginger Edwards (Michael Medwin), an East End rough diamond with a distinguished war record, returns home to find his girlfriend in bed with a spiv and his brother being beaten by his sadistic uncle whom he accidentally kills. Outside the law, Ginger is aided by comrades from his former regiment, especially his ex-commander, Colonel Wolf Merton (Jack Hawkins) with whom he shares a gradually intensifying bond; the adaptation removed the novel's homosexual overtones, apparently at Hawkins's request.[20] Although *The Intruder* allows Ginger's class anger and resentment to come through quite strongly on occasions, it opts for a reimposition of military paternalism. Ginger becomes a working-class version of the cadet who finally gives an unquestioning loyalty to his stern-but-loving father. The real animus is directed against the managerial class, represented by Captain Pirry (Dennis Price); a coward in war, now a successful businessman.

*The Intruder*'s faith in military paternalism was flatly opposed by *The Good Die Young* (1954), an Anglo-American crime thriller produced by Romulus. It showed a much bleaker and alienated society in which 'Four men, each from a different walk of life. A clerk, an airman, a prizefighter and a gentleman of leisure' – two American, two British – are united by a shared sense of failure and resentment. For the first three, played by Richard Basehart, John Ireland and Stanley Baker, civilian life has offered little except hardship, frustration and a sense of inadequacy in their jobs and their personal lives. They gather for consolatory lunchtime drinking and fall under the spell of Miles Ravenscourt – Rave – (Laurence Harvey), an aristocrat whose distinguished war record is bogus. Rave is a Mephistophelean Gothic villain, seducing these three frail egos into criminality by 'reminding' them that they fought for their country and deserve more than they have. When the raid he organises goes wrong, Rave has no compunction in shooting the police or his compatriots. *The Good Die Young* received very mixed reviews from 'pointless and squalid' to 'stark, occasionally terrifying, yet oddly tender'.[21] Rave was uniformly disliked as an implausibly melodramatic villain, but the other characters were thought to be convincing portraits of decent men made susceptible by their sense of the injustices of civilian life.

Korda's *The Deep Blue Sea* (1955), adapted by Terence Rattigan from his own successful stage and television play, retained Kenneth More as Freddie Page. Page's genesis may be traced back to the neurotic Flight Lieutenant Teddy Graham in *Flare Path*, transmuted via Wing Commander Archdale in *The Way to the Stars*, into the breezy test pilot Tony Garthwaite (Nigel Patrick) of *The Sound Barrier* who substitutes RAF slang – 'whanging around', 'piece of cake, darling' – for any attempt at understanding the principles of supersonic flight. Page is the next stage on, a womaniser and drunkard, getting too old to be a test pilot, the only way he can reclaim his identity: 'A month or two on the waggon and I'll be the old ace again – the old dicer with death.' Trapped in that Battle of Britain moment like a perpetual adolescent, Freddie is tormented by a sense of impotence and uselessness, but protects himself by a bantering insouciance from coming to terms with his own emotions and from his relationship with Hester (Vivien Leigh). She has left her husband to live with him but is driven to attempted suicide. Page's awareness of his deficiencies, and his inability to master them, are beautifully conveyed by More who draws on all the resources of his charismatic persona.

While critics responded warmly to his performance they all condemned the film's aesthetic that replaced the dingy, claustrophobic intensity of the play with an inappropriately glamorous internationalism. Shots of a Farnborough air display, winter sports in Switzerland and 'gaudy scenes of Soho night life' were clearly aimed at an American audience.[22] C. A. Lejeune suggested that 'this freedom of action would seem to defeat its own ends. The whole essence of the play is the characters' inability to move.'[23] This probably alienated the middle-class audience which had made the play such a success, and its emphasis on middle-class failure was unlikely to endear it to the predominantly working-class cinema audiences, who also failed to respond to Dearden and Relph's *The Ship That Died of Shame* (1955) with its maladjusted middle-class naval officer (George Baker) for whom the war was the time of moral certainty. Asquith's *Libel* (1959) boasted a riveting performance by Dirk Bogarde as an amnesiac aristocratic veteran, susceptible to the suggestion that he has returned from the war as a different man, a theme that recurs in *Tunes of Glory* (1960), in John Mills's suicidal colonel. But neither was conspicuously popular now that middle-class discomfiture not tragedy was popular. *Suspect*'s (1960) crippled psychotic, Alan Andrews (Ian Bannen), was a veteran of the Korean war.

However, this paradigm was continued in the 1960s by films adapted from the novels of John Le Carré where the type becomes the victim of the Cold War. The first, *The Spy Who Came in from the Cold* (1965), was adapted by Paul Dehn. Dehn co-wrote the screenplay for *Orders to Kill* (1958), which, along with Nigel Balchin's *Circle of Deception* (1960), provided the link with the previous cycle as both explore the betrayals perpetrated on decent servicemen during the Second World War. In taking up the theme of betrayal, Le Carré explicitly distanced himself from the black-and-white morality of the Bond universe which '[t]akes us away from moral doubt, banishes perplexity with action, morality with duty ... There is no victory in the Cold War, only a condition of human illness and a political misery.'[24] Le Carré, as Michael Denning has shown, inherited the sceptical questioning of Graham Greene's thrillers and the sense of Establishment treachery and decline that found its symbolic centre in the 'Philby Myth', the most celebrated and discussed defection of a member of the ruling class.[25] Despite their resonant Englishness, all three Le Carré adaptations in this period were directed by American left-liberals making sophisticated thrillers that showed the influence of the European art film.[26]

Producer-director Martin Ritt deglamorised *The Spy Who* at every opportunity: in the scripting, shooting and in the actors' performances. Oswald Morris's chillingly bleak, black and white photography creates an atmosphere of hopelessness and desperation in which Alec Leamas (Richard Burton) struggles to retain a sense of moral boundaries and the idea that 'our side' is better than its opponents. His boss, Control (Cyril Cusack), articulates the refined ruthlessness of the 'great game': 'Our methods can't afford to be any less ruthless than those of the opposition, can they?' Leamas is sent under deep cover to a shabby London with its drab Labour Exchange and the decaying Institute of

Psychical Research. His pretend defection is to a featureless seaboard landscape in Holland, where the ideological conflict is engulfed by a general hopelessness. In his frustration Leamas turns on his innocent, idealistic communist lover Nan (Claire Bloom): 'What the hell do you think spies are? ... They're just a bunch of seedy, squalid bastards like me.' Caught in a complex web of double bluff and betrayal in which she is an inconsequential pawn, Leamas finally makes a gesture of humanitarian defiance and dies trying to help her escape, a last throw of the honourable Englishman whose tragedy occupies the centre of Le Carré's fiction.

Leamas – grubby, disillusioned and defeated – was the third great male type spawned by post-war spy fiction. He took a slightly different shape as sad, middle-aged, lonely Charles Dobbs (James Mason) in Sidney Lumet's *The Deadly Affair* (1966), again adapted by Paul Dehn from Le Carré's first novel, *Call for the Dead* (1961). Lumet had wanted to make the film in black and white, but, as Columbia insisted on colour, he worked closely with cinematographer Freddie Young who 'pre-fogged' the film stock to produce a muted, rather bleached-out colour range, appropriate to another vision of a down-at-heel London, still gripped by austerity rather than affluence. In this world of decay and unseen menace littered with the detritus of war, Dobbs uncovers a complex web of duplicity and betrayal including his wartime colleague Dieter Frey (Maximilian Schell) who has also cuckolded him. Dobbs contains the dilemmas of the Le Carré world within himself, the gentle, perceptive, scholarly Englishman who wishes to preserve honour and decency, but whose final killing of Frey turns out to be needless.

Columbia's *The Looking Glass War* (1969), produced by Mike Franco-vich and writer-director Frank Pierson, was less successful in creating the atmosphere of shabby deceit that permeated the earlier films. It abandoned Le Carré's characterisation of Felix Leiser as a seedy middle-aged car salesman tempted into espionage by memories of his own wartime comradeship, by making him a Polish sailor, played by the new teenage heart-throb Christopher Jones whose loyalties are to his 'dolly bird' girlfriend (Susan George). It is through the relationship between John Avery (Anthony Hopkins) and Leclerc (Ralph Richardson) that the film sustains Le Carré's themes. Avery is a family man, but one whose marriage has gone stale. He has become introverted and alienated, sceptical about the meaning of their mission in putting Leiser over the Iron Curtain. But for Leclerc, whose marriage is a desiccated lie, it provides a means through which he can relive his finest hour, those glory days of the Second World War, when 'our generation was tried as never before and was not found wanting'. Avery gradually understands the callous brutality of these patriarchs: 'I always thought fathers were supposed to love their sons, now I know they don't. They hate them!' This overturns the loving relationship between the stern father and the 'cadet' that formed the symbolic centre of 1950s masculinity.

## The Criminal Veteran

The first wave of films about the criminal veteran – *Dancing with Crime* (1947), *They Made Me a Fugitive* (1947), *Night Beat* (1948) and *The Flamingo Affair* (1948) – showed restless and unsettled but fundamentally decent men turning to crime as a way of retaining the excitement, status and the opportunities for rapid success that war had provided. Their protagonists become engulfed in the murky waters of a London underworld rejuvenated by the black market. Three of the above were second features; it was the first feature, *They Made Me a Fugitive*, that had by far the most impact, as I have shown. Gang leader Narcy's latest recruit, newly demobbed RAF officer Clem Morgan (Trevor Howard), is bored, hard-drinking and cynical, addicted to excitement and action: 'What he needs is another war,' comments his girlfriend sourly. He takes to crime, the obvious substitute, as a drunken joke, decided on the toss of a coin. However, once enmeshed, Clem retains some scruples; when he shows a distaste for drug trafficking, he is framed for a policeman's murder. When Clem breaks gaol to clear his name he becomes more sympathetic, a tough version of the victim hero, not introspective and uncertain, but a British Bogart, mistrustful, hard-bitten and laconic, with a repertoire of mordant one-liners. In the film's most extraordinary scene he is propositioned by a young woman in an elegant house to murder her feckless husband. Clem explains he is not a hired killer, but a man out of joint with the times: 'The only reason I'm a fat-headed damn fool and not a hero is because I went on doing what the country put me in uniform to do after they'd taken it back.' In this Hobbesian world where the police use him as bait, Clem's only ally is Narcy's ex-girlfriend Sally (Sally Gray), alienated by her former lover's brutality. The scene in her flat where she removes the buckshot from Clem's back has a smouldering sensuality rare in British cinema. Her love and loyalty give poignancy to an otherwise bleak conclusion.

For critics, Clem was a more disturbing figure even than Narcy. He represented a deracinated middle-class unable to readjust, 'an unconscious personification of decent humanity demoralised by war and unfitted for peace'; such representations were 'socially dangerous in a world suffering from the severe after-effects of the moral distortions of war'.[27] An article in *Picture Post* concluded ominously: 'a class that is itself dispossessed is always easy game for exploitation. Hitlerism, for instance, grew out of the dispossessed middle classes of Germany after 1918.'[28]

Subsequent films were less prepared to sympathise with the criminal veteran. Nigel Patrick's maladjusted ex-officers in *Uneasy Terms* (1948), *The Jack of Diamonds* (1949), and *Silent Dust* (1949) were all weak and corrupt. *Silent Dust*, imaginatively directed by Lance Comfort, presented a Gothic figure.[29] Lieutenant Simon Rawley (Patrick) has had all the advantages which a wealthy background provided and reneged on them: 'I didn't fall in battle; I fell by the wayside.' A venal Enoch Arden, he returns from the 'dead' as a scarred deserter, black marketeer and murderer. His one thought is to blackmail his nearest and dearest into helping him escape capture. In a cleverly manipulated flashback sequence, he tries to elicit sympathy from his stepmother Joan with a tale of an inexperienced officer confused and adrift in the heat of battle; but the images start to show a womaniser and profiteer, a first glimpse of that 'other war', fought by cynical opportunists. Rawley takes a sadistic delight in tormenting his wife (Sally Gray) who has just remarried. But the film's climax is the 'reunion' with his blind and doting father Robert (Stephen Murray), the self-made man from a Leeds tenement, obsessed with creating a gentleman. Simon rejects his father's appeal to the officer's code, honourable suicide. In a macabre dénouement the two struggle together and Simon falls to his death from the balcony like a modern Lucifer.

The scandal of Simon's return is hushed up by the *savoir faire* of an aristocratic neighbour, Lord Clandon (Seymour Hicks), decaying but morally active, who urges all images of Simon be removed from the house; his return never happened. The price is a re-dedication of Robert's pavilion, intended to commemorate his 'lost' son, so that it becomes a communal monument to the fallen. In this way the film distances Simon as the rotten progeny of an overweening *arriviste*, especially as Clandon's nephew, Captain Oliver (Derek Farr), is the decent officer now married to Sally. But Oliver is the figure of dull virtue,

16. *Cage of Gold* – Jean Simmons confronts the criminal veteran, David Farrar: the *homme fatal* (BFI Stills, Posters and Designs. By courtesy of Canal +Image UK).

entirely lacking Simon's Byronic elan. The film's disturbing resonance is to suggest that Simon is the unacknowledged 'other', a Gothic monstrosity forged in the war's dark underside.

Dearden and Relph's *Cage of Gold* (1950) also used the Byronic figure, Wing Commander Bill Glennon (David Farrar), the corrupt version of Robert Dawson. Glennon returns after the war to haunt his former lover, young Judith Murray (Jean Simmons), who paints his portrait as a modern St George. Like Rawley, he is a womaniser, profiteer and blackmailer, whose post-war 'racket' is currency smuggling. But, like all Byronic males, he is really only obeying the dictates of his own nature, galvanised by war: 'If your trade is shooting down aeroplanes you have to make money the best way you can.' He can exist only in a world of excitement and adventure, bolstered by the admiration of a succession of beautiful women who will make no permanent demands on him. The film's moral schema – which offers solid and dependable Dr Alan

Kearn (James Donald) as the virtuous hero – is subverted by the charm of vice, Farrar's dark, thrilling eroticism as an *homme fatal*.

As has been noted, 1950 was a watershed after which representations of the veteran became infrequent, displaced by the hegemony of the cadet. Warwick, which often employed English stars as villains, used Nigel Patrick in a cameo role in *A Prize of Gold* (1955) as a corrupt ex-RAF pilot Brian Hammell – 'gone to seed since the war, quite a number of them around. Grand boys, who lived on excitement; they could never settle down to a humdrum life' – quite prepared to murder in cold blood. Rank's ambitious thriller *Tiger in the Smoke* (1956), adapted from Margery Allingham's influential crime novel which attempted to deepen the character of the criminal, developed the type.[30] Jack Cash/ 'Havoc' (Tony Wright) is a complex, hybrid figure: a delinquent from an impoverished background, a psychotic, an existentialist delineation of 'evil' and a maladjusted veteran. Roy Ward Baker's sophisticated direction, aided by Geoffrey Unsworth's accomplished cinematography, deploys point-of-view shots, *noir* lighting (including garish flashing neon lights) and unbalanced often tilted compositions shot at odd angles to create a menacing and macabre London underworld, enveloped in an ever-present fog; a world which might harbour such a figure as 'Havoc'. As both a character and an elemental force, he descends from nowhere, having escaped gaol and already committed murder twice, to take command of a grotesque gang of sturdy beggars and war relics who recall Brecht's *Die Dreigroschenoper*. The bomb-blasted Tom Gripper recognises his condition: 'Know you, Jack. Know the state you're in. Like you was in the war, time after you done those two sentries in.' And it was precisely that 'state' which made his commanding officer, Major Elkin, take him out of the detention centre where he was awaiting court martial to help secrete treasure in Elkin's Brittany home. Thus Havoc's sense of destiny, of having been chosen, stems from the corruption of the officer class fighting that 'other' war for its own gain.

The novel's ending is told from Havoc's point-of-view. He does not succeed in gaining the treasure, but neither is he captured. Seeking oblivion, he slips into a sunken water pipe so that his body is never found; this satisfyingly sustains the enigma of a figure who has wrenched free from all restraints. Unfortunately, Anthony Pelissier's adaptation lacked the courage of the film's visual style and allows the conventional hero, Geoffrey Levett (Donald Sinden), who has married Elkin's widow, to save the day by rescuing both the Nazi loot and bringing Havoc to justice. This ending was in line with Rank's commitment to 'wholesome family values', but it undermined and impoverished Allingham's study of evil.

*Tiger in the Smoke* was the last important film to dwell on this figure. In *West 11*, already discussed, Eric Portman gave a beautifully crafted swansong to the type as Major Dyce cruising the Notting Hill streets in search of a pliable young drifter who will murder his rich aunt. In Alfred Hitchcock's *Frenzy* (1972), Jon Finch's declassed squadron leader looks too young to have fought in the war.

## The Post-war Psychotic

The mental maladjustment of the veteran was mirrored and intensified in a closely related group of macabre films which rushed into the cultural space opened up by the lifting of the BBFC's prohibition on their production during the war.[31] British National's shoddy *Latin Quarter* (1945) was the first, eclipsed by Ealing's extraordinary *Dead of Night*, which mounted an extended critique of the scientific rationalism of psychologist Dr Van Straaten (Frederick Valk). The two most powerful episodes, Hamer's 'The Haunted Mirror' and Cavalcanti's 'The Ventriloquist's Dummy', both with screenplays by John V. Baines, explored a psycho-sexual terrain entirely absent from Ealing's wartime output.

In 'The Haunted Mirror', the epitome of middle-class respectability, Peter Courtland (Ralph Michael), a young accountant on the verge of matrimony, is presented as a rather passive, 'feminised' male. He becomes possessed by his *doppelgänger* reflection, a crippled, murderously jealous, Regency aristocrat who clearly represents a dark, violent sexuality he has repressed. This could be read symbolically as Ealing's fear and fascination with its own 'other', the Gothic sexuality of Gainsborough's costume films. The lure of this mirror world, presented as much more vibrant than the dull, sober anonymity of Courtland's modern flat, draws him very close to breakdown, attempting to strangle his fiancée Joan (Googie Withers), who has the determination and willpower to smash the mirror. Courtland has been identified as another maladjusted veteran, 'essentially, the officer of *San Demetrio*, demobbed and tested in a new context. The test opens up appalling conflicts and inadequacies.'[32]

In 'The Ventriloquist's Dummy' episode, Maxwell Frere (Michael Redgrave) suffers from a schizophrenia which becomes increasingly uncontrollable. He is possessed by his dummy, Hugo, whose leering sexuality and jeering contempt express the dark emotions which the

17. *Wanted for Murder*: mother and serial killer son, Barbara Everest
and Eric Portman (BFI Stills, Posters and Designs).

introverted Frere suppresses. They turn on his own insecurities and
weaknesses, a constant neurotic jealousy that Hugo will leave him and
go to some other man. This has been interpreted as a homosexual
relationship;[33] but it could also be understood more generally as the
eruption of a range of forbidden desires, including the licence to be
sexually provocative to women, to bully and dominate, which Frere can
articulate only through an interlocutor. In this case the outcome is
tragic. Frere's attempt to break free from Hugo/Hyde leads to im-
prisonment for the attempted murder of his rival and to his own
breakdown. He becomes a limp castrate able to speak only in Hugo's
strangulated falsetto. Redgrave's performance, aided by a visual style
which makes frequent use of Expressionist lighting and intense close-
ups, was extremely powerful. The actor became 'identified as a specialist
in the nerve-wracked, split-minded casualties of civilisation, men haunted
and obsessed'.[34]

The actor most identified with such types was Eric Portman, who
extended his portrayals of troubled, thwarted men begun during the

war. In Excelsior's *Wanted for Murder* (1946), he plays Victor Colebrook, a serial killer. His tormented mind is possessed by the legacy of his grandfather, a Victorian public hangman, whose waxworks effigy he smashes in an attempt to break free. Colebrook is an intelligent, cultivated and deeply sensitive middle-class professional, more tragic than monstrous, a sympathetic study of a man who feels an uncontrollable compulsion to dominate women through violence. Like Colpepper in *A Canterbury Tale*, he is a mother's boy who cannot form adult relationships with women.[35] The film is rather stagebound, compounded by Lawrence Huntington's ponderous direction, and is therefore at its most effective when the camera dwells on Portman's face, notably in the waxworks scene, which allows this gifted actor to construct a dominating performance as the 'soul in torment' who drowns himself in the Serpentine rather than face capture. One commentator celebrated Colebrook as 'one of the great aesthetic killers', the tormented artist whose exquisite sensibility determines his fate.[36]

*Picturegoer*'s readers responded strongly to Portman's performance.[37] He played similar roles in *Dear Murderer* (1947), *The Mark of Cain* (1948), *Corridor of Mirrors* (1948), and also *Daybreak* (1948) where he was, unusually, a working-class figure though one aestheticised through the film's conscious reconstruction of the ambience of the pre-war French Poetic Realist thrillers, with Portman as an English Jean Gabin. In each, his identity is riven between an exaggerated sensitivity and a capacity for violence. The star commented: 'People do like me as a murderer … Particularly the women. It's amazing how murderers seem to appeal to most of them.'[38] Portman's female fans responded to his ability to project, 'the strength of being harried and tested by circumstances … No-one is better than Portman at expressing with a haunted, tortured expression of the eyes in a face otherwise taut and immobile, the inner bitterness in a strong man's soul.'[39]

Robert Newton played the type in *Obsession* (1949) and *Temptation Harbour* (1949). In the former he plays a doctor determined that his wife's American lover must appreciate the artistic style, the beauty, of his fate at the hands of a man of far greater sensitivity and depth of feeling, which intensifies the strange intimacy between the murderer and his victim.[40] James Mason's psychotic brain surgeon in *The Upturned Glass* (1947) was another cultivated, fragile and unstable professional whose romanticised suffering mirrored Mason's tragic IRA terrorist in *Odd Man Out* (1947).

## The Damaged Young Man

Representations of these fractured and deranged thirtysomething aesthete-professionals, often a metaphor for damaged officers unsure of their peacetime role, were a symptom of the immediate post-war period and ceased at this point. There was an hiatus until the late 1950s when a cycle of horror films worked a series of variations on Stevenson's Jekyll and Hyde archetype. The key figure of this new cycle was the psychotic *young* man in films targeted at a predominantly male adolescent audience. They projected inner torments as sensational and safely distanced action. A Gothic-inflected psychological realism was replaced by a Grand Guignol visual style in which men's bodies are subject to frightening attacks, often undergoing graphic and hideous transformations. More visibly and spectacularly than their predecessors, these men act under compulsions they cannot control and which seal their fate. Part of the attraction of the archetype for audiences is that it offers the *experience* of evil's forbidden pleasures in the mind and body of the protagonist himself, even if they are ultimately censured. In the later films in particular, the possibilities of horror and violence within males are conceived as systemic; the problems lie as much with the social structure and the prevailing ideology as with the individual. Good and evil become, to some extent, interchangeable as they occupy the same space. Young men have no opportunity to mature successfully in a family or in a society led by a corrupt patriarchal establishment that is hypocritical and repressive.

The revival of the Jekyll and Hyde archetype began with two black and white films made back-to-back in 1958 by Producers Associates (John Croydon and Robert Day), *Grip of the Strangler* and *Corridors of Blood*, but they used the talents of Boris Karloff, the icon of the previous era. By contrast, Hammer employed an attractive young protagonist, beginning with *The Curse of the Werewolf* (1960), thoughtfully adapted from a serious literary text, Guy Endore's *The Werewolf of Paris* (1933). Oliver Reed is sympathetic as the tormented Leon, the helpless progeny of aristocratic corruption whose body contains 'a soul and a spirit constantly at war'. His wolfish self is released when he is 'weakened by vice': his first adult transformation takes place in a brothel. To the townsfolk he is simply a monster, but his release comes from the silver bullet fired by his foster father, the cultivated professional Don Alfredo Carido (Clifford Evans). Don Alfredo is another of director Terence

Fisher's celibate, untainted father figures, who covers the grotesque body with his cloak in the moving last moment.

Despite Fisher's direction, the dualistic paradigm was abandoned in *The Two Faces of Dr Jekyll* (1960). Wolf Mankowitz's ambitious screenplay reversed the Stevenson story. Paul Massie played an ugly, sepulchral Jekyll and a handsome Byronic Hyde, who looks much more youthful than his other half. Mankowitz was trying 'to get away from the hideous, violent drooling monster of previous versions', and to present evil as attractive.[41] 'That is why I made Hyde handsome instead of repulsive. This is not a horror film … It is a psychological thriller, but it is also a comment on the two-facedness of respectable society.'[42] This modern ambiguity fails to work because there is no counterpoint to Hyde's corruption. He simply becomes the most debauched rake in London, outdoing even the notorious libertine Paul Allen (Christopher Lee), his guide to London's underworld of boxing, East End night clubs and opium dens. In the end it matters little what Hyde or anyone else does. The film's modest popularity caused Hammer to abandon the type. The subsequent cycle of psychological thrillers, beginning with *Taste of Fear* (1961), took a naive young woman as their main protagonist; only Oliver Reed's supporting role in *Paranoiac* (1963) added anything to the development of the damaged young man.[43] When the studio returned to the archetype in 1971 with *Dr Jekyll and Sister Hyde*, Martine Beswick was one of Hammer's liberated anti-heroines enjoying the delights of her new body.

The most influential construction of the type was Michael Powell's *Peeping Tom* (1960), a singular film that, along with Hitchcock's *Psycho* (1960), has been identified as the birth of modern horror and its preoccupation with the psychotic young man.[44] *Peeping Tom* was part of what David Pirie calls Anglo-Amalgamated's 'Sadian trilogy' – the others were *The Horrors of the Black Museum* (1959) and *Circus of Horrors* (1960) – which all dealt with contemporary society and found their 'visual inspiration in 1950s pornography while their central preoccupation was with the British public's insatiable appetite for crimes of violence'.[45] All have schizophrenic anti-heroes, driven to murder what they use in their professional lives. The latter two were crass Grand Guignol, whereas *Peeping Tom* was much more analytical and disturbing. Its scriptwriter, Leo Marks, had created an original screenplay for Hammer in 1951 – *Cloudburst* – in which John Graham (Robert Preston), a wartime intelligence officer, becomes a cruel and brutalised figure beyond human appeal, as he pursues his wife's killers using all his training and expertise;

he seems to actively relish the torture and murder of his victims. Nine years later, Marks was still working through the intense and often tragic relationships he had with young women agents during the war as an intelligence officer for the Special Operations Executive: 'The idea of writing *Peeping Tom* was born in the briefing room of SOE.'[46] The script recalls the tragic victim-heroes of the post-war thrillers in its sensitive, shy, beautiful and pained serial killer, Mark Lewis (Carl Boehm), but he is much younger. His pathology, scopophilia, is clearly the result of the monstrous father (played by Powell), an obsessive Freudian psycho-analyst, whose desire to produce the definitive textbook on fear has created a murderous progeny. This turned the post-war vogue for Freudianism on its head, presenting it as a perverted science. Mark also has the traditional loathing of the glamorous young stepmother, wedded only six weeks after the death of his mother, and a macabre relish for ugliness and deformity. He is driven by the desire to produce an ultimate image of fear: 'I made them see their own terror as the spike went in. And if death has a face, they saw death too.' As a modern vampire he dies by impaling the spike of his tripod into his own neck, a grotesque parody of the officer's code.

*Peeping Tom* implicates rather than distances its audience. Mark is innocent, sympathetic, and his case explained in minute and compelling detail, so that he is understandable, not monstrous in the usual way. The film is also self-reflexive. It shows how Mark's pathology is related to a 'society of the spectacle' in which women are objectified as sex objects, not only as photographs in sleazy pornographic magazines, Mark's spare-time occupation, but in the film industry itself where he is employed as a focus-puller. An audience which delights in the inflicting of pain and terror in horror films are, by implication, themselves complicit voyeurs.

The film disturbed the censors and outraged critics, who were also dismayed by Powell's slumming foray into a genre associated with low-budget shockers, particularly as *Peeping Tom*, despite its restricted budget, was a very well produced film.[47] Otto Heller's photography nuances the usual garishness of 1950s Eastmancolor and Brian Easdale's chilling piano score underpins the key scenes that are handled with Powell's characteristic panache and audacity. The film's commercial chances were wrecked when Anglo responded to the assault of the reviewers by withdrawing the film after its first week in the West End and cancelling further British distribution.[48] In retrospect, *Peeping Tom* can be seen to have combined the strengths of both cycles: the compelling presentation of the sensitive hero of the psychological thrillers with the visceral visual style of the late 1950s horror films.

Subsequent contemporary versions were less powerful. MGM re-hashed their 1937 chiller *Night Must Fall* (1964), with Albert Finney as a serial killer, but it '[f]ell very heavily between two stools. We ruined the melodrama by trying to make it a psychological thriller, and couldn't pull that off either.'[49] Columbia's *The Collector* (1965) used another charismatic young star, Terence Stamp, as the twisted protagonist, a stalker obsessed with a young woman (Samantha Eggar). The Boultings' *Twisted Nerve* (1968), co-scripted by Marks, used biological imbalance, a damaged chromosome, to explain the psychopath Martin Durnley (Hywel Bennett) as a force of nature.[50]

The sustained evolution of the damaged young man came from further developments in low-budget Gothic horror, where the growth of new production companies – Amicus, Tigon and American Inter-national Pictures (AIP) – as rivals to Hammer, helped to attract new ideas and talent. David Pirie identifies the mid-1960s as a time when horror provided a space where 'the aspiring filmmaker could work within a tentative cultural tradition'.[51] The most notable of these were screen-writer Christopher Wicking and director Michael Reeves, both ardent *cinéastes*, who 'can be located within a growing cosmopolitan and counter-cultural fascination with Hollywood and genre cinema'.[52] Their work coupled the concern for damaged youth with a distrust of older male authority, seen as the agent of a corrupt and repressive state. Peter Hutchings has drawn attention to the popularisation of R. D. Laing's ideas of the family as the prime institution of patriarchal repression that is explored in these films.[53]

I have dealt with Reeves's key film *Witchfinder General*, with its damaged swashbuckler, in Chapter 4. Wicking's major contribution was his original screenplay for *Demons of the Mind* (1971), set in nineteenth-century Austria, whose cultural roots lay in Jacobean tragedy which Wicking admired.[54] In contradistinction to the earlier Hammer films, Arthur Grant's cinematography employs a more subdued, naturalistic colour range which, coupled with Peter Sykes's fluid camera work, complements a story that emphasises the ambiguous transference of desire and guilt. Wicking wanted to explore the scientific and psychological basis for apparently supernatural monsters: '*Demons* is like a werewolf story, but one that looks at the reality behind the legend.'[55] Baron Zorn (Robert Hardy) has immured himself in his isolated mansion after the death of

18. *Demons of the Mind* – Shane Briant as the damaged young man (BFI Stills, Posters and Designs. By courtesy of Canal +Image UK).

his wife, convinced that he is guilty of having violated her in making love when he saw her pain, the blood of her lost virginity and yet her desire for him to continue – 'it disgusted me'. *Demons* sees this disgust as the obverse of the Baron's idealism that is rooted in his dynastic obsessions, needing her pure peasant blood to cleanse the corruption of his aristocratic veins. His subsequent cruelty leads to her suicide, witnessed by the two children, Elizabeth (Gillian Hills) and Emil (Shane Briant). Convinced that 'the evil demon in my blood' is incurable and has transferred itself to them, Zorn keeps his children prisoners. Both have become passive, unnaturally pale and, kept apart, have developed incestuous longings. Emil, the sad aesthete-dandy with his ruffled orange shirt and tight trousers, is both Pre-Raphaelite and counter-cultural. In a desperate attempt to cure them, Zorn employs Dr Falkenberg (Patrick Magee), a proto-psychoanalyst hounded out of Vienna because of his advanced ideas. Falkenberg, the pure rationalist, learns to his horror that Zorn's children are 'extensions of your being in some grotesque way'. In a moment of Freudian insight he realises Emil's savage killings – he rapes his victims after strangling them, then scatters blood-red roses over their bodies – are willed and aided by Zorn himself. Falkenberg understands that Emil is 'the instrument of your lust' acting out Zorn's own violent hatred of women. Falkenberg is shot for this insight, and Zorn, after slashing the portrait of his wife in the womb, stalks his children, killing Emil in a final act of domination and possession. Elizabeth is saved inadvertently by the fearful villagers led by a mad priest (Michael Hordern), who stake Zorn with a flaming cross. Elizabeth, crazed by what has happened, becomes monstrous and lashes out at her former lover Carl (Paul Jones) who is powerless to reach her damaged mind. Her furious face is freeze-framed as the final image.

*Demons*' complexities, violence and highly ambivalent closure, its presentation of the young man as both victim and violator, link it with *Witchfinder* and back to *Peeping Tom*. They all establish a clear distance from the more typical films of the earlier period, such as *The Curse of the Werewolf*, that offered an isolatable evil and an uncorrupted patriarch. Their depiction of a depraved older generation wreaking havoc on the young links them to other films: AIP's *The Oblong Box* (1969) and *Cry of the Banshee* (1970) which Wicking co-wrote; Hammer's *Taste the Blood of Dracula* (1970), *Hands of the Ripper* (1971) and *Twins of Evil* (1971); Tigon's *The Creeping Flesh* (1972), Amicus's *And Now the Screaming Starts* (1973) and Tyburn's *The Ghoul* (1974).

In a British cinema habitually designated as itself repressed, the persistence and variety of the figure of the damaged man is eloquent testimony to the capacity of screenwriters, producers and directors to explore the dangerous terrain of unstable male sexuality, violence and psychological disorder. Both in the post-war cycle of maladjusted veterans and in the later psychological horror films, these films engaged with aspects of masculinity that were difficult, if not impossible, to discuss openly. The films create an often complex dialectic with Freudian ideas in an open-ended way that acknowledged the limitations of scientific rationality as well as its insights.

# 10

# Contemporary Types

One of the most striking features of masculinity in contemporary British cinema is its heterogeneity and hybridity: the range of male types is much wider than before and the types themselves more complex. A detailed account of masculine representations in recent British feature films would therefore require a separate book. What can be attempted here is an analysis of the major transformations that have taken place, seen from the historical perspective provided by the types analysed in the previous chapters. This focus reveals some continuities as well as profound changes and thus allows the current mix of male types to be better understood.

In part these changes reflect the present state of British film-making which has become decentred and eclectic, lacking the studio infrastructure or dominant producers of the earlier period. Although film production has recovered from the trough of the 1970s when television spin-offs dominated the box-office, it remains chronically unstable, films are often poorly distributed or never shown.[1] While aspects of the 1980s revival – literary adaptations or social realism – have been retained, a new generation of film-makers has emerged that embraces a more commercial, populist cinema.[2] This development has been possible because of a significant revival in cinema-going encouraged by the arrival of the multiplexes which, keyed into the growth of integrated leisure complexes, now account for just over half of all UK cinema admissions.[3] Cinema-going has remained a young persons' activity, but the ABC1 audience now comprises the majority of frequent cinema-goers, with a roughly equal balance of men and women.[4]

Cinema-going, despite this revival, will never return to its former importance as a leisure pursuit, but *film viewing* continues to be a significant part of popular culture with the majority of films watched on television (terrestrial or satellite) or on video (bought or rented).[5] The rising popularity of DVD and the anticipated advances in internet 'screenings' will increase this consumption. If these developments are taken into account, cinema remains a popular and influential medium, among all classes and age groups, and representations of masculinity derived from successful British feature films contribute to a national 'image culture'.[6] This shared image culture is characterised by the increasing interdependency of the media and leisure industries: films, television, advertising, male style magazines such as *Arena*, the popular music industry, sport and the national press. As commentators have pointed out, images of masculinity have never been so varied, so visible, so widely discussed or so self-conscious, becoming part of 'integrated lifestyle packages' in an increasingly consumer-orientated postmodern society.

## Heroic Masculinity: James Bond

James Bond has been *the* most enduring post-war British film hero in twenty films spanning thirty-eight years. As James Chapman has demonstrated, the figure has been continuously adjusted in response to cultural changes.[7] In his seven films, from *Live and Let Die* (1973) through to *A View to a Kill* (1987), Roger Moore re-created Bond as an old-style debonair hero, more polished and sophisticated than Connery's incarnation, using the mocking insouciance he had perfected in his role as Simon Templar in the television series, *The Saint*. Moore's humour was throwaway, and, certainly in the later films, verged on self-parody. It was an essential strand in the increasingly tongue-in-cheek direction of the series which became more light-hearted, knowing and playfully intertextual. There were strong continuities with Kenneth More's self-deprecating heroes, but the joke had gone further, a way of competing, by not competing, with the new generation of Hollywood hyper-masculine, stone-faced action men like Arnold Schwarzenegger or Sylvester Stallone.

Moore's successor in *The Living Daylights* (1987) and *Licence to Kill* (1989) was Timothy Dalton who played up the character's Byronic elements. His Bond was dark, morally ambiguous, self-critical and modern. Without Connery's leavening humour, the result was a claustro-phobic intensity that failed to win over the public.[8] It was six years before Bond returned in his current incarnation, Pierce Brosnan. Bros-nan's Bond is not modern but retro, a return to the style established by Connery and successful because Bond's brand-name sophistication fits perfectly into the world of postmodern consumerism. Brosnan's lean frame carries the 'Armani look' with its refined, understated Englishness, to perfection.[9] His lithe, sinuous athleticism is well suited to the fast-paced action and state-of-the-art gadgetry that retain the series' core appeal.

However, the writers were conscious that Brosnan's Bond could not simply return to the Connery mould.[10] The character's overt sexism was deflected by making 'M' a woman (Judi Dench), which was both topical (Stella Rimington's appointment as director-general of MI5) and also gave an apparently updated feminist take on Bond by having M denounce him as a 'sexist, misogynist dinosaur'. However, having nodded in the direction of political correctness, the films play out Bond's relationship to women in quite conventional ways, with the added frisson of the shifting sexual tension between Bond and M. The perceived need to give the new Bond depth and a sense of inner conflict was more difficult to achieve. *GoldenEye* (1995) uses the *doppelgänger* motif: the struggle with 006 Alec Trevelyan (Sean Bean), intent on revenging himself upon a British government that betrayed his parents, who mocks Bond's unswerving loyalty. In *The World is Not Enough* (1999) Bond's loyalty and ruthlessness are sufficiently unstable for the two villains, *femme fatale* and dying terrorist, to query his ability to kill and his fidelity to the cause.

This fine-tuning seems, at the time of writing, to have adjusted Bond to the temper of the age. He continues to function as a hero of consumption who retains the virile masculinity of the traditional male adventurer. Like Connery, Brosnan combines the character's debonair Englishness with a classless internationalism that is highly knowing. Audiences can enjoy the distinctive pleasures offered by a Bond film without necessarily investing the figure with idealised significance.

## The Everyman?

Within a heterogeneous postmodern consumer culture it is extremely difficult to offer a consensual figure of the ordinary Everyman. However, there are, I suggest, two antithetical versions, one that is resoundingly middle-class and therefore only partially representative; the other from an 'underclass' whose low status is an eloquent testimony to the ravages of Thatcherism. What has gone, almost completely, is the decent, respectable working-class paterfamilias or the boy-next-door.

## The Lovable New Man

The middle-class Everyman is woven into the fabric of the 'New Man', one of the most widely discussed recent constructions of masculinity. The New Man was an alternative image to the macho tough guy, embracing female roles and qualities, a vulnerable nurturer in touch with his emotions, but also rather narcissistic. He became a 'potent symbol for men and women searching for new images and visions of masculinity in the wake of feminism and the men's movement'.[11] Richard E. Grant's yuppie widower who discovers the joys of fatherhood in *Jack & Sarah* (1995) was clearly a New Man, but the key embodiment was Hugh Grant in two highly profitable romantic comedies: *Four Weddings and a Funeral* (1994) and its 'sequel', *Notting Hill* (1999). Grant's New Man was an updated version of Dirk Bogarde's Simon Sparrow from the 'Doctor' films, the gentle, low-rent Man About Town, lovably awkward, tongue-tied, endlessly self-deprecating and sexually naive. Grant's considerable skills of comic timing mean his understated bumbling never quite topples into risible 'silly assery'. In *Notting Hill* his bookshop assistant is even more prone to *faux-pas* than he is himself, and his slovenly Welsh flat-mate (Rhys Ifans) provides a vulgar comic foil. Grant stumbles his way though a love affair with a successful, sexually assured but impulsive American woman amid a commodified England: the upmarket Home Counties locations of *Four Weddings* and the genteel Bohemian chic of *Notting Hill*. The independence and strength of the women in these films allow Grant, like Bogarde, to adopt feminine qualities. This is manifested in his insecurity and compliance (though this has limits), his lack of ambition and his desire for stability and heterosexual union, thereby fulfilling his supportive New Man credentials.

Both films were produced by Working Title whose aim was to make 'stylish, commercial films aimed at a maturing yuppie audience, and upbeat enough to play on both sides of the Atlantic'.[12] For males in this target group, Grant's refined thirtysomething New Man persona offered a way of trying to come to terms with their masculinity in an era of casualisation and instability in the professions, where long-term security is unavailable and where work ceases to confer status and self-esteem.[13] This could also have a wider appeal as the comedy protects Grant's characters from becoming too precious. For women, perhaps from all classes and especially in America, Grant's quintessential diffident English charm proved particularly attractive, indicating the enduring appeal of that type.[14]

## The Underclass Everyman

Underclass males are a dominant feature of contemporary British cinema and take a variety of forms. The underclass male is a *paradoxical* Everyman as his representativeness comes through his social marginality, not, as in previous periods, through his ability to express an acceptable standard. Fears of social and sexual insecurity press much harder upon the underclass male disempowered by the Thatcher 'revolution' with its shift from a manufacturing to a service economy and concomitant high levels of unemployment. Underclass men are adrift in a society represented as hopelessly run-down. Their male confidence is eroded because they lack the traditional strengths of working-class masculinity: a secure place as the principal breadwinner and head of the family, and comradeship with mates at work or in a union.[15]

The most consistent chronicler of the underclass male is Ken Loach whose protagonists express 'the appalling cost in human misery that aggressive Thatcherite politics had brought on everybody'.[16] A steadfast Marxist, Loach remains committed to the working-class as the potential vehicle of change, but his films recognise the near impossibility of that change happening. The representative underclass Everyman Stevie (Robert Carlyle) in *Riff-Raff* (1991), newly released from prison, fantasises about petty entrepreneurialism, selling boxer shorts, as a way out of his work on the building site where he is degraded, exploited and lucky to escape the injuries sustained by many of his fellow labourers. His dreams, including the romance with a drifting New Age would-be singer Susan (Emer McCourt), collapse in disarray. The arson attack on the building site that concludes the film is a futile gesture that provides only momentary emotional relief. Loach's most recent film, *My Name is Joe* (1998), is set in a soulless Glasgow housing estate where unemployment, drug-taking and crime are endemic. Its underclass Everyman, Joe Kavanagh (Peter Mullan), is attempting to rebuild his life after a long bout of

19.  *Riff-Raff* – Robert Carlyle, the post-Thatcherite underclass
Everyman (BFI Stills, Posters and Designs. By courtesy of
FilmFour International/Paul Chedlow).

alcoholism caused by unemployment, and a marriage wrecked by his
drunken violence. He becomes a surrogate father to Liam, one of the
lads in the local football team he runs, but he cannot prevent Liam's
suicide to escape drug-related debts. At his funeral there may be the
possibility of a rapprochement with Joe's former lover, a social worker.
This muted, guarded valorisation of ordinary decency is the most that
Loach feels can be acknowledged in contemporary Britain.[17]

Loach retains a scrupulous honesty in depicting what he sees as the
severe difficulties contemporary working-class males have in trying to
forge a better life for themselves, or even surviving. Other film-makers
have found ways of offering a less bleak (in many ways much more

superficial) version of the underclass Everyman through wish-fulfilling comedy. *Brassed Off* (1996), *Up 'n' Under* (1998) and *The Match* (1999) were overtly sentimental, reviving an Ealingesque whimsy to deal with the problems of unemployment and the breakdown of communities. *The Full Monty* (1997) was more robust and wittier. The film's Sheffield is no longer the 'city on the move' of the early 1970s promotional rhetoric, but a run-down, post-industrial city, in which the beleaguered Everyman Gaz (Robert Carlyle) has lost his job, his self-respect and is fighting to retain joint custody of his son. His scheme is to train himself and five others, all 'scrap' from the steelworks, to become bargain basement Chippendales. The men's rehabilitation comes through stripping, an activity that has been for women a form of degradation in front of the male gaze. Screenwriter Simon Beaufoy wanted the men to be forced to discuss difficult issues, including their own insecurities about their bodies as the film was 'all about gender reversal and emasculation … Women are looking at men now in exactly the same way that men have looked at women (and cars) for years. Women now have the confidence, the money and the freedom to do it, and men just don't like it at all.'[18] What their rehearsals create is a joky, if nervous, camaraderie which allows each one of the heterogeneous group to become gradually more confident about their lives, their feelings and their sexuality, including Guy and Lomper who form a gay couple. This moral tale of male re-empowerment through a supportive homosocial community is handled with an ironic humour that made it palatable for audiences, including women, and its catharsis – workers who have nothing to lose but their underpants – neatly sidesteps any long term consequences.[19] The successful underclass Everyman is not, like his post-war predecessors, associated with the secure expectation of better times ahead, but with a feel-good fantasy.

## Fools and Rogues

Contemporary British cinema clearly retains an important cultural space for Fools and Rogues. The role of the Fool shows a continued need to poke fun at middle-class pretensions. The figure of the middle-class buffoon is embodied by John Cleese whose film characters derive from his wonderful creation of Basil Fawlty in the two BBC series of *Fawlty Towers* (1975/1979). Fawlty was a volatile mixture of obsequiousness and pomposity, both obsessive and dictatorial, but always discomfited and humiliated by circumstances. In *Clockwise* (1986) these traits are transferred to Cleese's self-congratulatory comprehensive school headmaster, whose craving for order and punctuality is wrecked. In *A Fish Called Wanda* (1988) Cleese plays a rather more sympathetic version. His timorous, repressed barrister, trapped in a loveless and stifling marriage, is desperate to cast care aside in the arms of a sexy and uninhibited American (Jamie Lee Curtis) who eventually betrays him. Nearly a decade later, the comedy of the 'sequel', *Fierce Creatures* (1997), was more strained and more sentimental. Cleese's repressed British decency is shown to be preferable to global corporate greed and the commodification of leisure.

The more manic buffoon is Mr Bean, the creation of *Four Weddings* writer Richard Curtis and actor Rowan Atkinson. *Bean* (1997), in order to accommodate this television character to the demands of a feature-length film narrative, casts Mr Bean as a bogus British art expert wreaking havoc upon his unsuspecting American hosts. One commentator identified Bean as 'the Everyman of nightmare: gauche, snivelling, maladroit and leeringly self-absorbed – yet somehow, after all the pratfalls, always triumphant. With his lisping gurgle of a voice … his continually contorting face, his awkward, stiff-limbed walk, and his elbow-patched tweed jacket and slacks, he looks like a cross between Man at C & A and a village idiot.'[20] As the latest in a long line of emotionally and socially arrested British comic grotesques, Bean is, in current idiom, the ultimate 'nerd', a disaster-prone and often disgusting skit on the expert, who makes viewers feel smarter and better able to cope.[21]

If contemporary Fools continue to deflate middle-class pretensions, the Rogue continues to celebrate working-class brains and entrepreneurial energy triumphing over circumstances. The 1980s version was the yuppie, the hero of Thatcherite enterprise whose lineaments hardened into a fixed stereotype: slicked hair, striped shirt, red braces, wide-shouldered suit and *de rigueur* accessories: Filofax, laptop computer and mobile phone. The yuppie announced his success through a loud, swaggering style as he leapt in and out of the ubiquitous Porsche.[22] As John Hill notes, 1980s British films were unsympathetic to the type, with the muted exception of Paul McGann's personable young City trader in *Dealers* (1989), a highly ambivalent film.[23] But, in the more commercial cinema of the 1990s, the type resurfaced in *Rogue Trader* (1999), starring the charismatic Ewan McGregor as Nick Leeson, the man who broke Barings

Bank. The film excuses his conduct by emphasising that this self-made son of a Watford plasterer was an inveterate gambler, always trying to salvage a desperate situation and acting partly in defence of his team of traders, rather than to accumulate wealth. Leeson's *gaucherie* and his unrepentant materialism are preferable to the upper-class greed of the petrified Barings' executives.

Although the real Leeson spoke in flat, neutral tones, McGregor's 'Mockney' aligned the portrait with the 'geezer', a contemporary version of the wide-boy/spiv which forms part of what has been dubbed 'New Laddism'. This boorish, retro-macho culture allows young men, who are well aware of the political incorrectness of their sexist attitudes, to insist on behaving badly, deriving immense pleasure from parading their veneration of football, lager and 'birds'. These attitudes have their roots in 1970s laddism which had its screen incarnation in Robin Askwith's Timmie Lea in the *Confessions of …* films. 'Randy Robin' became the darling of the *Sun* as his cheeky and libidinous persona fitted its vision of British culture.[24] Contemporary laddism is more ironic and self-reflexive, best exemplified in its own style magazine, *Loaded*, launched in 1994, for 'men who should know better'. New Laddism has been an influential backlash to the perceived effeminacy of the New Man, yet just as consumer conscious, knowing and narcissistic. Its uncomplicated, confident masculine style appealed to both working- and middle-class males.[25] As Claire Monk argues, laddism was one answer to current male fears of women, a misogynist response to a 'post-feminist male panic'.[26]

The big 'laddist' hit was *Lock, Stock and Two Smoking Barrels* (1998), whose target audience was defined as, 'Boys. Your average *Loaded* reader', but which also appealed to young women.[27] Its director, Guy Ritchie, gave the film the required rapid tempo, pop song sound-track and relentless, wise-cracking Mockney. Its four lovable and essentially in-nocent lads become embroiled in London's underworld in their attempt to create a brighter future for themselves. The film's highly allusive intertextuality and numerous bouts of stylised violence derive from Quentin Tarantino's influential *Reservoir Dogs* (1991) and *Pulp Fiction* (1994). But *Lock, Stock* Anglicised its ingredients, raiding the familiar elements of the British gangster tradition in its parade of lurid Cockney mobsters fighting it out with pastiche Scousers, catatonic middle-class dope dealers, and the dreadlocked black villains beloved of tabloid crime reporting. This heady mixture was topped off by casting pop star Sting as the father of one of the boys, and notorious soccer 'hard man' Vinnie Jones as the laconic hit man Big Chris. Jones's image dominated the film's publicity campaign, launched to coincide with the start of the new football season.

## Criminals

*Lock, Stock*'s confident use of London gangland mythology was indebted to Barrie Keeffe's *The Long Good Friday* (1981) which provided another image of the *fin-de-siècle* gangster, Harold Shand (Bob Hoskins), the East End godfather crushed by the IRA. The hard-man gangster retains a favoured place in popular mythology as shown by the cult status of *Get Carter* which enjoyed a recent cinematic re-release. J. K. Amalou's *Hard Men* (1997), or Anthony Neilson's *The Debt Collector* (1999) based on the story of reformed Glaswegian hard-man Jimmy Boyle, are indications of this continued fascination, as are *Circus*, *Rancid Aluminium* and *Gangster No. 1*, all released in 2000. However, the contemporary criminal is not confined to this one variety. Peter Medak's *The Krays* (1990) returned to *the* dominant post-war gangster story, in order to explore social and sexual pathology. Philip Ridley argued his screenplay was, 'a timeless moral tale … A poetical, mystical interpretation of a contemporary fable … about vulnerability'.[28] Although the film was accused of exploiting the Krays' legend in casting glamorous pop stars as gangsters, Martin and Gary Kemp from Spandau Ballet as Ronnie and Reggie, it actually shows their grubby viciousness. However, *The Krays* was much less concerned with what the twins did, or in the specificities of their milieu, as it was in tracing their pathological violence to complex causes. Two of these, wartime dislocation and a weak father, are familiar tropes from the 'delinquency' cycle. But the central source is the twins' symbolic castration by their strong-willed, over-protective mother, Violet (Billie Whitelaw), who despises men but idolises her darling boys. The twins' infantilism and their intense fear of women are depicted in the accumulating graphic intensity of Reggie's destruction of his wife Frances (Kate Hardie) and Ronnie's morbid, narcissistic and self-protective homosexuality. The pair's unnatural closeness as twins fuels a macabre competitiveness that leads inexorably to murder.

*The Krays* showed the potential of these periodic revistings of the gangster legend for an exploration of masculinity, but Claire Monk is right to argue that the main trajectory of 1990s crime films has been to help delineate the post-Thatcher underclass.[29] In Antonia Bird's popular *Face* (1997), Ray (Robert Carlyle) is the new type of criminal, no longer spiv, delinquent or gangster, but part of a disillusioned underclass in a society where corrupt policemen take a perverse pride in announcing the end of public service. Ray, a former activist who turned to crime after the defeat of the 1984–85 miners' strike, is burdened by guilt in dropping out of the Left's struggle for social change, continued by his mother and girlfriend Connie. Unlike the fading, overweight Dave (Ray Winstone), conscious of his failures as a criminal and a father, Ray is a sympathetic figure despite his violence, capable of sincere love for Connie and compassion for his trusting sidekick Stevie. Bird's use of London locations is unusual and imaginative and the film has an energy and a sardonic humour that can accommodate an upbeat ending without sentimentality.

## Rebels

Ray, like Jude Law's James Dean anti-hero Billy in *Shopping* (1994), is as much rebel as criminal showing how these two types have begun to merge. Its most celebrated incarnation was Mark Renton (Ewan McGregor) in *Trainspotting* (1996), adapted from Irvine Welsh's 1993 cult novel that delineated Edinburgh's heroin sub-culture with wit and energy.[30] The film matched the novel's linguistic 'excess' with an equally vigorous visual register, both fast-paced and innovatively stylised. Director Danny Boyle opined, 'We wanted the film to have a vibrancy – a humour, an outrageousness, we always wanted it to be larger than life.'[31] In a (much imitated) explosive opening, Renton and Spud (Ewen Bremner) hurtle down fashionable Princes Street, stolen goods falling out of their jackets, pursued by two store detectives. Renton's expression of exhilaration is held in freeze-frame as a car upends him, an image of a man committed to a life-affirming hedonism. This stylisation enabled the film-makers to eschew social realism with its cast of victims, 'the great post-war ideal that we can be communal'.[32] Renton, like an icono-clastic Pip, emerges as an inverted Everyman through whose eyes we understand events. His engaging voice-over monologues mock his own lack of ambition, his nationality and his self-dedication to a 'sincere and truthful drug habit'. The consequences of his addiction are not ignored, but neither are they condemned. His lifestyle and consciousness are what he chooses to embrace, and are preferable to the world of glib careerism and slowly rotting suburban respectability, surrounded by gadgets. Although the film shows the male camaraderie of the group – Sick Boy (Jonny Lee Miller), Spud, Tommy (Kevin McKidd) and Renton – it avoids the sentimentality of the conventional 'buddy' film. Tommy dies and Renton's fertile brain knows that in a competitive world the ruthless survive. He makes off with the proceeds of their drug deal, with Sick Boy stranded and the psychotic Begbie (Robert Carlyle) trashing the flat, but leaves some money for the hapless Spud.

According to its producer Andrew MacDonald, *Trainspotting* was aimed at the young multiplex audience, though with the sophistication and stylistic self-consciousness of the Hollywood 'Indie' cinema.[33] *Trainspotting*'s potential appeal was assisted by the skilful marketing campaign of the distributors Polygram which believed in its 'crossover' potential.[34] But the basis of its huge popularity was its celebration of the idiosyncratic energies of an underclass both poaching from and rejecting a decaying, post-welfarist society that offers nothing, and, in the process, trying to forge a new lifestyle that fits this changed situation. *Trainspotting*'s influence has been shown in a number of ways, not least in its highly ambivalent celebration of Celtic identity. This was an important element in the 'Welsh *Trainspotting*', *Twin Town* (1997), set in Swansea. *Human Traffic* (1999), set in Cardiff, was more concerned to pick up on the hedonism. It used a studio-based stylisation to create, 'a fantastical pseudo-documentary', and was greeted as the first film to deal centrally with club culture.[35] Its young men and women, including Jip (John Simm) the narrator, are shackled by dead-end jobs, have no investment in careers or social conformity, but enjoy a hedonistic lifestyle while recognising that it cannot last.

## Damaged Men

The figure of the damaged man is so frequent in recent British cinema that it could be said he has become its most representative image. Christopher Eccleston, with his gaunt features and suffering eyes, has been identified as a 'damaged Everyman' through his role as the Blitz-wrecked Derek Bentley in *Let Him Have It* (1991), and his later performances in *Shallow Grave* (1994), *Jude* (1996) and *Heart* (1998).[36] The underclass male is often irreparably damaged by social disintegration, most memorably shown in Mike Leigh's *Naked* (1993) which deepened this paradigm into an existentialist nightmare.[37] Its angst-ridden protagonist Johnny (David Thewlis), on the run from petty crime in his home city of Manchester, moves through an alienating and mournful twilight London landscape. Johnny is bright, well-read, a compulsive talker and philosophiser, but also violent and aggressively misogynist. Through his coruscating nihilism *Naked* shows a *Lear*-like determination to expose human nakedness, frailties and false hopes, particularly the fragile dreams of the security man who 'guards space'. Johnny is the most extreme example of a world where people cannot settle or find roots and where the wealthy, including a vicious yuppie, prey upon the weak. *Naked* offers no prospect of hope. Johnny rejects his former girlfriend's offer to accompany him in a return to Manchester.

Johnny has become estranged from any form of human contact, but Leigh's other films identify the key site of damage as the family. Not only have the cheery paterfamilias or the stern-but-loving surrogate father disappeared from British cinema, but their place has been taken by the monstrous father. What, in an earlier period, was confined to the Gothic mode, has now entered social realism, producing a contemporary landscape of violent and abusive working-class fathers, wrecking the lives of those around them including the traumatised son. Terence Davies's influential *Distant Voices, Still Lives* (1988) was the paradigm, continued in Ray Winstone's cameo role in Loach's *Ladybird, Ladybird* (1994), but most fully explored in Gary Oldman's *Nil by Mouth* (1997) and Tim Roth's *The War Zone* (1999), where Winstone was the central figure. In *Nil by Mouth*, Winstone's Raymond is the degraded image of the macho hard man, only comfortable in the company of other men, and violently misogynist. His brutal beating of his pregnant wife Valerie (Kathy Burke) is shocking and disgusting. Although Raymond's tearful confession that he was starved of affection by his father indicates the cause of his brutality, he shows no ability to break that vicious cycle. He has no compassion for his wife's younger brother Billy whom he beats up savagely. The film's reconciliatory ending seems contrived. Oldman's film showed the claustrophobic intensity of a South London estate, Roth's chilling film shows that same stifling intensity displaced to an isolated cottage in Devon. Winstone's character pretends to be a loving husband and father, perhaps even believes that he is one, but is revealed as chronically unstable, incapable of refraining from brutally abusing his daughter, thus scarring his son deeply as well, provoking a murderous assault on the monstrous paterfamilias.

These films imply that the father's inadequacies are part of the broken promise of post-war reconstruction. *Boston Kickout* (1996) makes this explicit by darkening the perky late 1960s optimism of *Here We Go Round the Mulberry Bush*. Life in 1990s Stevenage is a much grimmer affair for Phil (John Simm) who moved there with his father after his mother's suicide. His father degenerates into a useless alcoholic who attempts suicide, while Phil becomes an unemployed school-leaver whose friends are equally disaffected and purposeless; one ends up in an asylum. Phil's love affair is not with the sensible girl-next-door but Shona (Emer McCourt), a single parent who despises settling down. *Boston Kickout* ends optimistically: father and son are reconciled before Phil departs for university, but its painful rite of passage indicates the difficulties in finding a direction and purpose in the New Towns that were the post-war dream for urban regeneration and a better life.

In Shane Meadows's films this broken promise is bleaker. *Twenty FourSeven* (1998) is about the desperate need of underclass sons for their fathers, who are absent or violent abusers or callous wheeler-dealers obsessed by status symbols. This abandoned group of youths is trapped in a mean world of limited horizons, petty crime, drug abuse and aimless violence which stretches endlessly in front of them, living the same day every day as the title discloses. Their lives are given some meaning and purpose by the efforts of surrogate paterfamilias Darcy (Bob Hoskins) who uses the old-fashioned solution of a youth club, boxing and outward-bound weekends. But his efforts are sabotaged by the real fathers, the club disintegrates and Darcy declines into alcoholism. His death brings the group back together and seems to provoke some form of muted reconciliation and acceptance between fathers and sons.

*A Kind of Hush* (1999), set around the King's Cross area, was a detailed, sensitive and responsible look at child abuse. Writer-director Brian Stirner, like Meadows, works closely with unknown actors who gradually grow to understand their roles in depth. The film combines the observational strengths of the British social realist tradition with occasional lyrical passages, creating a delicate register appropriate to young men who are 'not kids of style'.[38] They form a fierce protective bond with each other based on their shared abuse, deeply mistrustful of any contact with outsiders. Their explosive violence and deep-rooted anger is mixed with an intense vulnerability in which each one breaks down at the moment they plan to exact revenge on their abusers. The central character Stu (Harley Smith) is the focus for the group's gradual attempt to form new relationships, guided by his surrogate father Chef (Roy Hudd).

But although Stu may have achieved a lasting relationship with a young Irish girl, the others remain insecure and uncertain. Producer Roger Randall-Cutler secured Lottery money and finance from British Screen for a film he believed would, 'appeal to audiences bored by formulaic, predictable, more escapist drama'.[39] However, it was dogged by distribution problems and achieved only a limited release, illustrating one of contemporary British cinema's most severe problems.

## Ethnic Hybridity and Gay Identities

Whereas in the 1940–70 period both blacks and gays were marginalised or stigmatised through a narrow range of demeaning stereotypes, and were often cast as victims, recent British cinema has challenged these prejudices in complex ways.[40] Their existence immediately questions the representativeness of the white, heterosexual Everyman. The so-called 'heritage' films were part of this process, providing an arena in which the social and sexual repression, including an undisclosed homoeroticism, of the gentlemanly ideal could be presented. Merchant-Ivory's *Maurice* (1987) rejected social conformity and sexual restraint in its celebration of gay desire, while *The Deceivers* (1988) critically examined the undisclosed racism of imperial archetypes. Major William Savage (Pierce Brosnan) of the British East India Company experiences, in disguise, the fascinating eroticism and violence of an alien culture. Unlike his predecessor, Harry Faversham, Savage can make no safe return to his own white culture when the job is completed. More recently, even obviously populist films like *Four Weddings and a Funeral* and *The Full Monty* have seen the need to include black and/or gay figures.

Black film-makers have played a key role in this process through their commitment to a plurality of representation and an insistence on the heterogeneity of black British experience. One of the great strengths of Hanif Kureishi's *My Beautiful Laundrette* (1985) was its willingness to problematise existing images. The Anglo-Pakistani Omar (Gordon Warnecke) was a culturally hybrid boy-next-door who embodied the author's own conflicted upbringing.[41] Omar is torn between his loyalty to the intellectual socialism of his alcoholic and bed-ridden father and the embrace of his uncle's Thatcherite entrepreneurialism in which Asians become winners not victims. The film was also a plea for spontaneity and honesty in sexual relationships which cut across boundaries of class and ethnicity, centrally Omar's gay love affair with the white skinhead Johnny (Daniel Day Lewis). Johnny is another hybrid boy-next-door, divided between his residual class loyalties and his desire for Omar. Isaac Julien's *Young Soul Rebels* (1992) was similarly hybrid, revisiting the time of Queen Elizabeth's Silver Jubilee in 1977 in order to prob-lematise the ethnic dimensions of that event and to celebrate not Punk but Soul as a utopian space where new forms of cross-class, gay and inter-racial identities can be forged. Both films used an eclectic visual style to distance themselves from what was perceived as the racist tradition of British social realism.

Both films were bids for black cinema to enter the mainstream; but, like much else in British cinema, this development remains precarious. Kureishi's most recent film, *My Son the Fanatic* (1998), reclaims the paterfamilias as a figure of admiration. Parvez (Om Puri) is bewildered by his son's desire for Muslim fundamentalism which makes him break off his engagement with a sensible white girl and invite a *mulvi* (holy man) over from Pakistan who dominates the household. Also increas-ingly estranged from his wife, Parvez forms a tentative, uncertain but honest relationship with a young white prostitute whom he tries to rescue from his son's vengeance and the abuse of German businessman Schitz. In this odd couple's precarious friendship lie the hopes of a more caring society. By contrast, *East is East* (1999), also set in the north but revisiting the 1970s, reverses audience sympathies. The at-tempts of paterfamilias George Khan (Om Puri), who has married a white woman, to impose Muslim orthodoxy on his recalcitrant family, finally force an open rebellion. The film's style is again hybrid, one which, like *Bhaji on the Beach* (1993), mixes social realism with sitcom as it weaves its way through an eclectic mix of identities.

Films about white gay identity have also shown an increasing diversity, 'acknowledging sexual plurality, fluidity and individuality'.[42] There have been biopics of radically different gay artists: Francis Bacon (*Love is the Devil*, 1998) and James Whale (*Gods and Monsters*, 1999); a wistful but moving tale of an elderly writer discovering his homosexuality (*Love and Death on Long Island*, 1998); a social realist film about a young gay Catholic clergyman (*Priest*, 1994); a rather precious romance between two young men on a South London estate (*Beautiful Thing*, 1996), and an appealingly downplayed one in *Madagascar Skin* (1995). The recent *Bedrooms and Hallways* (1999) is a romantic comedy dedicated to an eclectic sexual mix and mutable selves. Although its entertaining send-up of men's groups may be rather clichéd, the engaging central character Leo (Kevin

McKidd) is not a gay stereotype, but the boy-next-door who, in the modern world, is uncertain about his sexual orientation. By contrast, the camp queer Darren (Tom Hollander) is most directly in touch with his sexuality and the film has the confidence to play knowingly with this familiar stereotype, giving him the best lines. He dismisses Leo's discovery of his heterosexual impulses as a 'passing phase'. *Bedrooms and Hallways* is a smart, witty film that derives its fun precisely from an audience's ability to accept a range of different male identities without straining to be socially profound and without trying to foreclose alternatives and recommend one option as the preferred way.

*Bedrooms and Hallways* uses comedy and a mixture of realism and fantasy to depict a hybrid postmodern world of shifting identities. It suggests there is no real 'crisis' in contemporary masculinity as long as men are true to their impulses and are prepared to try a range of different selves. This living for the moment hedonism is an important component of British cinema, one that depoliticises the struggle over competing forms of masculinity. Indeed, I would suggest that this is one of the defining feature of the contemporary period. Within a commodified postmodern culture of relativity the male types no longer compete, they occupy separate spheres and audiences can pick and choose what takes their fancy. On one level this plurality is both admirable and a clear advance on the repression and marginalisation of the post-war period. On another it perhaps hides a profound crisis of male power, confidence and even identity caused by shifts in traditional male roles and the fear of women as more successful social and economic rivals. One response has been to retreat into an earlier period of security: the 'lad' with his knowingly retro masculinist confidence. Renton is, of course, partly a 'lad'. Another response, made by the *The Full Monty*, was to appropriate a form of female display as a form of male confidence-building in the face of fears that their sex, its sperm count dropping, might become 'obsolete'. Those fears, and the pervasive sense of damage to the lives of British films' young men, provide a reminder that men are living through often bewildering times.

# Conclusion

T*ypical Men*'s analysis of masculinity through types has revealed a series of complex and discontinuous rises and falls. After the detailed minutiae of the individual chapters, I offer here a overview of those changes and a brief consideration of their implications for the understanding of masculinity and British cinema history.

After the war there was a powerful move towards a consensual model of masculinity where British cinema and official discourses were closely aligned. The middle-class officer heroes of the war films, the civilian professionals and the 'well-spoken young' of the domestic comedies were very similar constructions of masculinity. Each displayed a more democratised version of gentlemanliness which absorbed its previously rival form, the ordinary Everyman, the hero of the People's War. The new consensus was a return to traditional values. These male types embodied duty, determination, restraint and responsibility. However, these post-war hegemonic figures were fundamentally less stable than their predecessor, the debonair gentleman, whose apparently effortless male confidence came from the profound certainty that the English were a chosen race which had created an empire. Therefore the post-war heroes had to work harder to maintain hegemony. Refighting the Second World War did not fully compensate for this loss of empire and gradually the officer hero was exposed as an anachronism or a neurotic. The figure of the decent boy-next-door lasted longer, having assimilated the new styles and energies of the emerging pop idols, but this too broke down in the face of renewed social change.

*Typical Men* has argued that hegemonic types always provoke challenge by alternative and oppositional forms of masculinity, male types that embody the repressed desires and transgressive pleasures that official culture has denied. Indeed, the centrality of the gentleman in this period is partly illustrated by the range and variety of inverted or parodic versions: dandies, rakes, cads, bounders, noodle officers, silly-asses, the working-class 'swell', the Byronic male, and the gangster as underworld Man About Town. These figures were drawn from two modes: comedy and the Gothic. Comedy, through its Fools and Rogues, consistently undermined middle-class respectability. Although Wisdom's Gump could be absorbed into a consensual paradigm, the popularity of the Rogue indicated the attractiveness of artful dodgers as an alternative to the puritanical paternalism of the professionals and the steady decency of the ordinary bloke. At times of relative cultural stability these figures could be tolerated if not accommodated. However, at times when the grip of the hegemonic form weakened, as at the end of the 1950s, the satiric Fools and Rogues of the Boultings' films or the renegade officers of *The League of Gentlemen* helped promote change by further undermining confidence in the framework of Victorian values that had underpinned post-war reconstruction. By contrast, the 'Carry Ons' were less socially subversive. But as the series developed, it created a space for ever more outrageously parodic versions of male sexuality.

The subversive function of the comic figures, however, was less marked than those drawn from British culture's Gothic 'heritage'. The eruptions of Gothic excess were unpredictable and explosive, but were associated with moments of change, when a space opened up for them to occupy. Thus Mason's Byronic aristocrats emerged in the middle of the war, when the debonair gentleman was challenged by the common man. At the end of the war, a time of intense instability, Gothic types became more complex and invasive. Byronic gangsters like Narcy in *They Made Me a Fugitive* joined forces with renegade middle-class veterans who themselves became psychotic and violent Gothic monsters, as in *Silent Dust*. The more sympathetic form was Eric Portman's tragically flawed victim-hero, the damaged man who had survived the war physically, but not emotionally. Between 1946 and 1950, this figure was the most representative image of masculinity. In the late 1950s Peter Cushing's Byronic Baron Frankenstein incarnated the threat of uncontrolled science, and Christopher Lee's Count Dracula, offered, like Mason, a forbidden eroticism. These Gothic figures had performed their most powerful ideological work by the early 1960s, but the generic space created by horror allowed the further development of extraordinarily varied representations of male psychosis throughout that decade.

The other engine of challenge and change came through the mode of social realism, which provided versions of unruly working-class masculinity that gained ground as the hegemonic form weakened. Stanley Baker was a kind of cultural battering ram as the modern tough guy. Baker's working-class truculence was mirrored in the figure of the Angry Young Man which, both for a dissident intelligentsia and for cinema-goers, was an attractively iconoclastic image of *rebellious* working-class ordinariness. Albert Finney's Arthur Seaton provided another key ingredient, an unashamed youthful hedonism; Tom Courtenay's Borstal boy was a third figure, no longer the delinquent but the rebel. It was these figures that were developed in the 1960s, in Michael Caine's Harry Palmer, or his Alfie, which replaced the wartime stereotype of the cheery Cockney by the cool, modern anti-hero. Except Bond, the most interesting, charismatic and glamorous male figures were now oppositional, at odds with the state and preoccupied with personal gratifications. In this increasingly volatile situation, a more complex and fragmented youth culture threw up images of alienated young men, refusing to accept the standards of their elders and experimenting with alternative lifestyles.

The complicating factor was James Bond. Sean Connery's screen incarnation synthesised the tough guy's violence and competitive individualism, the impeccable stylishness of the clubland gentleman and a Byronic eroticism, to produce *the* modern English folk hero. Bond combined the traditional hero's secure masculine purpose with a re-configured hedonism, making the gentleman a contemporary, sexy and guiltless sensualist. He enjoyed all the pleasures the puritanical heroes of the 1950s had denied or repressed. Bond was packaged in ways that were exciting, spectacular and playful, allowing audiences to enjoy a commodified and knowing fantasy.

It is this potent mixture that ensures Bond's continued popularity, the one form of masculinity that has survived in the midst of the fundamental changes that have taken place since the end of the 1960s. But beyond Bond, as I have discussed, contemporary types of masculinity differ radically from their predecessors. In particular, the ordinary Everyman is now an impossible construction, present in only a vestigial way in Hugh Grant's Mr Nice. The legacy of Thatcherism has created a degraded underclass and a pervasive sense of social and psychological damage. Not only is the hegemony of the idealised gentleman over, but also the other post-war ideal of the (white, heterosexual) common man. This is, I submit, a profound change, one whose repercussions are only just becoming visible. 'Crisis in masculinity' is a tired cliché, but the phrase does seem appropriate to the contemporary moment with its pervasive sense of male insecurity and uncertain identity. However, as *Typical Men* has insisted throughout, moments of cultural change are highly complex, the product of different dynamics and different audience allegiances. Contemporary British cinema is quite capable of producing positive figures. Mark Renton in *Trainspotting* is perhaps the most representative contemporary male: young, alienated, but also a chameleon, neither hero or villain, conformist or rebel. He is the product of a culture that is decentred and heterogeneous, no longer recognising clear national, ethical or sexual boundaries, where forms of masculinity are becoming increasingly hybrid and audiences delight in the knowingness and self-referentiality of popular culture.

Naturally, any analysis of the current situation must be provisional. Future historians of masculinity, from the other side of the millennium, will need to examine these developments in a fuller historical perspective, giving a detailed account of what I can only sketch in a preliminary way as the spur to future work. What I hope this study has shown is not only the range and variety of masculinity, but the interest and importance of the consensual figures of the 1950s, a period conventionally considered in the historiography of British cinema as the doldrums era with its cast of dull and boring 'tweed men'. We are now, I think, able to give these figures their weight and even their dignity as the products of a particular historical moment, the aftermath of the war, where they embodied stability and the need for reassurance. As that moment changed, and audience tastes shifted, they lost authority and identity, becoming troubled and even damaged men, exemplified by John Mills's suicidal colonel in *Tunes of Glory*.

Historians are never neutral and while I have endeavoured to be balanced, doubtless many who read *Typical Men* will dispute many points or draw very different conclusions. But however one interprets these male cultural types, the project of understanding masculinity historically, the long process of making masculinity visible and therefore available for analysis and reflection, has really only just begun.

# Notes

Only the author, main title and date of books listed in the select bibliography are given in the chapter notes; all other titles are given in full. Where film reviews or newspaper articles are cited without a page reference, the source is the British Film Institute's microfiche collection, which does not usually include page numbers. References to Press Books are those held in the BFI library. The date of the film (in brackets) is the release date as given in Denis Gifford's *The British Film Catalogue 1895–1985: A Guide to Entertainment Films* (Newton Abbot: David and Charles, 1986). Dates for films after 1985 are those given in *Sight and Sound*.

## Introduction

1. Richard Dyer, 'The Role of Stereotypes', in his *The Matter of Images* (1993), pp. 11–18.

2. See Raphael Samuel, 'Figures of National Myth', in R. Samuel (ed.), *Patriotism: The Making and Unmaking of British National Identity. Vol. III, National Fictions* (London: Routledge, 1989), pp xi–xxxvi; Graham Dawson, *Soldier Heroes* (1993), pp. 11–18.

3. R. W. Connell, *Masculinities* (1995), pp. 76–80.

4. For a general discussion of hegemony, see Raymond Williams, 'Base and Superstructure in Marxist Cultural Theory', in his *Problems in Materialism and Culture* (London: Verso, 1980), pp. 31–49.

5. See Judith Butler, *Gender Trouble* (1990).

6. See Richard Dyer, *Stars* (1979), pp. 53–67.

7. See Geoffrey Macnab, *Searching for Stars* (2000). Macnab's study includes a discussion of 'stock types', but his understanding of the ways in which these operate differs significantly from my own.

8. *Picturegoer*'s readership may have been as high as 1,430,000, the figure given in the *Hulton Readership Survey No. 1* (London: Hulton Press, 1947), Table 13, p. 26. It is a valuable source for popular taste as its readers came predominantly from the 'DE' group, mainly women. As an index of cinema's decline, the magazine metamorphosed into *Date* in April 1960.

9. For discussion see Janet Thumim, 'The "Popular", Cash and Culture in the Postwar British Cinema Industry', *Screen*, 32/3 (Autumn 1991), pp. 245–71; Andrew Spicer, 'Male Stars, Masculinity and British Cinema, 1945–1960', in Robert Murphy (ed.), *The British Cinema Book* (1997), pp. 144–53; Robert Murphy, 'Popular British Cinema', *Journal of Popular British Cinema*, 1 (1998), pp. 6–12.

10.  Peter Burke, *Popular Culture in Early Modern Europe* (rev. edn, 1994).

11.  For discussion of the representation of gay men in British cinema see Richard Dyer, '*Victim*: Hegemonic Project', *Film Form*, 2 (1977), reprinted in his *The Matter of Images*, pp. 93–110; Andy Medhurst, '*Victim*: Text as Context', *Screen*, 25/4–5 (Winter 1984), reprinted with a new preface in Andrew Higson (ed.), *Dissolving Views* (1996), pp. 117–32; and Stephen Bourne, *Brief Encounters* (1996); for an informative overview see Alan Sinfield, *The Wilde Century* (1994). For the representation of black masculinity see Kobena Mercer, *Welcome to the Jungle* (1994); Karen Ross, *Black and White Media: Black Images in Film and Television* (Cambridge: Polity Press, 1996); Lola Young, *Fear of the Dark: 'Race', Gender and Sexuality in Cinema* (London: Routledge, 1996).

12.  Eve Kosofsky Sedgwick, *Between Men* (1985).

13.  Sue Harper, *Women in British Cinema* (2000). I am extremely grateful to Dr Harper for allowing me to read this important work in manuscript.

# 1. The War Years

1.  Jeffrey Richards, *The Age of the Dream Palace* (London: Routledge and Kegan Paul, 1984), pp. 191–206, 225–41; Kenton Bamford, *Distorted Images: British National Identity and Film in the 1920s* (London: I.B.Tauris, 1999), pp. 51–69.

2.  See Angus Calder, *The People's War: Britain 1939–1945* (London: Jonathan Cape, 1969), pp. 337–8; Paul Addison, *The Road to 1945: Britain and the Second World War* (London: Jonathan Cape, 1975), pp. 162–229.

3.  Robert Murphy, 'The British Film Industry: Audiences and Producers', in Philip M. Taylor (ed.), *Britain and the Cinema in the Second World War* (London: Macmillan, 1988), pp. 31–41.

4.  Attendances rose from 990 million in 1939 to 1,635 million in 1946; *Kinematograph and Television Year Book* (1955), p. 381.

5.  In the 1947 Bernstein Questionnaire to Granada cinema-goers, 96 per cent of respondents thought that British films had 'got better' during the war; copy in BFI library, p. 8.

6.  Martin Wiener, *English Culture and the Decline of the Industrial Spirit* (Harmondsworth: Penguin, 1992), p. 11.

7.  See Mark Girouard, *The Return to Camelot* (1981); Philip Mason, *The English Gentleman* (1982).

8.  Christine Heward, *Making a Man of Him: Parents and their Sons' Education at an English Public School 1929–50* (London: Routledge, 1988); Jonathan Rutherford, *Forever England* (1997), pp. 11–38.

9.  Jeffrey Richards, *Happiest Days: The Public Schools in English Fiction* (Manchester: Manchester University Press, 1988), p. 13.

10.  Harold Laski, 'The Danger of Being a Gentleman: Reflections on the Ruling Class in England', in his *The Danger of Being a Gentleman and Other Essays* (London: Allen and Unwin, 1939), pp. 13–31, at p. 20.

11.  Jeffrey Richards, 'The Cinema of Empire', in his *Visions of Yesterday* (1973), pp. 2–221; John Bristow, *Empire Boys* (1991).

12.  See Richards, *The Age of the Dream Palace*, pp. 225–41.

13.  Peter Burnup, *Motion Picture Herald*, 2 January 1943, p. 13.

14.  See respondents' comments in Jeffrey Richards and Dorothy Sheridan (eds), *Mass-Observation at the Movies* (1987), pp. 225, 233, 241, 258, 264, 267, 271.

15.  *The Times*, 20 May 1943.

16.  See Geoffrey Macnab, *J. Arthur Rank and the British Film Industry* (1993), pp. 90–110.

17. See David Mellor (ed.), *A Paradise Lost* (1987).

18. See Arthur Koestler, 'The Birth of a Legend', *Horizon* (April 1943); Eric Linklater, *The Art of Adventure* (London: Macmillan, 1947), pp. 73–98; Sebastian Faulks, *The Fatal Englishman: Three Short Lives* (London: Hutchinson, 1996), pp. 111–208.

19. Sue Harper, *Picturing the Past* (1994), pp. 86–94.

20. Del Giudice believed in films achieving 'the dignity of theatre', finding their audience through extended 'repertory' runs; see John Baxter, *The Leader*, 9 November 1946 and 21 June 1947.

21. For this construction see Alan Sinfield, 'History and Ideology, Masculinity and Miscegenation: The Instance of *Henry V*', in his *Faultlines: Cultural Materialism and the Politics of Dissident Reading* (Oxford: Clarendon Press, 1992), pp. 109–42.

22. See Felix Barker, *The Oliviers* (London: Hamish Hamilton, 1953), esp. pp. 240–1.

23. See Peter Burnup, '*Henry V* Goes to Market in Britain', *Motion Picture Herald*, 14 July 1945, p. 30.

24. See C. A. Lejeune's review, *Observer*, 4 April 1943.

25. See Granger's autobiography, *Sparks Fly Upward* (London: Granada, 1982), pp. 62–3.

26. The film's Press Book announced that Granger's Nino was, 'back to the red-blooded love of Valentino'.

27. J. P. Mayer, *British Cinemas and their Audiences* (London: Dennis Dobson, 1948), p. 187.

28. Marjorie Deans, *Meeting at the Sphinx: Gabriel Pascal's Production of 'Caesar and Cleopatra'* (London: Macdonald, n.d. [?1946]), p. 76.

29. For a recent discussion see James Chapman, *The British at War* (1998), esp. pp. 58–85.

30. *Picture Post*, 2 January 1943.

31. *Manchester Guardian*, 28 December 1943.

32. See John Ellis, 'Made in Ealing', *Screen*, 16/1 (Spring 1975), pp. 79–127.

33. Charles Barr, *Ealing Studios* (1993), pp. 23–38; see also Jeffrey Richards, 'Wartime British Cinema Audiences and the Class System: The Case of *Ships with Wings* (1941)', *Historical Journal of Film, Radio and Television*, 7/2 (1987), pp. 129–41.

34. Michael Balcon, *Realism and Tinsel* (London: Workers Film Association, 1944), p. 11.

35. In his article 'A Tribute to Britain', Priestley wrote, 'After the victory we still want – and it is what we have always wanted – a steady and firmly rooted life, with plenty of fun and cosiness and a kind of domestic poetry inside it.' *Picture Post*, 28 April 1945, p. 16.

36. See Geoff Brown (with Anthony Aldgate), *The Common Touch: The Films of John Baxter* (London: BFI, 1989), pp. 7–13, 81.

37. Ibid., p. 96.

38. Press Book.

39. Vincent Porter and Chaim Litewski, '*The Way Ahead*: Case History of a Propaganda Film', *Sight and Sound* (Spring 1981), p. 112.

40. Eric Ambler, *Here Lies: An Autobiography* (London: Weidenfeld and Nicolson, 1985), p. 187.

41. See Julian Poole, 'British Cinema Attendance in Wartime: Audience Preference at the Majestic, Macclesfield, 1939–46', *Historical Journal of Film, Radio and Television*, 7/1 (1987), pp. 15–34, at p. 25.

42. Jeffrey Richards, 'Basil Dearden at Ealing', in Alan Burton, Tim O'Sullivan and Paul Wells (eds), *Liberal Directions* (1997), pp. 24–5.

43. Steven Fielding, Peter Thompson and Nick Tiratsoo, '*England Arise!*': The Labour Party and Popular Politics in 1940s Britain* (Manchester: Manchester University Press, 1995), pp. 1–45.

44. See Roger Bromley, *Lost Narratives: Popular Fictions, Politics and Recent History* (London: Routledge, 1988), pp. 109–56. See also Fred Miller Robinson, *The Man in the Bowler Hat* (1993).

45. Raphael Samuel, 'The Middle Class Between the Wars', pt 3, *New Socialist* (May/June 1983), p. 29.

46. Geoffrey Gorer, *Exploring English Character* (London: Cresset Press, 1955), p. 291.

47. C. A. Lejeune, 'A Word in Friendship', in P. Noble (ed.), *British Film Yearbook 1947–48* (London: Skelton Robinson, 1948), p. 31.

48. See *Picture Post*, 26 April 1941, pp. 30–1; *Picturegoer*, 29 September 1946, p. 6.

49. Gareth Stedman Jones, 'The "Cockney" and the Nation, 1780–1988', in David Feldman and Gareth Stedman Jones (eds), *Metropolis London: Histories and Representations since 1800* (London: Routledge, 1989), pp. 312–15.

50. Enid Welsford, *The Fool* (1935), pp. 315, 320.

51. George Orwell, 'The Art of Donald McGill', in *Collected Essays* (London: Secker and Warburg, 1961), pp. 167–78, at pp. 176, 178.

52. Robert M. Torrance, *The Comic Hero* (1978), p. 7.

53. See Anthony Aldgate's discussion, 'Raise a Laugh: Let George Do It', in Anthony Aldgate and Jeffrey Richards, *Britain Can Take It* (1986), pp. 76–95.

54. According to the *Motion Picture Herald*'s star polls, Formby was Britain's most popular star from 1938 to 1943 inclusive. In 1944 he came third, and he dropped to ninth in 1946. Askey had been third in 1941, fifth in 1942, ninth in 1943 and out of the top ten in 1944 and 1945. Trinder had been twelfth in 1942 but was not mentioned after that point.

55. Aldgate, 'Raise a Laugh', p. 88.

56. David Bret, *George Formby: A Troubled Genius* (London: Robson Books, 1999), pp. 111–12.

57. Richards, *The Age of the Dream Palace*, p. 206.

58. See Robert Hirst, *Three Men and a Gimmick* (Kingswood, Surrey: World's Work, 1957), pp. 87–101.

59. M. E. J., 'A "Silly Little Man" Grows Up', *Picturegoer*, 5 September 1942, p. 6.

60. See Sue Harper, '"Nothing to Beat the Hay Diet": Comedy at Gaumont and Gainsborough', in Pam Cook (ed.), *Gainsborough Pictures* (1997), pp. 80–98.

61. John Fisher, *Funny Way to be a Hero* (1973), pp. 178–84.

62. Peter Bailey, 'Champagne Charlie: Performance and Ideology in the Music Hall Swell Song', in J. S. Bratton (ed.), *Music Hall: Performance and Style* (Milton Keynes: Open University Press, 1986), pp. 49–69.

63. Harper, *Picturing*, p. 110.

64. See Michael Booth, *English Melodrama* (1965).

65. Mario Praz, *The Romantic Agony* (1970), pp. 55–93.

66. P. L. Thorslev Jnr, *The Byronic Hero* (1962).

67. *Kinematograph Weekly*, 8 January 1942, p. 85.

68. R. J. Minney, *Talking of Film* (London: Home and Van Thal, 1947), pp. 4, 16, 35, 43.

69. *Daily Telegraph*, 22 July 1943.

70. Sue Harper, 'Historical Pleasures: Gainsborough Costume Melodrama', in Christine Gledhill (ed.), *Home is Where the Heart is* (London: BFI, 1987), pp. 166–70.

71. Harper, *Picturing*, p. 190.

72. J. P. Mayer, *Sociology of Film* (London: Faber and Faber, 1946), p. 213.

73. *Picturegoer*, 4 September 1943, p. 9. See my 'Male Stars, Masculinity and British Cinema, 1945–1960', in Robert Murphy (ed.), *The British Cinema Book* (1997), p. 145.

74. See Robert Murphy, 'A Brief Studio History', in Sue Aspinall and Robert Murphy (eds), *Gainsborough Melodrama* (London: BFI, 1983), p. 5.

75. In the readers' poll for 1945, Mason gained 16.3 per cent of the votes for his

role in *The Seventh Veil*, just behind Olivier's 19.1 per cent for *Henry V*; *Picturegoer*, 16 July 1946, p. 9. In the 1946 poll he was in eleventh place with 3.2 per cent of the votes for *The Wicked Lady*; ibid., 19 July 1947, p. 7.

76. Kevin Macdonald, *Emeric Pressburger: The Life and Death of a Screenwriter* (London: Faber and Faber, 1994), p. 236.

77. See Martin Petter, '"Temporary Gentlemen" in the Aftermath of the Great War: Rank, Status and the Ex-Officer Problem', *Historical Journal*, 37 (1994), pp. 127–52.

78. See the recollections of John Basnett, quoted in Paul Addison, *Now the War is Over: A Social History of Britain 1945–51*, rev. edn (London: Pimlico, 1995), p. 47.

79. See John Baxendale, '"You and I – All of Us Ordinary People": Renegotiating "Britishness" in Wartime', in Nick Hayes and Jeff Hill (eds), *'Millions Like Us'? British Culture in the Second World War* (Liverpool: Liverpool University Press, 1999), pp. 295–322.

## 2. The Twilight of the English Gentleman

1. See Searle Kochberg, 'The London Films of Herbert Wilcox', unpublished MA dissertation (Polytechnic of Central London, 1990).

2. Ewart Hodgson, *Evening Standard*, 23 August 1946.

3. See Colin McDowell, *The Man of Fashion* (1997).

4. *Sunday Times*, 25 August 1946.

5. *Kinematograph Weekly*, 18 December 1947, p. 19.

6. Raymond Leader, 'The Light Touch of the Englishman', *ABC Film Review* (October 1954), pp. 10–11.

7. See my 'Prince Charming in a Top Hat: The Debonair Man About Town in British Romantic Musical Comedy', in Ian Conrich and Estella Tincknell (eds), *Film's Moments of Musical Performance* (Trowbridge: Flicks Books, forthcoming).

8. *Picturegoer*, 13 April 1946, p. 14.

9. Karol Kulik, *Alexander Korda: The Man Who Could Work Miracles* (London: W. H. Allen, 1975), p. 135.

10. *Film Weekly*, 4 May 1934.

11. Sue Harper, *Picturing the Past* (1994), pp. 25–6.

12. Robin Nash, *Daily Star*, 11 November 1955.

13. *Picturegoer*, 3 July 1957, p. 6; original emphasis.

14. Ibid., 31 May 1958, p. 5. Bogarde may also have had a gay fan base; see Richard Dyer, 'Coming Out as Going In: The Image of the Homosexual as a Sad Young Man', in his *The Matter of Images* (1993), pp. 73–92.

15. Press Book for *The Wind Cannot Read*, author's collection.

16. Derek Monsey, *Sunday Express*, 18 June 1958.

17. *Picturegoer*, 23 May 1959, p. 5.

18. C. A. Lejeune, *Observer*, 10 February 1958.

19. See Sue Harper and Vincent Porter, 'Cinema Audience Taste in 1950s Britain', *Journal of Popular British Cinema*, 2 (1999), pp. 66–82.

20. Beau Riffenburgh, *The Myth of the Explorer* (Oxford: Oxford University Press, 1994), pp. 2–7, 34–5.

21. See Michael Balcon, *Michael Balcon Presents ... A Lifetime of Films* (London: Hutchinson, 1969), pp. 171–5.

22. David James, *'Scott of the Antarctic': The Film and its Production* (London: Convoy Publications, 1948), pp. 36–8, 136–7.

23. Charles Frend, *'Scott of the Antarctic*: The Making of the Film', *Photographic Journal* (1949), p. 193.

24. Kenneth More recorded that he had wept at this point but this had been cut

from the final film: *More or Less* (London: Hodder and Stoughton, 1978), p. 132. Such an overt display of emotion may have been thought insufficiently 'manly' at Ealing; see Hawkins's recollections about filming *The Cruel Sea*, discussed below.

25. Roger Manvell (ed.), *Three British Screenplays* (London: Methuen, 1950), p. 292.

26. *Sunday Dispatch*, 5 December 1948.

27. *Kinematograph Weekly*, 15 December 1949, p. 13.

28. James Robertson Justice as Petty Officer Evans in *Scott* was the paradigm.

29. See Neil Rattigan, 'The Last Gasp of the Middle Class: British War Films of the 1950s', in W. W. Dixon (ed.), *Re-viewing British Cinema, 1900–1992* (New York: State University of New York Press, 1994), pp. 143–53.

30. Raymond Durgnat, *A Mirror for England* (1970), pp. 142–3.

31. See Jack Hawkins's recollections, *Anything for a Quiet Life* (London: Elm Tree Books, 1973), pp. 106–7.

32. Andy Medhurst, '1950s War Films', in Geoff Hurd (ed.), *National Fictions* (London: BFI, 1985), p. 37.

33. This male comradeship continues the 'Graeco-Medieval' chivalric code of knightly love; see Jeffrey Richards, '"Passing the Love of Woman": Manly Love and Victorian Society', in J. A. Mangan and J. Walvin (eds), *Manliness and Morality* (1987), pp. 92–122.

34. Ray Stephens, *ABC Film Review* (February 1957), pp. 12–13.

35. Robert Otway, *Sunday Graphic*, 10 January 1953.

36. Angus Calder, *The Myth of the Blitz* (1991), pp. 1–19f.

37. William Whitebait, 'The Great Squeeze – or When Will British Films Grow Up?', in William Whitebait (ed.), *International Film Annual no. 2* (London: John Calder, 1958), p. 23.

38. See Marketing Trends Limited, *Cinema Going in Greater London 1963: A Study of Attitudes and Behaviour* (London: Federation of British Film Makers, 1963), pp. 62–3.

39. Cited in Herbert Gans, *American Films and TV Programs on British Screens* (1959), pp. 38–9.

40. C. A. Lejeune, *Observer*, 11 October 1959.

41. Thomas Spencer, *Daily Worker*, 17 May 1953.

42. For the growth of the executive class in the 1950s, see Ralph [*sic*] Samuel, '"Bastard" Capitalism', in E. P. Thompson (ed.), *Out of Apathy* (London: New Left Books/Stevens and Sons, 1960), pp. 19–55.

43. Gans, *American Films and TV Programs*, Table 7, p. 38 and note 1, p. 149. The film appealed much more strongly to the AB and C1 groups.

44. Derek Granger, *Financial Times*, 19 March 1954.

45. *Films and Filming* (April 1955), p. 3.

46. *Sunday Times*, 22 June 1956.

47. 'Josh' Billings, *Kinematograph Weekly*, 12 December 1957.

48. Kenneth More, *Happy Go Lucky: My Life* (London: Robert Hale, 1959), pp. 163–4.

49. *Daily Star*, 12 March 1959.

50. *Tribune*, 16 October 1959.

51. Ivor Adams, 'More the Magnificent', *Daily Star*, 8 October 1959.

52. *Manchester Guardian*, 10 October 1959.

53. Campbell Dixon, '"Old Boy" More Puts His Feet Up', *Daily Herald*, 13 March 1959.

54. *Spectator*, 14 November 1958.

55. L. A. Siedentop, 'Mr Macmillan and the Edwardian Style', in V. Bogdanor and R. Skidelsky (eds), *The Age of Affluence* (London: Macmillan, 1970), pp. 17–54.

56. More, quoted in the *Sunday Graphic*, 3 November 1957.

57. More parodied 'Kenneth Moreness' in *Man in the Moon* (1960), to little effect.

58. Dilys Powell, *Sunday Times*, 20 January 1952.

59. *Tribune*, 9 September 1957.

60. *Sunday Times*, 1 June 1958.

61. Foreman left when Lean insisted the adaptation be made less unpatriotic; Kevin Brownlow, *David Lean* (London: Richard Cohen Books, 1996), pp. 345–57.

62. Quotations from the Press Book for·*Sea of Sand*.

63. John Mills, *Up in the Clouds, Gentlemen Please* (London: Penguin, 1980), p. 341.

64. Lawrence James, *The Golden Warrior: The Life and Legend of Lawrence of Arabia* (London: Weidenfeld and Nicolson, 1990).

65. See Adrian Turner, *The Making of David Lean's 'Lawrence of Arabia'* (London: Dragon's World, 1994), pp. 23–40. Rank made a substitute version, *The Black Tent*, in 1955, starring Anthony Steel.

66. See Brownlow, *David Lean*, pp. 402–91; Steven C. Caton, *Lawrence of Arabia: A Film's Anthropology* (Berkeley, Los Angeles and London: University of California Press, 1999).

67. Epigraph to Turner, *The Making*, p. 1.

68. Graham Dawson, *Soldier Heroes* (1994), pp. 167–230.

69. *Evening Standard*, 13 December 1962.

70. Dawson, *Soldier Heroes*, pp. 226–7.

## 3. Heroes of Modernity: Civilian Professionals

1. Roger Lewis and Angus Maude, *The English Middle Classes* (London: Phoenix House, 1949), p. 122. Ronald W. Clark, *The Rise of the Boffins* (London: Phoenix House, 1962).

2. Jeffrey Weeks, *Sex, Politics and Society* (1989), p. 233.

3. Harold Perkin, *The Rise of Professional Society: England Since 1800* (London: Routledge, 1989), pp. 3–4, 117, 405–54; Michael Roper, *Masculinity and the British Organization Man since 1945* (1994).

4. For an overview, see Rosamund Haynes, *From Faustus to Strangelove* (1994).

5. Ibid., p. 110.

6. Gareth Stedman Jones, *Languages of Class: Studies in English Working Class History 1832–1982* (Cambridge: Cambridge University Press, 1983), p. 246.

7. See Pat Jackson, *A Retake Please!* (Liverpool: Royal Naval Museum Publications/ Liverpool University Press, 1999), pp. 300–8.

8. Fred Majdalayny, *Daily Mail*, 15 June 1951; original emphasis.

9. Michael Frayn, 'Festival', in Michael Sissons and Philip French (eds), *Age of Austerity* (Oxford: Oxford University Press, 1986), pp. 305–26. See also Ross McKibbin, *Classes and Cultures* (1998), pp. 44–9, 528–33.

10. Herbert Gans, *American Films and TV Programs on British Screens* (1959), p. 33.

11. See Martha Wolfenstein and Nathan Leites, *Movies: A Psychological Study* (Glencoe, IL: Free Press, 1950), esp. pp. 179, 201.

12. Geoffrey Gorer, *Exploring English Character* (London: Cresset Press, 1955), p. 296.

13. Compare Hawkins as a news editor in *Front Page Story* (1954) and as a freighter pilot in *The Man in the Sky* (1957).

14. 'Josh' Billings, *Kinematograph Weekly*, 28 February 1957, p. 11.

15. See Dearden and Relph's letter to the *Sunday Times*, 13 October 1957.

16. Waxman's comments, quoted in *Kinematograph Weekly*, 25 December 1958, p. 15.

17. John Hill, *Sex, Class and Realism* (1986), pp. 80–1.

18. In *Sapphire* (1959), Dearden and Relph reverted to the earlier paternalist paradigm.

19. See Losey's comments in Michel Ciment, *Conversations with Losey* (London: Methuen, 1985), pp. 174–8.

20. Guest, interviewed in Brian McFarlane (ed.), *An Autobiography of British Cinema* (1997), p. 259.

21. Robert Murphy, *Sixties British Cinema* (1992), pp. 201–35.

22. For a fuller analysis see ibid., pp. 232–4.

23. Noel Annan, *Our Age* (1991), p. 509; see also pp. 379–82.

24. Peter Ustinov, *Dear Me* (London: Mandarin, 1992), pp. 199–201.

25. Robert A. Jones, 'The Boffin: A Stereotype of Scientists in Post-war British Films (1945–1970)', *Public Understanding of Science*, 6 (1997), pp. 31–48. Oddly, Jones does not mention *School for Secrets*.

26. The Mass-Observation report *Where is Science Taking Us?* described widespread public anxiety about atomic bombs, a feeling that science was now out of control whereas it had formerly been a blessing; M-O Report 2489, May 1947, held in the Mass-Observation Archive, University of Sussex. British National's early science fiction film *Counterblast* (1948) was advertised as 'Man of Science or Menace to Society?'; *Kinematograph Weekly*, 13 May 1948, pp. 8–9. For an overview see Andrew Tudor, *Monsters and Mad Scientists* (1989).

27. See Harry Hopkins, *The New Look: A Social History of the Forties and Fifties in Britain* (London: Secker and Warburg, 1963), pp. 277, 385.

28. Lean, quoted in London Films publicity material, included in the microfiche for *The Sound Barrier*.

29. Rattigan recounted his meeting with test pilots at Farnborough, 'quiet young men, absolutely unlike the types I had known during the war'. Interview with Charles Hamblett, *John Bull*, 6 December 1952; quoted in Michael Darlow and Gillian Hodson, *Terence Rattigan: The Man and His Work* (London: Quartet, 1979), p. 195.

30. Asquith's film was made in haste, the director piqued at Rattigan's 'desertion' to Lean; R. J. Minney, *Puffin Asquith* (London: Leslie Frewin, 1973), pp. 150–1.

31. Fred Majdalayny, *Daily Mail*, 30 January 1953.

32. *Manchester Guardian*, 26 July 1952.

33. It was eighth in the *Motion Picture Herald*'s rankings, 3 January 1953, p. 22.

34. Hopkins, *The New Look*, pp. 390–1.

35. John Baxter, *Science Fiction and the Cinema* (London: Barnes/Zwemmer, 1970), p. 95.

36. See I. Q. Hunter, 'Introduction: The Strange World of the British Science Fiction Film', in Hunter (ed.), *British Science Fiction Cinema* (London: Routledge, 1999), pp. 6–7.

37. Joy Leman, 'Wise Scientists and Female Androids: Class and Gender in Science Fiction', in John Corner (ed.), *Popular Television in Britain: Studies in Cultural History* (London: BFI, 1991), p. 110.

38. Paul Wells, 'Apocalypse Then!: The Ultimate Monstrosity and Strange Things on the Coast … an Interview with Nigel Kneale', in Hunter (ed.), *British Science Fiction Cinema*, pp. 48–56, at p. 56.

39. Kneale was sharply critical of Donlevy's performance; ibid., p. 51.

40. See David Pirie, *Hammer: A Cinema Case Study* (London: BFI, 1980), pp. 39–40.

41. Peter Hutchings, '"We're the Martians Now": British sf Invasion Fantasies of the 1950s and 1960s', in Hunter (ed.), *British Science Fiction Cinema*, p. 46.

42. See Steve Chibnall, 'Alien Women: The Politics of Sexual Difference in British SF Pulp Cinema', in ibid., pp. 65–6.

43. See Chris Baldick, *In Frankenstein's Shadow: Myth, Monstrosity and Nineteenth-century Writing* (Oxford: Oxford University Press, 1987); Fred Botting, *Making Monstrous: Frankenstein, Criticism, Theory* (Manchester: Manchester University Press, 1991).

44. Jon Turney, *Frankenstein's Footsteps: Science, Genetics and Popular Culture* (New Haven and London: Yale University Press, 1998), pp. 35, 42, 92–111, 121–8.

45. David Pirie, *A Heritage of Horror* (1973), pp. 69–70.

46. Sue Harper, 'The Scent of Distant Blood: Hammer Films and History', in Tony Barta (ed.), *Screening the Past: Film and the Representation of History* (Westport, CT: Praeger, 1998), pp. 109–25.

47. Pirie, *A Heritage*, p. 82.

48. Derek Hill, 'The Face of Horror', *Sight and Sound* (Winter 1959–60), pp. 7–9.

49. Pirie, *A Heritage*, p. 78.

50. Peter Hutchings, *Hammer and Beyond* (1993), pp. 70–86f.

# 4. The Action Adventurer

1. See John G. Cawelti, *Apostles of the Self-Made Man: Changing Concepts of Success in America* (Chicago: University of Chicago Press, 1965).

2. Paul Zweig, *The Adventurer* (1974).

3. '*Saraband for Dead Lovers': The Film and its Production* (London: Convoy Publications, 1949), p. 20; my emphasis.

4. Granger was popular with girls, but especially with boys: he was their favourite star. See the Mass-Observation Survey, 'Children's Cinema Going in Coventry' (17 July 1947) in Box File 15, Mass-Observation Archive, University of Sussex.

5. This was reinforced by the film's publicity, see the Press Book.

6. *Daily Graphic*, 14 April 1946.

7. See Jeffrey Richards, *Swordsmen of the Screen* (1984).

8. See the comments of producer Bernard Smith quoted in Derek Elley, *The Epic Film: Myth and History* (London: Routledge and Kegan Paul, 1984), p. 155.

9. Harry Watt, 'You Start from Scratch Down Under', *Picturegoer*, 22 June 1946, p. 9.

10. *Daily Express*, 7 July 1950.

11. *News Chronicle*, 20 September 1948.

12. Rank publicity material for *Where No Vultures Fly*; BFI microfiche on Steel.

13. *Daily Mail*, 6 November 1951.

14. 'Steel Man', *Films and Filming* (April 1956), p. 5.

15. Jympson Harman, *Daily Express*, 28 March 1954. Other reviewers were equally sceptical.

16. Herbert Gans, *American Films and TV Programs on British Screens* (1959), p. 28.

17. See Jeffrey Richards, *The Age of the Dream Palace* (London: Routledge and Kegan Paul, 1984), p. 167.

18. See 'The Warwick Story', *Kinematograph Weekly*, 31 May 1956, pp. 12–17.

19. See Vincent Porter, 'Methodism versus the Market-place: The Rank Organisation and British Cinema', in Robert Murphy (ed.), *The British Cinema Book* (London: BFI, 1997), pp. 129–30.

20. Jympson Harman, *Evening News*, 25 October 1956.

21. *Kinematograph Weekly*, 25 October 1956, p. 16.

22. See Donovan Pedelty, *Picturegoer*, 17 August 1957, p. 10.

23. *Picturegoer*, 17 November, 1956, pp. 10–11, 31, and 24 November, p. 20.

24. See my 'The Emergence of the British Tough Guy: Stanley Baker, Masculinity and the Crime Thriller', in Steve Chibnall and Robert Murphy (eds), *British Crime Cinema* (1999), pp. 81–93.

25. Sarah Stoddart, 'Don't be a Softie Baker – We Like You This Way', *Picturegoer*, 19 November 1955, p. 21.

26. Reported in *Kinematograph Weekly*, 20 March 1958, p. 25.

27. Gans, *American Films and TV Programs*, pp. 60–8.

28. See Geoffrey Gorer, *Exploring English Character* (London: Cresset Press, 1955), p. 298.

29. David Conrad, 'Stanley Baker: Tough at the Top', *Films and Filming* (November 1959), p. 5.

30. Exhibitors campaign booklet.

31. Jay Hyams, *War Movies* (New York: Gallery Books, 1984), pp. 152–3, 164.

32. Cubby Broccoli (with Donald Zec), *When the Snow Melts* (London: Boxtree, 1998), pp. 165–6, 171.

33. For discussion of Connery's persona and performance see my, 'Sean Connery: Loosening His Bonds', in Bruce Babington (ed.), *British Stars and Stardom* (Manchester: Manchester University Press, 2001), pp. 218–30.

34. David Cannadine, 'James Bond and the Decline of England', *Encounter* (September 1979), pp. 46–55, at p. 55. See also, Michael Denning, *Cover Stories* (1987), pp. 91–113.

35. See Bill Osgerby, '"Bachelors in Paradise": Masculinity, Lifestyle and Men's Magazines in Post-war America', *Media Arts Working Papers*, 6 (Southampton: Southampton Institute, 1999).

36. Kingsley Amis, *The James Bond Dossier* (London: Jonathan Cape, 1965), pp. 36, 42.

37. Penelope Houston, '007', *Sight and Sound* (Winter 1964–65), pp. 14–16.

38. Tony Bennett and Janet Woollacott, *Bond and Beyond* (1987); James Chapman, *Licence to Thrill* (1999).

39. Alexander Walker, *Hollywood, England* (1986), p. 198.

40. See, *inter alia*, John Parker, *Sean Connery* (London: Gollancz, 1993), pp. 171–88.

41. Michael Caine, quoted in Philip Judge, *Michael Caine* (Tunbridge Wells: Spellmount, 1985), p. 33; this was Saltzman's conception, see p. 34.

42. See Dudley Jones, 'The Great Game? The Spy Fiction of Len Deighton', in Clive Bloom (ed.), *Spy Thrillers: From Buchan to Le Carré* (London: Macmillan, 1990), pp. 100–12.

43. John Coleman, *New Statesman*, 26 March 1965.

44. Deighton had been educated at the ICA and had written *London Dossier* (1964), a 'hepcat' guide to the new bohemia; see Alex Seago, *Burning the Box of Beautiful Things: the Development of a Postmodern Sensibility* (Oxford: Oxford University Press, 1995), pp. 144–5, 148, 178–85.

45. Caine recalled that in order to remove any hint of homosexuality from the role, Palmer's shopping had to include a trolley joust with Ross and his preparation of the meal had to become a seduction; *What's It All About?* (London: Century, 1992), pp. 207–08.

46. Isabel Quigly, *Spectator*, 19 March 1965.

47. *Observer*, 20 October 1966.

48. See Robert Hewison, *Too Much: Art and Society in the Sixties 1960–1975* (London: Methuen, 1986), pp. 74–7.

49. Elaine Gallagher, *Candidly Caine* (London: Guild/LWT, 1990), pp. 102–3.

# 5. The Everyman

1. The major exception was *Dunkirk* (1958) with John Mills as Corporal 'Tubby' Binns.

2. See Franco Moretti, *The Way of the World: The 'Bildungsroman' in European Culture* (London: Verso, 1987).

3. See R. Gilmour, *The Idea of the Gentleman in the Victorian Novel* (London: Allen and Unwin, 1981), pp. 105–48.

4. For details see Cineguild publicity included on the microfiche for *Great Expectations*.

5. Raphael Samuel, 'Docklands Dickens' and '"Who Calls So Loud?"': Dickens on Stage and Screen', in his *Theatres of Memory, Vol. 1* (1994), pp. 411, 424.

6. Research Services Ltd, *Film Star Poll, RS 64* (May 1948), p. 2. I am grateful to Professor Vincent Porter for supplying this reference.

7. His role as a mildly rebellious Everyman in Two Cities' *The History of Mr Polly*

(1949) failed to enthuse audiences, partly because its mixed mode of realism and slapstick failed to gel.

8. See Martha Vicinus, *The Industrial Muse* (London: Croom Helm, 1974), p. 273.

9. See Colin Ward and Dennis Hardy, *Goodnight Campers* (London: Mansell, 1986).

10. Ted Willis, *Evening All: Fifty Years Over a Hot Typewriter* (London: Macmillan, 1991), p. 125.

11. *Kinematograph Weekly*, 7 August 1947, p. 17.

12. Double page advertisement, *Cinema Today*, 14 October 1948.

13. See Mabel Constanduros's autobiography, *Shreds and Patches* (London: Lawson and Dunn, 1946), pp. 125, 131.

14. Jeffrey Richards, *Films and British National Identity* (1997), pp. 139–43. See also letters from *Picturegoer*'s readers, 3 September 1949, p. 7.

15. See Steven Fielding, Peter Thompson and Nick Tiratsoo, *'England Arise!': The Labour Party and Popular Politics in 1940s Britain* (Manchester: Manchester University Press, 1995).

16. Ken Annakin, interview in Brian McFarlane, *An Autobiography of British Cinema* (1997), p. 25.

17. Henry Raynor, 'Nothing to Laugh At', *Sight and Sound* (April 1950), p. 67.

18. Dixon's shooting, and his wife's reactions to the news of his death, produced strong emotional reaction in audiences; see Sue Harper and Vincent Porter, *Weeping in the Cinema in 1950*, Mass-Observation Occasional Paper 3 (Falmer: University of Sussex, 1995), p. 10.

19. Clive Emsley, 'The English Bobby: An Indulgent Tradition', in Roy Porter (ed.), *Myths of the English* (Cambridge: Polity Press, 1993), p. 126. See also, Jeffrey Richards, 'The Thin Blue Line: *The Blue Lamp*', in Anthony Aldgate and Jeffrey Richards, *Best of British*, rev. edn (London: I.B.Tauris, 1999), pp. 125–47.

20. Geoffrey Gorer, *Exploring English Character* (London: Cresset Press, 1955), p. 35.

21. See Jack Warner, *Jack of All Trades* (London: W. H. Allen, 1975), p. 127; Stanley Holloway, *Wiv a Little Bit o' Luck* (London: Leslie Frewin, 1967), p. 134.

22. Charles Barr, *Ealing Studios* (1993), p. 104.

23. In this respect these films' sexual politics were deeply conformist. Only ACT's *Second Fiddle* (1958) even raised the issue of what happens if both partners pursue professional careers, only to conclude that a woman's true vocation is motherhood!

24. McFarlane, *An Autobiography*, p. 558.

25. I base this observation on Andrew Britton, 'Cary Grant: Comedy and Male Desire', *CineAction!* (December 1986), pp. 37–51.

26. Janet Finch and Penny Summerfield, 'Social Reconstruction and the Emergence of the Companionate Marriage, 1945–59', in David Clark (ed.), *Marriage, Domestic Life and Social Change* (London: Routledge, 1991), pp. 7–32.

27. *Sunday Times*, 21 March 1954.

28. Both Box and Thomas thought that this was a key ingredient for audience appeal; see McFarlane, *An Autobiography*, pp. 87 and 557.

29. 'Josh' Billings, *Kinematograph Weekly*, 22 April 1954, p. 5.

30. Roy Nash, *Daily Star*, 19 March 1954.

31. *Sunday Times*, 21 March 1954.

32. See Box's comments to Geoffrey Macnab in *J. Arthur Rank and the British Film Industry* (1993), pp. 223–4.

33. John Davis, 'Intermission: The British Film Industry', *National Provincial Bank Review* (August 1958), p. 5.

34. Cited in Herbert Gans, *American Films and TV Programs on British Screens*, pp. 38–9.

35. Thomas considered that the subsequent 'Doctor' films were far less realistic than *Doctor in the House*; 'My Way with Screen Humour', *Films and Filming* (February 1959), p. 5.

36. Interview with David Spiers, *Screen*, 11/3 (Summer 1970), p. 6.

37. For a detailed discussion see Anthony Aldgate, *Censorship and the Permissive Society* (1995), pp. 147–8.

38. For discussion and Dudley Sutton's comments see Stephen Bourne, *Brief Encounters* (1996), pp. 177–9.

39. Mark Abrams, *The Teenage Consumer* (London: London Press Exchange, 1959), p. 9.

40. Ibid., p. 13. Abrams also argued that the welfare state had eroded traditional class differences but exaggerated differences of taste. These new consumers were indifferent to the cultural capital of their 'betters' because they were the target of an array of cultural material including tabloid newspapers and commercial television. 'Social Change in Modern Britain', *Political Quarterly*, 30 (1959), pp. 149–56.

41. Abrams, *The Teenage Consumer*, pp. 14, 17.

42. Stuart Levy, interviewed in *Kinematograph Weekly*, 7 March 1957, p. 21.

43. *Monthly Film Bulletin* (July 1957), p. 91.

44. Colin MacInnes, 'Young England, Half English: The Pied Piper from Bermondsey', *Encounter* (December 1957); reprinted in his *England Half English* (London: Hogarth Press, 1986), pp. 11–19; at p. 16.

45. Colin MacInnes, 'Pop Songs and Teenagers', *Twentieth Century* (February 1958), reprinted in ibid., pp. 45–59; at p. 50.

46. Tommy Steele, *My Own Story* (London: Pemrow Publications, n.d. [?1958]), p. 59.

47. Full page pin-up, *Kinematograph Weekly*, 5 September 1957, p. 34.

48. See, *The Frankie Vaughan Story, By Himself* (London: Pemrow Publications, n.d. [? 1958]), esp. p. 62.

49. See Nick Cohn, *Pop from the Beginning* (London: Weidenfeld and Nicolson, 1969), pp. 60–2.

50. John Hill, 'Television and Pop: The Case of the 1950s', in John Corner (ed.), *Popular Television in Britain* (London: BFI, 1991), pp. 101–3.

51. Quoted in Steve Turner, *Cliff Richard: The Biography* (London: Lion Books, 1993), p. 163.

52. Cohn, *Pop from the Beginning*, p. 73.

53. See Kurt Gänzl, *The British Musical Theatre, Vol. ii: 1915–1984* (London: Macmillan, 1986), pp. 715–19.

54. Turner, *Cliff*, pp. 190–1.

55. Neil Sinyard, *The Films of Richard Lester* (London: Croom Helm, 1985), pp viii, 5–6, 9, 14, 19, 21–2.

# 6. Fools and Rogues

1. See J. P. Mayer, *British Cinemas and their Audiences* (London: Dennis Dobson, 1948), pp. 172, 173, 182, 208, 222, 228; Roger Manvell, 'Critical Survey', *Penguin Film Review*, 4 (October 1947), p. 15.

2. Brenda Cross, 'Wotcha Slash!', *Picturegoer*, 29 March 1947, p. 9.

3. See Kenneth Tynan's 1950 essay 'Sid Field', reprinted in *Profiles* (London: Nick Hern Books, 1989), pp. 11–13.

4. See the '*London Town* Questionnaire 2', September 1946, in Film Box File 15, Mass-Observation Archive, University of Sussex; Peter Noble (ed.), *British Film Yearbook 1947–48* (London: Skelton Robinson, n.d. [?1948]), pp. 19–20.

5. John Fisher, *What a Performance: The Life of Sid Field* (London: Seeley, Service and Co., 1975), pp. 178f.

6. For details see Richard Dacre, *Trouble in Store: Norman Wisdom – a Career in Comedy* (Dumfries: T. C. Farries, 1991).

7. Norman Wisdom, *Don't Laugh at Me* (London: Arrow Books, 1992), p. 109.

8.  See Louis Marks, 'Top Billing', *Sight and Sound* (December 1954), p. 11.

9.  Interview in *Kinematograph Weekly*, 26 April 1956, p. 17.

10.  It was Wisdom's decision to make the scene riotous; Carstairs had wanted a 'restrained' scene; see Dacre, *Trouble in Store*, p. 34.

11.  Derek Grainger, *Financial Times*, 15 December 1953.

12.  Margaret Hinxman, 'Where Does Wisdom Go From Here?', *Picturegoer*, 5 February 1954, pp. 8–9. All three rejected the idea that 'Norman' should become the 'smart guy'.

13.  John Grierson, '"Physical Wallop" Can Lift Box-Office to New Heights', letter in *Kinematography Weekly*, 14 January 1954, p. 6.

14.  See Herbert Gans's tabulations in his *American Films and TV Programs on British Screens* (1959), p. 38.

15.  *The Times*'s review of *Petticoat Pirates*, 1 December 1961. Drake's control over his films was greater than Wisdom's; see his autobiography, *Drake's Progress* (London: Robson Books, 1986).

16.  Michael Balcon, 'Let's Stop This Moaning About British Films', *Daily Mail*, 14 March 1956.

17.  See Philip Kemp, *Lethal Innocence: The Cinema of Alexander Mackendrick* (London: Methuen, 1991).

18.  Mackendrick, quoted in ibid., p. 46.

19.  Kenneth Tynan, *Alec Guinness* (London: Barrie and Rockliff, 1953), p. 93.

20.  *ABC Review* (August 1952), pp. 4–5.

21.  Freddie Hancock and David Nathan, *Hancock* (London: BBC, 1986), p. 74.

22.  See Roger Wilmut, *Tony Hancock 'Artiste'* (London: Methuen, 1978), p. 116.

23.  Ibid., p. 124.

24.  See my 'Misfits and the Marginalised: Gender in the Boultings' Feature Films', in Alan Burton, Tim O'Sullivan and Paul Wells (eds), *The Family Way* (2000), pp. 68–80.

25.  Alexander Walker, *Peter Sellers* (London: Coronet, 1982), p. 159.

26.  Quoted in ibid., p. 45.

27.  See Colin Watson, *Snobbery With Violence: English Crime Stories and Their Audience* (London: Eyre and Spottiswoode, 1971), pp. 186–7.

28.  Denis Gifford, *The Golden Age of Radio* (London: Batsford, 1985), p. 189.

29.  Especially as the hapless bungler Dewberry in *We Joined the Navy* (1962).

30.  See Dick Hobbs, *Doing the Business: Entrepreneurship, the Working Class, and Detectives in the East End of London* (Oxford: Oxford University Press, 1988), esp. pp. 84–107.

31.  Geoffrey Gorer, *Exploring English Character* (London: Cresset Press, 1955), p. 229.

32.  Paul Addison, *Now the War is Over: A Social History of Britain 1945–51*, rev. edn (London: Pimlico, 1995), p. 49.

33.  See David Hughes, 'The Spivs', in Michael Sissons and Philip French (eds), *Age of Austerity 1945–1951* (Oxford: Oxford University Press, 1986), pp. 69–88.

34.  R. F. Delderfield, *Worm's Eye View* (London: Samuel French, 1948), p. 14.

35.  *Picturegoer*, 19 May 1951, p. 15.

36.  Shiner stated that his films were aimed at suburban and provincial audiences and were often not showcased in the West End where they might attract critics' opprobrium; 'I play to the masses and they take me for what I am.' *Picturegoer*, 29 March 1958, p. 14.

37.  *Kinematograph Weekly*, 24 July 1952, p. 17.

38.  *Monthly Film Bulletin* (Autumn 1961), p. 157.

39.  Alexander Walker, *Hollywood, England* (1986), p. 138.

40.  Ibid., pp. 144–5.

41.  Quoted in the Press Book for *Tom Jones*.

42.  Michael Caine, *What's It All About?* (London: Arrow, 1992), p. 216.

43.  Walker, *Hollywood, England*, pp. 306–8.

44.  Isabel Quigly, *Spectator*, 1 April 1966.

45.  Mary Binnington and Duncan Blair, 'What Is It About Sexy Rexy?', *Picturegoer*,

17 March 1951, pp. 16–17.

46. See *Picturegoer*, 17 August 1958, p. 7; Robert Hirst, *Three Men and a Gimmick* (Kingswood, Surrey: World's Work, 1957), pp. 45–86.

47. *Motion Picture Herald*, 5 January 1961, p. 23.

48. See 'Cash and Carry On', *Sunday Times*, 22 May 1977; see also Morris Bright and Robert Ross, *Mr Carry On: The Life and Work of Peter Rogers* (London: BBC, 2000).

49. Marion Jordan, 'Carry On ... Follow That Stereotype', in James Curran and Vincent Porter (eds), *British Cinema History* (London: Weidenfeld and Nicolson, 1983), pp. 317–27.

50. See Sally and Nina Hibbin, *What a Carry On: The Official Story of the Carry On Films* (London: Hamlyn, 1988), p. 9.

51. Ibid., p. 12.

52. Quoted in Kenneth Easthaugh, *The Carry-On Book* (Newton Abbot: David and Charles, 1978), p. 30.

53. Margaret Anderson, '"Stop Messing About!": The Gay Fool of the "Carry On" Films', *Journal of Popular British Cinema*, 1 (1998), pp. 37–47.

54. Pierre Duchartre, *The Italian Comedy*, trans. Randolph T. Weaver (New York: Dover, 1966), p. 230.

# 7. Criminals: Spivs, Delinquents and Gangsters

1. Andrew Spicer, 'The Emergence of the British Tough Guy: Stanley Baker, Masculinity and the Crime Thriller', in Steve Chibnall and Robert Murphy (eds), *British Crime Cinema* (1999), pp. 81–93.

2. See 'Arresting the Crime Wave', *Picture Post*, 4 August 1945, pp. 16–20; Edward Smithies, *Crime in Wartime* (London: Allen and Unwin, 1982).

3. Robert Warshow, 'The Gangster as Tragic Hero', *Partisan Review* (February 1948); reprinted in his *The Immediate Experience* (New York: Doubleday, 1962), pp. 127–33.

4. See Stella Bruzzi, 'The Instabilities of the Franco-American Gangster', in *Undressing Cinema: Clothing and Identity in the Movies* (London: BFI, 1997), pp. 67–94.

5. Doré Silvermann, *Express and Star* (Wolverhampton), 18 January 1949.

6. Colin McArthur, *Underworld U.S.A.* (London: Secker and Warburg, 1972), p. 100.

7. Ken Hughes, 'Those Nutty Intellectuals', *Films and Filming* (January 1963), p. 10.

8. For contemporary discussion see *Picture Post* (December 1945), pp. 15–19; H. D. Willcock, *Report on Juvenile Delinquency* (London: Mass-Observation, Falcon Press, 1949).

9. See Stephen Humphries, *Hooligans or Rebels? An Oral History of Childhood and Youth 1889–1939* (Oxford: Basil Blackwell, 1981).

10. Geoffrey Pearson, *Hooligan* (1983).

11. John Hill, *Sex, Class and Realism* (1986), pp. 101–2.

12. I am indebted here to Steve Chibnall, 'The Teenage Trilogy: *The Blue Lamp, I Believe in You* and *Violent Playground*', in Alan Burton, Tim O'Sullivan and Paul Wells (eds), *Liberal Directions* (1997), p. 142.

13. Dilys Powell, *Britain Today* (April 1950), p. 36.

14. *Picturegoer*, 1 July 1950, p. 7.

15. Raymond Durgnat, *A Mirror for England* (1970), p. 145.

16. *Films and Filming* (August 1955), p. 3.

17. *Kinematograph Weekly*, 15 January 1953, p. 14.

18. *Evening Standard*, 5 February 1953.

19. See Anthony Aldgate, '*Women of Twilight*, *Cosh Boy* and the Advent of the "X" Certificate', *Journal of Popular British Cinema*, 3 (January 2000), pp. 59–68.

20. See Jon Clarke, Stuart Hall, Tony Jefferson and Brian Roberts, 'Subcultures, Cultures and Class', in Hall and Jefferson (eds), *Resistance Through Rituals* (1976), pp. 9–75.

21. See Stanley Cohen, *Folk Devils and Moral Panics: The Creation of the Mods and Rockers* (Oxford: Basil Blackwell, 1972).

22. See James Robertson, *The Hidden Cinema: British Film Censorship in Action* (London: Routledge, 1989), p. 105.

23. See Anthony Aldgate, *Censorship and the Permissive Society* (1995), pp. 13–31.

24. See *Picturegoer*, 15 September 1956, p. 11. In publicity photographs McCallum displayed the trademark slouch. Paul Dehn entitled his review of *Violent Playground*, 'Is This Our James Dean?', *News Chronicle*, 28 February 1958.

25. George Melly, *Revolt into Style* (Oxford: Oxford University Press, 1970), p. 30. See also Clayton Cole, 'The Dean Myth', *Films and Filming* (January 1957), p. 17.

26. Editorial, *Man About Town* (Autumn 1957), p. 9. See also Nick Cohn, *Today There are No Gentlemen: The Changes in Englishmen's Clothes Since the War* (London: Weidenfeld and Nicolson, 1971), pp. 43–9.

27. For Faith's obsession with emulating Dean, see his autobiography, *Acts of Faith* (Bantam, 1996), pp. 19–20, 40, 86.

28. Beat was essentially an American cultural phenomenon; see the editors' introduction to Gene Feldman and Max Gartenberg (eds), *Protest* (London: Souvenir Press, 1959), pp. 15–17.

29. Alfred Hitchcock noted gnomically, 'if you ... make your villain a foreigner – officialdom raises no objection'. 'The Censor Wouldn't Pass It', interview with J. Danvers Williams, *Film Weekly*, 5 November 1938, quoted in Stephen C. Shafer, *British Popular Films 1929–1939* (London: Routledge, 1997), p. 198.

30. *Kinematograph Weekly*, 19 December 1946, p. 203.

31. *New Statesman*, 2 November 1946.

32. A. E. Wilson, *Daily Star*, 25 October 1946.

33. Donald McFadden, 'Tough Guy Billy Hartnell Comes of Age', *Film World*, 2/3 (1950), p. 20.

34. Roger Manvell noted this dandyism, including Narcy's 'carefully polished nails'; *Contemporary Cinema*, 1/7 (August 1947), p. 176.

35. Arthur Vesselo, 'Films of the Quarter', *Sight and Sound* (Autumn 1947), p. 120.

36. Patrick Rice, 'When Sadism Becomes British', in J. Cross and A. Rattenbury (eds), *Screen and Audience* (London: Saturn Press, 1947), p. 4.

37. *Picturegoer*, 3 July 1948, p. 18.

38. Leonard Wallace, 'Dark Man, Dark Horse', ibid., 24 February 1951, p. 13.

39. See J. A. Gomez, 'The Theme of the Double in *The Third Man*', *Film Heritage*, vi (Summer 1971), pp. 7–12.

40. Steve Chibnall, 'Ordinary People: "New Wave" Realism and the British Crime Film 1959–1963', in Chibnall and Murphy (eds), *British Crime Cinema*, pp. 94–109.

41. See Losey's comments in his interview for *Oxford Opinion*, 18 February 1960.

42. Michel Ciment, *Conversations with Losey* (London: Methuen, 1985), p. 186.

43. Seth Holt stated that the adaptation had deliberately excluded any explanation of Gregory's actions, including the novel's one of maladjustment after the war. Interview with Kevin Gough-Yates, *Screen*, 10/6 (November–December 1969), p. 7.

44. Ibid., p. 10.

45. Robert Murphy, *Sixties British Cinema* (1992), pp. 211–17.

46. 'Mike Hodges Discusses *Get Carter*', NFT, 23 September 1997, reprinted in Chibnall and Murphy (eds), *British Crime Cinema*, pp. 116–22; at p. 120.

47. Mike Hodges, 'Interview', *Cinema Rising*, 3/2 (1972), p. 2.

48. Robert Murphy, 'A Revenger's Tragedy – *Get Carter*', in Chibnall and Murphy (eds), *British Crime Cinema*, pp. 123–33.

49. Ibid., pp. 127–9.

50. See Colin MacCabe, *Performance* (London: BFI, 1998).

51. Ibid., pp. 13–18, 24–7.

52. Peter Wollen, 'Possession', *Sight and Sound* (September 1995), p. 20.

53. See Cammell's letter to the producer Sandy Lieberson, quoted in MacCabe, *Performance*, p. 79.

54. Ibid., pp. 61–2.

# 8. Rebel Males

1. See Robert Murphy, 'Gainsborough after Balcon', in Pam Cook (ed.), *Gainsborough Pictures* (1997), pp. 148–52.

2. See Vincent Porter, 'The Context of Creativity: Ealing Studios and Hammer Films', in James Curran and Vincent Porter (eds), *British Cinema History* (London: Weidenfeld and Nicolson, 1983), p. 187.

3. See Pierre Bourdieu, *Distinction* (1984).

4. See Charles Drazin, *The Finest Years: British Cinema of the 1940s* (London: André Deutsch, 1998), pp. 71–88.

5. Review of *Queen of Spades*, *Daily Mail*, 18 March 1949.

6. Michael Powell, *A Life in Movies* (London: Heinemann, 1986), p. 579.

7. Sue Harper, *Picturing the Past* (1994), p. 173.

8. C. A. Lejeune, *Observer*, 24 September 1950; Leonard Mosley, *Daily Express*, 22 September 1950; *Sunday Pictorial*, 24 September 1950; *News of the World*, 24 September 1950; *Sunday Dispatch*, 24 September 1950; *Daily Graphic*, 22 September 1950.

9. *Kinematograph Weekly*, 5 June 1958, p. 11.

10. See Ken Gelder, *Reading the Vampire* (1994).

11. Franco Moretti, *Signs Taken for Wonders: Essays in the Sociology of Literary Forms* (London: Verso, 1983), p. 100.

12. Terence Fisher, interview in A. Eyles, R. Adkinson and N. Fry (eds), *House of Horror: The Complete Hammer Films Story* (London: Creation Books, 1994), p. 17.

13. See Lee's autobiography, *Tall, Dark and Gruesome* (London: W. H. Allen, 1975), p. 212.

14. Lawrence Alloway, 'Monster Films', *Encounter* (January 1960), p. 71.

15. Profile in *Picturegoer*, 1 November 1958, p. 5. This whole issue was a 'Horror Special'.

16. *Blood of the Vampire* had been scheduled for a six-week run at the London Pavilion, but was taken off after four weeks; Derek Hill, 'The Face of Horror', *Sight and Sound* (Winter 1959/60), p. 11.

17. The convincing contemporary Dracula is Turner in *Performance*, as I have shown.

18. Frank Hilton, 'The New Class', *Encounter* (February 1958), pp. 59–63.

19. See Harry Ritchie, *Success Stories: Literature and the Media in England, 1950–1959* (London: Faber and Faber, 1988).

20. 'Room at the Top?', *Sight and Sound* (Spring 1959), p. 56.

21. Ibid., p. 59.

22. See John Trevelyan, *What the Censor Saw* (London: Michael Joseph, 1973), pp. 106f.

23. Richard Hoggart, *The Uses of Literacy* (Harmondsworth: Penguin, 1958), pp. 291–316.

24. David Storey, 'Journey through a Tunnel', *The Listener*, 1 August 1963, p. 161.

25. Dirk Bogarde, *Snakes and Ladders* (Harmondsworth: Penguin, 1988), p. 170.

26. Tony Richardson, quoted in 'The Man Behind an Angry Young Man', *Films and Filming* (February 1959), p. 9.

27. See Alexander Walker, *Hollywood, England* (1986), pp. 57–8.

28. See, for instance, Stuart Hall, 'Jimmy Porter and the Two-and-Nines', *Cinema Studies*, 1 (1960), pp. 10–11.

29. Braine, quoted in Robert Murphy, *Sixties British Cinema* (1992), p. 13.

30. Braine, quoted in Kenneth Allsop, *The Angry Decade* (London: Peter Owen, 1958), p. 84.

31. See Walker, *Hollywood, England*, p. 59.

32. See Anthony Aldgate and Jeffrey Richards, *Best of British* (1983), p. 141.

33. *Spectator*, 4 November 1960; original emphasis.

34. *Manchester Guardian*, 29 October 1960.

35. See Walker, *Hollywood, England*, p. 88.

36. *Daily Cinema*, 26 October 1960.

37. See Alan Sillitoe, *Life without Armour* (London: HarperCollins, 1995), pp. 272–3.

38. See Jeffrey Richards, *Films and British National Identity* (1997), p. 152.

39. Bill Harding, *The Films of Michael Winner* (1978), p. 22.

40. Studio publicity, microfiche for *West 11*.

41. Draper, quoted in Harding, *Michael Winner*, p. 47; the third film in a projected trilogy was never made.

42. Ibid., pp. 27–9.

43. Ibid., p. 44.

44. John Boorman, quoted in Michel Ciment, *John Boorman* (London: Faber and Faber, 1986), p. 56.

45. See Catherine Itzin, *Stages in the Revolution: Political Theatre in Britain Since 1968* (London: Eyre Methuen, 1980), pp. 91–101.

46. Geoffrey Gorer, 'The Perils of Hypergamy', *New Statesman*, 4 May 1957, pp. 566–8.

47. Michael Kustow, *Sight and Sound* (Summer 1966), p. 144.

48. Murphy, *Sixties British Cinema*, p. 157.

49. Erik Hedling, *Lindsay Anderson: Maverick Film-Maker* (London: Cassell, 1998), pp. 80–104.

50. Quoted in Elizabeth Sussex, *Lindsay Anderson* (London: Studio Vista, 1969), p. 91.

51. Hedling, *Lindsay Anderson*, pp. 104–6.

# 9. Damaged Men

1. See Judith Halberstam, *Skin Shows* (1995), esp. pp. 19–24.

2. For historical overviews see Peter Reese, *Homecoming Heroes: An Account of the Reassimilation of British Military Personnel into Civilian Life* (London: Leo Cooper, 1992); Anthony Babington, *Shell Shock: A History of Changing Attitudes to War Neurosis* (London: Leo Cooper, 1997). See also Brian McFarlane, 'Losing the Peace: Some British Films of Postwar Adjustment', in Tony Barta (ed.), *Screening the Past: Film and the Representation of History* (Westport, CT: Praeger, 1998), pp. 93–107. For full references to the contemporary sources see my PhD thesis, 'The Representation of Masculinity in British Feature Films, 1943–1960', University of Westminster, October 1998.

3. G. W. B. James, 'Psychological Lessons from Active Service', *The Lancet*, 22 December 1945, p. 805.

4. P. and L. Bendit, *Living Together Again* (London: Gramol Press, 1946), p. 13.

5. A. T. M. Wilson, *The Serviceman Comes Home*, Pilot Papers 1 (Pilot Press, 1946), pp. 13–14.

6. Sydney Jacobson, 'The Problem of the Demobbed Officer', *Picture Post*, 26 January 1946, pp. 19–20.

7. Mass-Observation, *The Journey Home* (February 1944), pp. 47, 116.

8. H. M. D. Parker, *Manpower: A Study of Wartime Policy* (London: HMSO/Longmans Green, 1957), pp. 256–7.

9. See the Press Book for ABPC's *Man on the Run* (1949), a sympathetic study.

10. See Martha Wolfenstein and Nathan Leites, *Movies: A Psychological Study* (Glencoe, IL: Free Press, 1950).

11. For a recent study see Joanna Bourke, *An Intimate History of Killing: Face-to-Face Killing in Twentieth Century Warfare* (London: Granta, 1999).

12. 'Finding that wife or fiancée had become more mature, more sophisticated, or had developed new and wider interests demanded readjustments which some found impossible'; M. H. Whiles, 'A Study of Neurosis Among Prisoners of War', *British Medical Journal*, 17 November 1945, p. 697. For an overview see John Costello, *Love, Sex and War: Changing Values 1939–1945* (London: Collins, 1985).

13. *Sunday Express*, 26 May 1946. Paul Holt's review in the *Daily Express* (25 May 1946) was entitled, 'Your hero is a bit of a prig!'

14. *Daily Mail*, 24 May 1946.

15. Quotation from *Frieda*'s Press Book, which claimed *Frieda* was, 'the first of what may be a post-war cycle of films aiming at a return to intimate normality'.

16. See Ambler's autobiography, *Here Lies Eric Ambler* (London: Weidenfeld and Nicolson, 1985), pp. 221–2.

17. See D. R. MacCalman, 'A Psychologist Looks at Stress', *The Practitioner* (January 1946), p. 56.

18. For Anderson's comments see *Sequence*, 7 (Spring 1949), p. 11.

19. Robin Maugham, 'Preface' to the reissue of his 1949 novel *Line on Ginger* as *The Intruder* (London: W. H. Allen, 1974), p. 7.

20. See the comments of director Guy Hamilton in Brian McFarlane, *An Autobiography of British Cinema* (1997), p. 274.

21. Dilys Powell, *Sunday Times*, 7 March 1954; Peter Burnup, *News of the World*, 7 March 1954.

22. Reg Whiteley, *Daily Mirror*, 26 August 1955.

23. *Observer*, 28 August 1955.

24. John Le Carré, 'To Russia with Greetings', *Encounter* (May 1966), p. 6.

25. Michael Denning, *Cover Stories* (1987), pp. 117–21.

26. Brian Neve, *Film and Politics in America: A Social Tradition* (London: Routledge, 1992), pp. 212–13.

27. Arthur Vesselo, 'Films of the Quarter', *Sight and Sound* (Autumn 1947), p. 120.

28. Jacobson, 'The Problem of the Demobbed Officer', p. 20.

29. For detailed analysis see Brian McFarlane, *Lance Comfort* (Manchester: Manchester University Press, 1999), pp. 89–94.

30. See Julian Symons, *Bloody Murder*, rev. edn (Harmondsworth: Penguin, 1985), p. 141.

31. See Robert Murphy, *Realism and Tinsel* (1989), pp. 169–71. For discussion of the role of the BBFC, which actively prevented more such films from being produced, see my, 'The British Board of Film Censors Scenario Reports at the BFI: The Case of the Macabre Film', *Journal of Popular British Cinema*, 3 (January 2000), pp. 121–4.

32. Charles Barr, *Ealing Studios* (1993), p. 57.

33. Peter Hutchings, *Hammer and Beyond* (1993), p. 33.

34. Richard Findlater, *Michael Redgrave: Actor* (London: Heinemann, 1956), p. 59.

35. A version of *Wanted for Murder* had been written by Pressburger in 1938, see Kevin Macdonald, *Emeric Pressburger: The Life and Death of a Screenwriter* (London: Faber and Faber, 1994), p. 138.

36. A. Crooks Ripley, *Vaudeville Patterns* (London: Brownlee, 1946), pp. 96–110, at p. 106.

37. *Picturegoer*, 19 July 1947, p. 11. Gregory Peck came first that year for his performance in *Spellbound*, indicating a public taste for the damaged male.

38. Quoted in H. Cole, 'Making Murder Pay', *Picturegoer*, 4 January 1947, p. 7.

39. *Picturegoer*, 17 December 1949, p. 8.

40. Wolfenstein and Leites, *Movies*, p. 212.

41. Interview with Felix Barker, *Evening News*, 3 October 1960.

42. Quotation from the Columbia Pictures' Press Book included on the microfiche for the film.

43. The unsympathetic *Monthly Film Bulletin* described these films as 'Hammer Mark II, i. e. the quasi-*Diaboliques* exercise as opposed to the Transylvanian blood-bath' (Spring 1963, p. 90).

44. Andrew Tudor, *Monsters and Mad Scientists* (1989), pp. 192f.

45. David Pirie, *A Heritage of Horror* (1973), p. 99.

46. Leo Marks, Introduction to the screenplay of *Peeping Tom* (London: Faber and Faber, 1998). Marks returned to this theme in *Sebastian* (1968).

47. For censorship problems see Anthony Aldgate, *Censorship and the Permissive Society* (1995), pp. 53–7. For the critical reception see Ian Christie, 'The Scandal of Peeping Tom', in I. Christie (ed.), *Powell, Pressburger and Others* (London: BFI, 1978), pp. 53–8; and Michael Powell, *Million Dollar Movie* (London: Heinemann, 1992), pp. 400–2.

48. Powell, *Million Dollar Movie*, p. 402.

49. Finney, quoted in Quentin Falk, *Albert Finney: In Character* (London: Robson Books, 1992), pp. 72–3.

50. For a perceptive reading of the film and its context see I. Q. Hunter, '*Twisted Nerve*: "a good dose of S and V"', in Alan Burton, Tim O'Sullivan and Paul Wells (eds), *The Family Way* (2000), pp. 227–37.

51. Pirie, *A Heritage*, pp. 155–6.

52. Hutchings, *Hammer and Beyond*, p. 136.

53. Ibid., pp. 166f.

54. See the interview with Wicking by Julian Petley, *Journal of Popular British Cinema*, 1 (January 1998), pp. 142–50.

55. Ibid., pp. 148–9.

# 10. Contemporary Types

1. See Geoffrey Macnab, 'Unseen British Cinema', in Robert Murphy (ed.), *British Cinema of the 90s* (2000), pp. 135–44; see also Peter Todd, 'The British Film Industry in the 1990s', in ibid., pp. 17–26.

2. Xan Brooks, *Choose Life: Ewan McGregor and the British Film Revival* (London: Chameleon Books, 1998), pp. 25–6.

3. Karsten-Peter Grummit and Katharine Couling, *Cinemagoing Europe 1999* (Leicester: Dodona Research, April 1999), pp. 19–20. For an overview see Stuart Henson, 'Spoilt for Choice? Multiplexes in the 90s', in Murphy (ed.), *British Cinema of the 90s*, pp. 48–59.

4. Eddie Dyja (ed.), *BFI Film and Television Handbook 2000* (London: BFI, 1999), p. 31. For discussion see Claire Monk, 'Heritage Films and the British Cinema Audience in the 1990s', *Journal of Popular British Cinema*, 2 (1999), pp. 22–38.

5. A point well made by John Hill, 'British Cinema as National Cinema: Production, Audience and Representation', in Robert Murphy (ed.), *The British Cinema Book* (1997), pp. 244–54.

6. For this term see Thomas Elsaesser, 'Images for Sale: The "New" British Cinema', in Lester Friedman (ed.), *British Cinema and Thatcherism* (1993), pp. 59f.

7. See James Chapman, *Licence to Thrill* (1999), pp. 149–229.

8. Ibid., pp. 230–47.

9. For the 'Armani Look' see Sean Nixon, *Hard Looks* (1996), pp. 37–9.

10. See the comments of screenwriter Bruce Feirstein, quoted in Iain Johnstone, '*The World Is Not Enough': A Companion* (London: Boxtree Books, 1999), p. 19.

11. Rowena Chapman, 'The Great Pretender: Variations on the New Man Theme', in R. Chapman and J. Rutherford (eds), *Male Order* (1988), pp. 225–48, at p. 226.

12. Producer Tim Bevan, quoted in the *Observer Magazine*, 20 March 1994, p. 14.

13. For a general discussion see Jonathan Rutherford, *Forever England* (1997), pp. 139–68.

14. Julie Burchill, *Sunday Times*, 15 May 1994, section 10, pp. 2–3. Grant played exactly the same role in costume in the highly successful *Sense and Sensibility* (1996).

15. John Hill, *British Cinema in the 1980s* (1999), p. 167.

16. Graham Fuller (ed.), *Loach on Loach* (London: Faber and Faber, 1998), p. 111.

17. *My Name is Joe* found a wide public, judging by its UK box-office returns; Dyja (ed.), *BFI Film and Television Handbook 2000*, p. 33.

18. 'The Naked Truth' – interview with Syrie Johnson, *Evening Standard*, 26 August 1997, p. 2.

19. The film's British promotional campaign traded on the (ungratified) expectation of penis display.

20. Quentin Curtis, 'The Funny Thing about Mr Bean', *Daily Telegraph*, 8 August 1997, p. 22.

21. See Bryan Appleyard, 'Why Does Mr Bean Travel so Well?', *Sunday Times*, 20 July 1997, section 11, pp. 6–7.

22. Frank Mort, *Cultures of Consumption* (1996), pp. 170–5.

23. Hill, *British Cinema in the 1980s*, pp. 18–19.

24. See Leon Hunt, *British Low Culture* (1998), pp. 63–5, 114–27.

25. Tim Edwards, *Men in the Mirror* (1997), pp. 81–3.

26. Claire Monk, 'Men in the 90s', in Murphy (ed.), *British Cinema of the 90s*, pp. 156–66, at p. 157.

27. Julia Short, an executive for Polygram which distributed the film; quoted in Nick Roddick, 'Shotguns and Weddings', *Mediawatch 99–Sight and Sound*, 9/3 (March 1999) p. 13.

28. Quoted in Hugo Davenport, 'Soft-pedalling the Violence', *Daily Telegraph*, 26 April 1990.

29. Claire Monk, 'From Underworld to Underclass: Crime and British Cinema in the 1990s', in Steve Chibnall and Robert Murphy (eds), *British Crime Cinema* (1999), pp. 172–88.

30. For a general discussion see Matthew Collin, *Altered State: The Story of Ecstasy Culture and Acid House* (London: Serpent's Tail, 1997).

31. Quoted in Maria Alvarez, 'Screen Chic Hits the Streets', *Moving Pictures* (December 1996), p. 11.

32. Boyle, quoted in Brooks, *Choose Life*, p. 68.

33. Interview by Graham Jones in Lucy Johnson (ed.), *Talking Pictures* (London: BFI, 1997), pp. 86–9.

34. See Alice Rawsthorn, 'Small Budget Movie with Big Ambitions', *Financial Times*, 27 January 1996, p. 5.

35. Dan Rider, 'Club Nation', *Total Film – the Brit Issue* (June 1999), pp. 82–4.

36. See Lizzie Francke, 'Ready to Explode', *Sight and Sound* (October 1996), pp. 6–8.

37. See Leigh's introduction to *Naked and Other Screenplays* (London: Faber and Faber, 1995).

38. Stirner, quoted in *Televisual* (October 1997), p. 22.

39. Publicity material supplied by the distributors, Metrodome, dated 4 September 1998.

40. For an overview see Sarita Malik, 'Beyond "The Cinema of Duty"? The Pleasures of Hybridity: Black British Film of the 1980s and 1990s', in Andrew Higson (ed.), *Dissolving Views* (1996), pp. 202–25.

41. See Hanif Kureishi, 'The Rainbow Sign', in *My Beautiful Laundrette and The Rainbow Sign* (London: Faber and Faber, 1986), pp. 7–38.

42. Stella Bruzzi, 'Two Sisters, the Fogey, the Priest and his Lover', in Murphy (ed.), *British Cinema of the 90s*, pp. 125–34.

# Select Bibliography

This Bibliography lists only the principal sources; references to specific articles given in the chapter notes are not repeated here. I have also confined the secondary sources to those concerned with cultural history, studies of British cinema, or masculinity.

## Unpublished Material

### British Film Institute Library (London)

British Board of Film Censors: Scenario Reports 1941–47, 1949.

Film Scripts – S10453: *The Deep Blue Sea*; S12843: *The Fool and the Princess*; S13351: *He Snoops to Conquer*; S6456: *I'll Turn to You*; S13227: *Little Big Shot*; S14924: *Reluctant Heroes*; S15195: *Worm's Eye View*.

Microfiches on individual films discussed; on male stars, producers, screenwriters and directors referred to (where available); Press Books on films discussed (where available).

### Mass-Observation Archive (University of Sussex)

M-O 1341 (July 1942) *Social Climbing*; M-O 1789 (January 1943) *Demobilisation*; M-O 2120 (January 1944) *Film and Family Life*; M-O 2467 (April 1947) *Saturday Night*; M-O 2489 (May 1947) *Where is Science Taking Us?*; M-O 2491 (May 1947) *Deserters*; M-O 3058 (November 1948) *Good Men and Bad Men*; M-O 3073 (December 1948) *Middle Class: Why?*; M-O 3110B (April 1949) *A British Sex Survey*; M-O 3192 (December 1949) *Man and His Cigarette*; M-O 3194 (December 1949) *Hours Away from Work – Boys in Mixed Clubs: A Study of Interests*.

Bulletin New Series no. 18, 'Domestic Male', 1948; Bulletin New Series no. 22, 'Not Angels but Angles'; Reprint vol. 1 no. 19, 'Why Do They Go to the Pictures?'

Box File 15 containing unsorted manuscript material, including 'Cinema-Going 1946–50'.

## Published Sources

### Books

Aitken, Ian, *Alberto Cavalcanti: Realism, Surrealism and National Cinemas* (Trowbridge: Flicks Books, 2000).

Aldgate, Anthony, *Censorship and the Permissive Society: British Cinema and Theatre 1955–1965* (Oxford: Clarendon Press, 1995).

Aldgate, Anthony, James Chapman and Arthur Marwick (eds), *Windows on the Sixties* (London: I.B.Tauris, 2000).

Aldgate, Anthony and Jeffrey Richards, *Britain Can Take It: The British Cinema in the Second World War* (Oxford: Blackwell, 1986).

— *Best of British: Cinema and Society from 1930 to the Present*, rev. edn (London: I.B.Tauris, 1999).

Allsop, Kenneth, *The Angry Decade: a Survey of the Cultural Revolt of the Nineteen-fifties* (London: Peter Owen, 1958).

Annan, Noel, *Our Age: The Generation that Made Post-war Britain* (London: Fontana, 1991).

Babington, Bruce, *Launder and Gilliat* (Manchester: Manchester University Press, 2002).

Baillieu, Bill and John Goodchild, *The British Film Business* (Chichester: John Wiley & Sons, 2002).

Barefoot, Guy, *Gaslight Melodrama: From Victorian London to 1940s Hollywood* (New York and London: Continuum, 2001).

Barr, Charles, *Ealing Studios* (London: Studio Vista, 1993).

Bennett, Tony and Janet Woollacott, *Bond and Beyond: The Political Career of a Popular Hero* (London: Macmillan, 1987).

Booth, Michael, *English Melodrama* (London: Herbert Jenkins, 1965).

Boscagli, Maurizia, *Eye on the Flesh: Fashions of Masculinity in the Early Twentieth Century* (Boulder, CO and Oxford: Westview Press/HarperCollins, 1996).

Bourdieu, Pierre, *Distinction: A Social Critique of the Judgment of Taste* (London: Routledge and Kegan Paul, 1984).

— *The Field of Cultural Production* (Cambridge: Polity Press, 1993).

Bourne, Stephen, *Brief Encounters: Lesbians and Gays in British Cinema 1930–1971* (London: Cassell, 1996).

— *Black in the British Frame: Black People in British Film and Television 1896–1996* (London: Cassell, 1998).

Breward, Christopher, *The Hidden Consumer: Masculinities, Fashion and City Life 1860–1914* (Manchester: Manchester University Press, 1999).

Bristow, Joseph, *Empire Boys: Adventure in a Man's World* (London: HarperCollins, 1991).

Brosnan, John, *The Horror People* (London: Macdonald and Jane's, 1976).

Brown, Geoff, *Launder and Gilliat* (London: BFI, 1977).

Burke, Peter, *Popular Culture in Early Modern Europe*, rev. edn (Aldershot: Scolar Press, 1994).

Burton, Alan, Tim O'Sullivan and Paul Wells (eds), *Liberal Directions: Basil Dearden and the Postwar British Film Culture* (Trowbridge: Flicks Books, 1997).

— (eds), *The Family Way: The Boulting Brothers and British Film Culture* (Trowbridge: Flicks Books, 2000).

Butler, Judith, *Gender Trouble: Feminism and the Subversion of Identity* (London: Routledge, 1990).

Calder, Angus, *The Myth of the Blitz* (London: Jonathan Cape, 1991).

Cawelti, John G., *Adventure, Mystery and Romance: Formula Stories as Art and Popular Culture* (Chicago: Chicago University Press, 1976).

Chapman, James, *The British at War: Cinema, State and Propaganda, 1939–1945* (London: I.B.Tauris, 1998).

— *Licence to Thrill: A Cultural History of the James Bond Films* (London: I.B.Tauris, 1999).

— *Saints and Avengers: British Adventure Series of the 1960s* (London: I.B.Tauris, 2002).

Chapman, Rowena and Jonathan Rutherford (eds), *Male Order: Unwrapping Masculinity* (London: Lawrence and Wishart, 1988).

Chibnall, Steve, *J. Lee Thompson* (Manchester: Manchester University Press, 2000).

Chibnall, Steve and Robert Murphy (eds), *British Crime Cinema* (London: Routledge, 1999).

Clare, Anthony, *On Men: Masculinity in Crisis* (London: Chatto & Windus, 2000).

Cohan, Steven, *Masked Men: Masculinity and the Movies in the Fifties* (Bloomington, IN: Indiana University Press, 1997).

Cohan, Steve and Ina Rae Hark (eds), *Screening the Male: Exploring Masculinities in Hollywood Cinema* (London: Routledge, 1993).

Connell, R. W., *Masculinities* (Cambridge: Polity Press, 1995).

Cook, Pam (ed.), *Gainsborough Pictures* (London: Cassell, 1997).

Curtis, Anthony (ed.), *The Rise and Fall of the Matinée Idol* (London: Weidenfeld and Nicolson, 1974).

David, Hugh, *Heroes, Mavericks and Bounders: The English Gentleman from Lord Curzon to James Bond* (London: Michael Joseph, 1991).

Davidoff, Leonore and Catherine Hall, *Family Fortunes: Men and Women of the English Middle Class 1780–1850* (London: Hutchinson, 1987).

Dawson, Graham, *Soldier Heroes: British Adventure, Empire and the Imagining of Masculinities* (London: Routledge, 1994).

Denning, Michael, *Cover Stories: Narrative and Ideology in the British Spy Thriller* (London: Routledge and Kegan Paul, 1987).

Dickinson, Margaret and Sarah Street, *Cinema and State: The Film Industry and the British Government 1927–84* (London: BFI, 1985).

Docherty, David, David Morrison and Michael Tracey, *The Last Picture Show? Britain's Changing Film Audience* (London: BFI, 1987).

Dollimore, Jonathan, *Sexual Dissidence: Augustine to Wilde, Freud to Foucault* (Oxford: Oxford University Press, 1991).

Durgnat, Raymond, *A Mirror for England: British Movies from Austerity to Affluence* (London: Faber and Faber, 1970).

Dyer, Richard, *Stars* (London: BFI, 1979).

— *The Matter of Images: Essays on Representations* (London: Routledge, 1993).

Easlea, Brian, *Fathering the Unithinkable: Masculinity, Scientists and the Nuclear Arms Race* (London: Pluto Press, 1983).

Easthope, Anthony, *What a Man's Gotta Do: The Masculine Myth in Popular Culture* (London: Grafton Books, 1986).

Edwards, Tim, *Men in the Mirror: Men's Fashion, Masculinity and Consumer Society* (London: Cassell, 1997).

Faludi, Susan, *Stiffed: The Betrayal of the Modern Man* (London: Chatto and Windus, 1999).

Farrell, Kirby, *Post-traumatic Culture* (Baltimore and London: Johns Hopkins University Press, 1998).

Fisher, John, *Funny Way to be a Hero* (London: Muller, 1973).

Fluegel, Jane (ed.), *Michael Balcon: The Pursuit of British Cinema* (New York: Museum of Modern Art, 1984).

Friedman, Lester (ed.), *British Cinema and Thatcherism: Fires were started* (London: UCL Press, 1993).

Gans, Herbert, *American Films and TV Programs on British Screens: A Study of the Function of American Popular Culture Abroad* (Pennsylvania: University of Pennsylvania Institute for Urban Studies, 1959).

Gelder, Ken, *Reading the Vampire* (London: Routledge, 1994).

Geraghty, Christine, *British Cinema in the Fifties: Gender, Genre and the 'New Look'* (London: Routledge, 2000).

Ghaill, Máirtín Mac an (ed.), *Understanding Masculinities: Social Relations and Cultural Arenas* (Buckingham: Open University Press, 1996).

Girouard, Mark, *The Return to Camelot: Chivalry and the English Gentleman* (New Haven, CT and London: Yale University Press, 1981).

Glancy, Mark, *When Hollywood loved Britain: The Hollywood 'British' film 1939-1945* (Manchester: Manchester University Press, 1999).

Gledhill, Christine (ed.), *Stardom: Industry of Desire* (London: Routledge, 1991).

Gorer, Geoffrey and Ronald Searle, *Modern Types* (London: Cresset Press, 1955).

Green, Martin, *A Mirror for Anglo-Saxons* (London: Chatto and Windus, 1960).

— *Dreams of Adventure, Deeds of Empire* (London: Routledge and Kegan Paul, 1980).

— *Children of the Sun: A Narrative of 'Decadence' in England After 1918* (London: Pimlico, 1992).

Halberstam, Judith, *Skin Shows: Gothic Horror and the Technology of Monsters* (Durham and London: Duke University Press, 1995).

Hall, Leslie, *Hidden Anxieties: Male Sexuality, 1900–1950* (Cambridge: Polity Press, 1991).

Hall, Stuart and Tony Jefferson (eds), *Resistance Through Rituals: Youth Subcultures in Post-War Britain* (London: Hutchinson, 1976).

Harding, Bill, *The Films of Michael Winner* (London: Frederick Müller, 1978).

Harper, Sue, *Picturing the Past: The Rise and Fall of the British Costume Film* (London: BFI, 1994).

— *Women in British Cinema: Mad, Bad and Dangerous to Know* (London: Continuum, 2000).

Haynes, Rosamund, *From Faust to Strangelove: Representations of the Scientist in Western Literature* (Baltimore and London: Johns Hopkins University Press, 1994).

Hewison, Robert, *In Anger: Culture in the Cold War, 1945–60*, rev. edn (London: Methuen, 1988).

— *Culture and Consensus: England, Art and Politics since 1940* (London: Methuen, 1995).

Higgins, Peter, *Heterosexual Dictatorship: Male Homosexuality in Postwar Britain* (London: Fourth Estate, 1997).

Higson, Andrew, *Waving the Flag: Constructing a National Cinema in Britain* (Oxford: Oxford University Press, 1995).

— (ed.), *Dissolving Views: Key Writings on British Cinema* (London: Cassell, 1996).

Hill, John, *Sex, Class and Realism: British Cinema 1956–1963* (London: BFI, 1986).

— *British Cinema in the 1980s* (Oxford: Clarendon Press, 1999).

Horrocks, Roger, *Male Myths and Icons: Masculinity in Popular Culture* (London: Macmillan, 1995).

Hunt, Leon, *British Low Culture: From Safari Suits to Sexploitation* (London: Routledge, 1998).

Hunter, I. Q. (ed.), *British Science Fiction Cinema* (London: Routledge, 1999).

Hutchings, Peter, *Hammer and Beyond: The British Horror Film* (Manchester: Manchester University Press, 1993).

— *Terence Fisher* (Manchester: Manchester University Press, 2001).

Jeffords, Susan, *Hard Bodies: Hollywood Masculinity in the Reagan Era* (New Brunswick, NJ: Rutgers University Press, 1994).

Kane, Michael, *Modern Men: Mapping Masculinity in English and German Literature, 1880–1930* (London: Cassell, 1999).

Kelly, Terence (with Graham Norton and George Perry), *A Competitive Cinema* (London: Institute of Economic Affairs, 1966).

Kimmel, Michael, *Manhood in America: A Cultural History* (New York: The Free Press, 1996).

Kirkham, Pat and David Thoms (eds), *War Culture: Social Change and Changing Experience in World War Two Britain* (London: Lawrence and Wishart, 1995).

Kirkham, Pat and Janet Thumim (eds), *You Tarzan: Masculinity, Movies and Men* (London: Lawrence and Wishart, 1993).

— (eds), *Me Jane: Masculinity, Movies and Women* (London: Lawrence and Wishart, 1995).

Klapp, Orrin, *Heroes, Villains and Fools* (Englewood Cliffs, NJ: Prentice Hall, 1962).

Laing, Stuart, *The Representation of Working-class Life 1957–1964* (London: Macmillan, 1986).

Landy, Marcia, *British Genres: Cinema and Society, 1930–1960* (Princeton, NJ: Princeton University Press, 1991).

Lehman, Peter (ed.), *Masculinity: Bodies, Movies, Culture* (London: Routledge, 2001).

Leigh, Jacob, *The Cinema of Ken Loach: art in the service of the people* (London: Wallflower Press, 2002).

Lichtenstein, Claude, *As Found: The Discovery of the Ordinary: British Architecture and Art of the 1950s* (London: Lars Muller, 2002).

McDowell, Colin, *The Man of Fashion: Peacock Males and Perfect Gentlemen* (London: Thames and Hudson, 1997).

McFarlane, Brian, *An Autobiography of British Cinema* (London: Methuen, 1997).

— *Lance Comfort* (Manchester: Manchester University Press, 1999).

MacKenzie, S.P., *British War Films 1939-1945* (London: Hambledon and London, 2001).

McKibbin, Ross, *Class and Cultures: England 1918–1951* (Oxford: Oxford University Press, 1998).

McLaren, Angus, *The Trials of Masculinity: Policing Sexual Boundaries 1870–1930* (Chicago: Chicago University Press, 1997).

Macnab, Geoffrey, *J. Arthur Rank and the British Film Industry* (London: Routledge, 1993).

— *Searching for Stars: Stardom and Screen Acting in British Cinema* (London: Cassell, 2000).

Mangan J. A. and J. Walvin (eds), *Manliness and Morality: Middle Class Masculinity in Britain and America 1800–1940* (Manchester: Manchester University Press, 1987).

Marwick, Arthur, *The Sixties: Cultural Revolution in Britain, France, Italy, and the United States, c.1958–c.1974* (Oxford: Oxford University Press, 1998)

Mason, Philip, *The English Gentleman: The Rise and Fall of an Ideal* (London: André Deutsch, 1982).

Mellor, David (ed.), *A Paradise Lost: The Neo-Romantic Imagination in Britain, 1935–55* (London: Lund Humphries/Barbican Art Gallery, 1987).

Mercer, Kobena, *Welcome to the Jungle: New Positions in Black Cultural Studies* (London: Routledge, 1994).

Minghall, R., *A Geography of Victorian Gothic Fiction: Mapping History's Nightmares* (Oxford: Oxford University Press, 1999).

Moers, Ellen, *The Dandy: Brummell to Beerbohm* (London: Secker and Warburg, 1960).

Mort, Frank, *Cultures of Consumption: Masculinities and Social Space in Late Twentieth Century Britain* (London: Routledge, 1996).

Murphy, Robert, *Realism and Tinsel: Cinema and Society in Britain 1939–49* (London: Routledge, 1989).

— *Sixties British Cinema* (London: BFI, 1992).

— (ed.), *The British Cinema Book* (London: BFI, 1997).

— *British Cinema and the Second World War* (London: Continuum, 2000).

— (ed.), *British Cinema of the 90s* (London: BFI, 2000).

Nixon, Sean, *Hard Looks: Masculinities, Spectatorship and Contemporary Consumption* (London: UCL Press, 1996).

Osgerby, Bill, *Youth in Britain Since 1945* (Oxford: Blackwell, 1998).

— *Playboys in Paradise: Masculinity, Youth and Leisure-style in Modern America* (Oxford: Berg, 2001).

Osgerby, Bill and Anna Gough-Yates (eds), *Action TV: Tough Guys, Smooth Operators and Foxy Chicks* (London: Routledge, 2001).

Paris, Michael, *Warrior Nation: Images of War in British Popular Culture, 1850-2000* (London: Reaktion Books, 2000).

Parish, James and Don Stanke, *The Debonairs* (New York: Arlington House, 1975).

Pearson, Geoffrey, *Hooligan: A History of Respectable Fears* (London: Macmillan, 1983).

Petrie, Duncan, *Creativity and Constraint in the British Film Industry* (London: Macmillan, 1991).

— (ed.), *New Questions of British Cinema* (London: BFI, 1992).

Pirie, David, *A Heritage of Horror: The English Gothic Cinema, 1946–1972* (London: Gordon Fraser, 1973).

Polhemus, Ted, *Street Style: From Sidewalk to Catwalk* (London: Thames and Hudson, 1994).

Political and Economic Planning, *The British Film Industry* (London: PEP, 1952; *Supplement*, 1958).

Porter, Roy (ed.), *Myths of the English* (Cambridge: Polity Press, 1992).

Porter, Vincent, *On Cinema* (London: Pluto Press, 1985).

Potter, Dennis, *The Glittering Coffin* (London: Gollancz, 1960).

Praz, Mario, *The Romantic Agony* (Oxford: Oxford University Press, 1970).

Punter, David, *The Literature of Terror: A History of Gothic Fictions from 1765 to the Present Day, Vol. 1: The Gothic Tradition; Vol. 2: The Modern Gothic* (Harlow: Longman, 1996).

Rattigan, Neil, *This Is England: British Film and the People's War, 1939-1945* (London: Associated University Presses, 2001).

Raven, Simon, *The English Gentleman: An Essay in Attitudes* (London: Anthony Blond, 1961).

Richards, Jeffrey, *Visions of Yesterday* (London: Routledge and Kegan Paul, 1973).

— *Swordsmen of the Screen: From Douglas Fairbanks to Michael York* (London: Routledge and Kegan Paul, 1977).

— *Films and British National Identity: From Dickens to 'Dad's Army'* (Manchester: Manchester University Press, 1997).

Richards, Jeffrey and Dorothy Sheridan (eds), *Mass-Observation at the Movies* (London: Routledge and Kegan Paul, 1987).

Robertson, James, *The Hidden Cinema: British Film Censorship in Action, 1913–1972* (London: Routledge, 1989).

Robinson, Fred Miller, *The Man in the Bowler Hat: His History and Iconography* (Chapel Hill and London: University of North Carolina Press, 1993).

Roper, Michael, *Masculinity and the British Organization Man since 1945* (Oxford: Oxford University Press, 1994).

Roper, Michael and John Tosh (eds), *Manful Assertions: Masculinities in Britain since 1800* (London: Routledge, 1991).

Rutherford, Jonathan, *Forever England: Reflections on Masculinity and Empire* (London: Lawrence and Wishart, 1997).

Samuel, Raphael, *Theatres of Memory Vol. I: Past and Present in Contemporary Culture* (London: Verso, 1994).

— *Theatres of Memory, Vol. II: Island Stories: Unravelling Britain* (London: Verso, 1998).

Schoene-Harwood, Berthold, *Writing Men: Literary Masculinities from 'Frankenstein' to the New Man* (Edinburgh: Edinburgh University Press, 2000).

Sedgwick, Eve K., *Between Men: English Literature and Male Homosocial Desire* (New York: Columbia University Press, 1985).

Sedgwick, John, *Popular Filmgoing in 1930s Britain: A Choice of Pleasures* (Exeter: Exeter University Press, 2000).

Segal, Lynne, *Slow Motion: Changing Masculinities, Changing Men* (London: Virago, 1990).

Shaw, Tony, *British Cinema and the Cold War: The State, Propaganda and Consensus* (I.B.Tauris, 2001).

Silverman, Kaya, *Male Subjectivity at the Margins* (London: Routledge, 1992).

Simpson, Mark, *Male Impersonators: Men Performing Masculinity* (London: Cassell, 1995).

Sinfield, Alan, *Literature, Politics and Culture in PostWar Britain* (Oxford: Blackwell, 1989).

— *The Wilde Century: Effeminacy, Oscar Wilde and the Queer Movement* (London: Cassell, 1994).

Sinyard, Neil, *The Films of Richard Lester* (London: Croom Helm, 1985).

— *Jack Clayton*, (Manchester: Manchester University Press, 2000).

Sklar, Robert, *City Boys: Cagney, Bogart, Garfield* (Princeton, NJ: Princeton University Press, 1992).

Smith, Murray, *Trainspotting* (London: BFI, 2002).

Spicer, Andrew, *Film Noir* (Harlow: Longman, 2002).

— *Sydney Box* (Manchester: Manchester University Press, forthcoming).

Spraos, John, *The Decline of Cinema: An Economist's Report* (London: Allen and Unwin, 1962).

Stallybrass, Peter and Allon White, *The Politics and Poetics of Transgression* (London: Methuen, 1986).

Street, Sarah, *British National Cinema* (London: Routledge, 1997).

Studlar, Gaylyn, *The Mad Masquerade: Stardom and Masculinity in the Jazz Age* (New York: Columbia University Press, 1996).

Sussman, Herbert, *Victorian Masculinities: Manhood and Masculine Poetics in Early Victorian Literature and Art* (Cambridge: Cambridge University Press, 1995)

Tasker, Yvonne, *Spectacular Bodies: Gender, Genre and the Action Cinema* (London: Comedia/ Routledge, 1993).

Thorslev, P. L. Jnr, *The Byronic Hero: Types and Prototypes* (Minneapolis: University of Minnesota Press, 1962).

Threadgold, Derek, *Shepperton Studios: An Independent View* (London: BFI, 1994).

Torrance, Robert M., *The Comic Hero* (Cambridge, MA and London: Harvard University Press, 1978).

Tosh, John, *A Man's Place: Masculinity and the Middle-class Home in Victorian England* (New Haven and London: Yale University Press, 1999).

Tudor, Andrew, *Monsters and Mad Scientists: A Cultural History of the Horror Movie* (Oxford: Blackwell, 1989).

Walker, Alexander, *National Heroes: British Cinema in the Seventies and Eighties* (London: Harrap, 1985).

— *Hollywood, England: The British Film Industry in the Sixties* (London: Harrap, 1986).

Weeks, Jeffrey, *Sex, Politics and Society: The Regulation of Sexuality since 1800*, 2nd edn (London: Longman, 1989).

— *Coming Out: Homosexual Politics in Britain from the Nineteenth Century to the Present*, rev. edn (London: Quartet, 1990).

Welsford, Enid, *The Fool: His Social and Literary History* (London: Faber and Faber, 1935).

Williams, Tony, *Structures of Desire: British Cinema, 1939–1945* (New York: State University of New York Press, 2000).

Zijderveld, A. C., *Reality in a Looking-glass: Rationality through an Analysis of Traditional Folly* (London: Routledge and Kegan Paul, 1982).

Zweig, Paul, *The Adventurer* (Princeton, NJ: Princeton University Press, 1974).


**Journal Articles and Chapters in Collections**

Barr, Charles, 'Introduction: Amnesia and Schizophrenia', in C. Barr (ed.), *All Our Yesterdays: 90 Years of British Cinema* (London: BFI, 1986), pp. 1–30.

Bennett, Tony, 'Introduction: Popular Culture and the "Turn to Gramsci"' in T. Bennett, C. Mercer and J. Woollacott (eds), *Popular Culture and Social Relations* (Milton Keynes: Open University Press, 1986), pp. xi–xix.

Brown, Geoff, 'Which Way to the Way Ahead? Britain's Years of Reconstruction', *Sight and Sound* (Autumn 1978), pp. 242–7.

Browning, H. E. and A. A. Sorrell, 'Cinemas and Cinema-going in Great Britain', *Journal of the Royal Statistical Society*, series A, 117/2 (1954), pp. 133–70.

Burton, Alan and Steve Chibnall, 'Promotional Activities and Showmanship in British Film Exhibition', *Journal of Popular British Cinema*, 2 (1999), pp. 83–99.

Chapman, James, 'Action, Spectacles and the *Boy's Own* Tradition in British Cinema' in Robert Murphy (ed.), *The British Cinema Book* rev. edn (London: BFI, 2001), pp. 217–25.

Chibnall, Steve, 'Travels in Ladland: The British Gangster Film Cycle, 1998-2001', in Robert Murphy (ed.), *The British Cinema Book* rev. edn (London: BFI, 2001), pp. 281–91.

Clay, Andrew, 'When the Gangs Came to Britain: the Postwar British Crime Film', *Journal of Popular British Cinema*, 1 (1998), pp. 76–86.

— 'Men, Women and Money: Masculinity in Crisis in the British Professional Crime Film 1946–1965', in Steve Chibnall and Robert Murphy (eds), *British Crime Cinema* (London: Routledge, 1999), pp. 51–65.

Cooper, D. E., 'Looking Back in Anger', in Victor Bogdanor and Robert Skidelsky (eds), *The Age of Affluence* (London: Macmillan, 1970), pp. 154–87.

Corrigan, Philip, 'Film Entertainment as Ideology and Pleasure: Towards a History of

Audiences', in James Curran and Vincent Porter (eds), *British Cinema History* (London: Weidenfeld and Nicolson, 1983), pp. 24–38.

Eley, Geoff, 'Finding the People's War: Film, British Collective Memory, and World War II', *American Historical Review* 1006/3 (2001), pp. 818–28.

Eyles, Allen, 'A Passion for Cinema: Ken Hughes', *Focus on Film*, 6 (Spring 1971), pp. 42–51.

Gledhill, Christine, 'Signs of Melodrama', in Christine Gledhill (ed.), *Stardom: Industry of Desire* (London: Routledge, 1991), pp. 207–29.

Glover, David, 'The Stuff that Dreams are Made of: Masculinity, Femininity and the Thriller', in Derek Longhurst (ed.), *Gender, Genre and Narrative Pleasure* (London: Unwin Hyman, 1989), pp. 67–83.

Gough-Yates, Kevin, 'The Hero' [four parts], *Films and Filming* (December 1965–March 1966).

Green, Ian, 'Malefunction', *Screen*, 25/4–5 (July–October 1984), pp. 36–49.

Hall, Stuart, 'The Social Eye of Picture Post', *Birmingham Working Papers in Cultural Studies*, 2 (Birmingham: CCCS, 1972).

— 'Cultural Identity and Diaspora', in J. Rutherford (ed.), *Identity: Community, Culture and Difference* (London: Lawrence and Wishart, 1990), pp. 222–37.

Harper, Sue, 'The Years of Total War: Propaganda and Entertainment', in Christine Gledhill and Gillian Swanson (eds), *Nationalising Femininity: Culture, Sexuality and British Cinema in the Second World War* (Manchester: Manchester University Press, 1996), pp. 193–212.

— 'Popular Film, Popular Memory: The Case of the Second World War', in Martin Evans and Ken Lunn (eds), *War and Memory in the Twentieth Century* (Oxford: Berg, 1997), pp. 163–76.

Healy, Murray, 'Were We Being Served? Homosexual Representation in Popular British Comedy', *Screen*, 36/3 (Autumn 1995), pp. 243–56.

Hebdige, Dick, 'Towards a Cartography of Taste 1935–1962', in *Hiding in the Light: On Images and Things* (London: Comedia/Routledge, 1988), pp. 45–76.

Higson, Andrew, 'A Diversity of Film Practices: Renewing British Cinema in the 1970s', in Bart Moore-Gilbert (ed.), *The Arts in the 1970s: Cultural Closure?* (London: Routledge, 1994), pp. 216–39.

Hill, John, 'British Film Policy', in Albert Moran (ed.), *Film Policy: International, National and Regional Perspectives* (London: Routledge, 1996), pp. 101–13.

— 'Allegorising the Nation: British Gangster Films of the 1980s', in Steve Chibnall and Robert Murphy (eds), *British Crime Cinema* (London: Routledge, 1999), pp. 160–71.

— 'Failure and Utopianism: Representations of the Working Class in British Cinema of the 1990s', in Robert Murphy (ed.), *British Cinema of the 90s* (London: BFI, 2000), pp. 178–87.

Kemp, Philip, 'New Maps of Albion', *Film Comment*, 35/3 (May–June 1999), pp. 64–9.

LeMathieu, D. L., 'Imagined Contemporaries: Cinematic and Televised Dramas about the Edwardians in Great Britain and the US, 1967–1985', *Historical Journal*, 10/3 (1990), pp. 243–56.

Longhurst, Derek, 'Sherlock Holmes: Adventures of the English Gentleman 1887–1894', in Derek Longhurst (ed.), *Gender, Genre and Narrative Pleasure* (London: Unwin Hyman, 1989), pp. 51–66.

McCrillis, Neal R., ' "Simply try for one hour to behave like gentlemen": British Cinema during the early Cold War, 1945-1960', *Film and History* 31/2 (2001), pp. 6-12.

McFarlane, Brian, 'Pulp Fictions: The British B Film and the Field of Cultural Production', *Film Criticism*, 21/1 (Autumn 1996), pp. 48–70.

McKendrick, Neil, '"Gentlemen and Players" Revisited: the Gentlemanly Ideal, the Business Ideal and the Professional Ideal in English Literary Culture', in N. McKendrick and R. Outhwaite (eds), *Business Life and Public Policy: Essays in Honour of D. C. Coleman* (Cambridge: Cambridge University Press, 1986), pp. 93–136.

Medhurst, Andy, 'Can Chaps be Pin Ups? The British Male Film Star of the 1950s', *Ten-8*, 17 (February 1985), pp. 3–8.

— 'Dirk Bogarde', in Charles Barr (ed.), *All Our Yesterdays* (London: BFI, 1986), pp. 346–54.

— 'Negotiating the Gnome Zone: Versions of Suburbia in British Popular Culture', in Roger Silverstone (ed.), *Visions of Suburbia* (London: Routledge, 1997), pp. 240–68.

Murphy, Robert, 'Citylife: Urban Fairytales in Late 90s British Cinema', in Robert Murphy (ed.) *The British Cinema Book* rev. edn (London: BFI, 2001), pp. 292–300.

— 'Another false dawn? The Film Consortium and the franchise scheme', *Journal of Popular British Cinema* 5 (2002), pp. 31–6.

— 'British *Film Noir*' in Andrew Spicer (ed.), *European Film Noir* (Manchester: Manchester University Press, forthcoming).

Neale, Steve, 'Masculinity and Spectacle', *Screen*, 24/6 (November–December 1983), pp. 2–16.

Newman, Kim, 'Psycho-thriller, qu'est-ce que c'est?', in Steve Chibnall and Julian Petley, (eds), *British Horror Cinema* (London: Routledge, 2002), pp. 71–81.

O'Sullivan, Tim, '*Suspect*: in Search of the "Superior Support"', in Alan Burton, Tim O'Sullivan and Paul Wells (eds), *The Family Way: The Boulting Brothers and British Film Culture* (Trowbridge: Flicks Books, 2000), pp. 200–14.

Petley, Julian, 'The Lost Continent', in Charles Barr (ed.), *All Our Yesterdays: 90 Years of British Cinema* (London: BFI, 1986), pp. 98–119.

Porter, Vincent, 'Between Structure and History: Genre in Popular British Cinema', *Journal of Popular British Cinema*, 1 (1998), pp. 25–36.

— 'Outsiders in England: The Films of the Associated British Picture Corporation, 1949–1958', in Justine Ashby and Andrew Higson (eds), *British Cinema Past and Present* (London: Routledge, 2000), pp. 152–65.

— 'The Robert Clark Account: Films Released in Britain by Associated British Pictures, British Lion, MGM, and Warner Bros., 1946–1957', *Historical Journal of Film, Radio and Television*, 20/4 (2000), pp. 469–511.

— 'All Change at Elstree: Warner Bros., ABPC and British Film Policy, 1945–1961', *Historical Journal of Film, Radio and Television* 21/1 (2001), pp.5–35.

— 'The hegemonic turn: film comedies in 1950s Britain', *Journal of Popular British Cinema* 4 (2001), pp. 81–94.

Pronay, Nicholas, '"The Land of Promise": The Projection of Peace Aims in Britain', in K. R. M. Short (ed.), *Feature Films as History* (London: Croom Helm, 1981), pp. 51–77.

— 'Post-bellum Cinema: A Survey of Films Relating to World War II Made in Britain Between 1945–1960', *Historical Journal of Film, Radio and Television*, 8/1 (1988), pp. 39–54.

— 'British Film Sources for the Cold War: The Disappearance of the Cinema-going Public', *Historical Journal of Film, Radio and Television*, 3/1 (1993), pp. 7–17.

Ramsden, John, 'Refocusing "The People's War": British War Films of the 1950s', *Journal of Contemporary History*, 33/1 (1998), pp. 35–63.

Richards, Jeffrey, 'From Christianity to Paganism: The New Middle Ages and the Values of "Medieval" Masculinity', *Cultural Values*, 3/2 (April 1999), pp. 213–34.

Roper, Michael and John Tosh, 'Introduction: Historians and the Politics of Masculinity', in M. Roper and J. Tosh (eds), *Manful Assertions: Masculinities in Britain since 1800* (London: Routledge, 1991), pp. 1–24.

Ryall, Tom, 'One Hundred and Seventeen Steps Towards Masculinity', in Pat Kirkham and Janet Thumim (eds), *You Tarzan: Masculinity, Movies and Men* (London: Lawrence and Wishart, 1993), pp. 153–66.

— 'New Labour and the cinema: culture, politics and economics', *Journal of Popular British Cinema* 5 (2002), pp. 5-20.

Spicer, Andrew, 'British *Neo-Noir*', in Andrew Spicer (ed.), *European Film Noir* (Manchester: Manchester University Press, forthcoming).

— 'Fisher and Genre II: The Crime Films', in James Chapman (ed.), *Fantastic Visions: Terence Fisher and British Film Culture* (London: Wallflower, forthcoming).

— 'The Reluctance to Commit: Hugh Grant and the New British Romantic Comedy', in Bruce Babington, Ann Davies and Phil Powrie (eds), *Masculinities and Film* (London: Wallflower, forthcoming).

Stafford, Roy, '"What's showing at the Gaumont?": rethinking the study of British cinema in the 1950s', *Journal of Popular British Cinema* 4 (2001), pp. 95–111.

Williams, Christopher, 'The Social Art Cinema: A Moment in the History of British Film and Television Culture', in C. Williams (ed.), *Cinema: the Beginnings and the Future* (London: University of Westminster Press, 1996), pp. 192–200.

Williams, Michael, 'War-Torn Dionysus: The Silent Passion of Ivor Novello', in Andrew Higson (ed.) *Young and Innocent? The Cinema in Britain, 1896-1930* (Exeter: Exter University Press, 2002), pp. 256–70.

Williams, Tony, 'British *Film Noir*', in Alain Silver and James Ursini (eds), *Film Noir Reader – 2* (New York: Limelight Editions, 1999), pp. 243–69.

Wollen, Peter, 'Riff-raff Realism', *Sight and Sound* (April 1998), pp. 18–22.

# Film Index

# General Index

Grant, Arthur, 60, 181
Grant, Hugh, 187, 203
Grant, Richard E., 187
Graves, Peter, 30
Gray, Dulcie, 49
Gray, Sally, 171, 172
Green, Guy, 81
Green, Nigel, 77
Greene, Graham, 130, 169
Greene, Max, 128
Greenwood, Joan, 109, 146, 165
Greenwood, Robert, 17
Greenwood, Walter, 15
Gregson, John, 35, 45, 54, 89, 92
Grenfell, Joyce, 119
Greville, Edmond T., 127, 135
Grierson, John, 106
Guest, Val, 54, 59, 116, 117
Guinness, Alec, 35, 44, 46, 108, 109, 146
Gump, 104–6, 202

Haigh, Kenneth, 100
Hamer, Robert, 146, 147, 175
Hamilton, Guy, 78
Hammer Films, 45, 54, 58, 61, 62–3, 71, 116, 148–50, 179, 181, 183; 'Mummy' films, 64
HammerScope, 60
*Hancock's Half Hour*, 125
Hancock, Tony, 102, 110–11
Handl, Irene, 110
Handley, Tommy, 19
Hanley, Jimmy, 17, 82, 84, 86, 131, 132
Hardie, Kate, 193
Hardy, Robert, 181
Hare, Robertson, 17, 20
Harlow, John, 136
Harper, Kenneth, 99
Harper, Sue, 5
Harris, Richard, 155
Harrison, Kathleen, 83
Harrison, Rex, 11, 28, 120
Hartnell, William, 16, 136, 137
Harvey, Laurence, 116, 117, 129, 133, 151, 152, 154, 167
Havelock-Allan, Anthony, 166
Hawkins, Jack, 35, 36, 38, 44, 46, 48, 51, 52, 69, 70, 121, 167
Hawtrey, Charles, 123–4
Hay, Will, 19
Hayes, Melvyn, 136
Headley, Jack, 67
hedonism, 200, 203

Heller, Otto, 155, 180
Hemmings, David, 67, 94, 157
Hendry, Ian, 117, 142
Henson, Gladys, 83, 86
heroic masculinity, 185–6
heroin, culture of, 194
Heywood, Anne, 52
Hicks, Seymour, 172
Hill, Benny, 102
Hill, Derek, 42, 43
Hill, John, 191
Hillier, Erwin, 26
Hills, Gillian, 182
Hitchcock, Alfred, 175
Hobson, Valerie, 146, 163, 166
Hodges, Mike, 141
Hoggart, Richard, 150
Holden, William, 44
Hollander, Tom, 200
Holloway, Stanley, 18, 23, 86–7, 108
Hollywood, 7, 67, 68, 70, 71, 103, 128; Indie cinema, 195
Hollywood Majors, 141
Holt, Seth, 141
homosexuality, 94, 123–4, 130, 142, 176, 193
homosociality, 5, 121, 140
Hopkins, Anthony, 170
Hordern, Michael, 183
Horniman, Roy, 146
horror films, 4
Hoskins, Bob, 193, 197
Houghton, Don, 149
Houston, Donald, 90, 93, 152
Houston, Penelope, 150
Howard, Leslie, 8, 9, 29, 31, 32, 39, 45, 55
Howard, Ronald, 48
Howard, Trevor, 43–4, 138, 171
Howerd, Frankie, 102, 116
Hudd, Roy, 197
Hudis, Norman, 92, 96, 122
Hughes, Ken, 128, 129, 139
Hulbert, Jack, 115
Hutchings, Peter, 181
Hylton, Jane, 84

Ifans, Rhys, 187
Imperial Adventurer, 68–71
Independent Artists, 140
Independent Producers, 7, 10, 81–2
Individual Pictures, 66
Internet, films watched on, 185
Ireland, John, 167